The History of Law in Europe

The History of Law in Europe

An Introduction

Bart Wauters

Professor of Law, IE University, Spain

Marco de Benito

Professor of Law, IE University, Spain

Edward Elgar
PUBLISHING

Cheltenham, UK • Northampton, MA, USA

Published by
Edward Elgar Publishing Limited
The Lypiatts
15 Lansdown Road
Cheltenham
Glos GL50 2JA
UK

Edward Elgar Publishing, Inc.
William Pratt House
9 Dewey Court
Northampton
Massachusetts 01060
USA

A catalogue record for this book
is available from the British Library

Library of Congress Control Number: 2016957253

This book is available electronically in the **Elgar**online
Law subject collection
DOI 10.4337/9781786430762

MIX
Paper from
responsible sources
FSC® C013604

ISBN 978 1 78643 075 5 (cased)
ISBN 978 1 78643 076 2 (eBook)

Typeset by Columns Design XML Ltd, Reading
Printed and bound by CPI Group (UK) Ltd, Croydon, CR0 4YY

Cupidae legum iuventuti

Contents

Introduction

The History of Law in Europe: An Introduction is written for students and all those readers – whether legal students, scholars, lawyers, or the general public – interested in this essential aspect of European history. The book describes the different ways in which law has been understood in the context of Europe's political, economic, social and cultural development. It does not seek to be encyclopedic. Rather, it aims to offer a synthesis of the key developments and most crucial points in European legal history.

Legal history as an autonomous academic discipline developed in nineteenth-century Germany, when Carl Friedrich von Savigny (d. 1861) advanced the idea that ancient Roman law had been the backbone of legal doctrine in Europe ever since, in the eleventh century, jurists at the law school in Bologna began methodically to study Justinian's codification. While fundamentally correct, Savigny's view of the past was hardly unbiased. He saw himself and his fellow German professors as the natural culmination, the zenith, of a succession of glorious periods of Roman legal doctrine: from eleventh-century Bologna to Humanist France and the elegant Roman-Dutch School. Savigny's proposition also allowed Roman law to be identified with German history, right at a time when Germany as a unified state was coming into being. Bologna's medieval university, which so many German students attended that they were organized as a separate Teutonic nation, had been actively sponsored by the German Emperor Frederick Barbarossa; the supreme court of the Empire, the *Reichskammergericht*, declared Roman law to apply on a suppletive basis starting 1495; and the Holy Roman Empire, entrenched in its German heartland, was seen as the natural successor to Ancient Rome.

Savigny's views, though, did not go unchallenged. European scholars, also in Germany, underscored the historical importance of indigenous, non-Roman legal institutions. And with more than a little national chauvinism, English legal historians flatly denied any influence of Roman law, past or present, on their own legal system. On the Continent, Savigny was said to overstate the role of Roman law in history, since – it was argued – Roman law had not been applied directly by the courts and generally had not been received to the extent that it had been in Germany. The largely Romantic trend to focus on the study of national legal history continued into the twentieth century, peaking during the paroxysm of nationalism between the world wars.

With the founding of the European Coal and Steel Community in 1951, which, step by step, evolved into the European Union that we know today, the national approach to European legal past gave way to a broader perspective based on *families* or *traditions*: a Continental family based on the *ius commune* (or Roman and medieval canon law) and the English tradition of "common law." A third legal family, that of the Soviet republics, was often considered alongside the other two.

The fall of the Berlin Wall in 1989 marked yet another shift in the approach to European legal history. Suddenly Europe was much larger, as it naturally included the diverse legal traditions that had nearly been strangled under the Soviet yoke. This multiformity blurred the dichotomy of common law versus civil law systems and attracted interest in legal traditions that did not easily fit into the common or civil law families, such as those of the Scandinavian countries, Scotland, Greece, and the Balkans.

Where does this book stand, then, in the context of this scenario? First of all, as mentioned, it is meant to constitute a short introduction, not an encyclopedic overview of the legal traditions of every single European country. Aside from the titanic nature of such an enterprise, we seriously doubt that the sum-of-the-parts approach – a national one, after all – is necessarily the most enlightening. We shall be content if we manage to spark the reader's curiosity and spur him to understand Europe's legal past as a shared language, of which its different national laws – particularly on the Continent – are but dialectical expressions. While this focus on the shared language of law should not blind us to the importance of its local or national expressions, we argue that even these local and national expressions possess some common features that allow for a common understanding. In the book, when we describe items of local or national legal history, we do so in order to illustrate this more general point. They are offered as *examples*. As such, others could easily have been cited, but we believe that those chosen illustrate a certain point particularly well. Though we have tried to include examples from all over Europe, those from Western Europe predominate. We trust that the intelligent reader will, in any event, be able to place a certain local expression of the law in a useful framework.

Secondly, our narrative is built upon the pillars of the civil law and common law families. The export of these two traditions to countries and regions all around the world and their impact on today's global legal and economic relations, in and of itself justify this decision. It is true that there have been moments in history when, for example, the Vikings or Byzantines exported their customs to other places, or their economies were more powerful than the Western ones. For this reason we have included brief accounts of Scandinavian, Greek, and Eastern European law, but we have refrained from covering them comprehensively and separately. Hence, discussion of the Scottish "mixed" system is succinct, and falls in the chapter on the history of the common law.

Thirdly, even if recent scholarship has uncovered some cross-pollination of ideas between the civil and common law traditions, and concepts and institutions share similar features on both sides of the Channel, this separation is still largely valid, based on history stemming back to the twelfth century. Thus, we opted to make this divide structurally visible by addressing the common law separately instead of integrating it into each of the chapters, organized chronologically. We are aware that some readers might find this approach awkward, as at times they will be forced to check points appearing in previous chapters, but in a book so concise, and with the help of its index, we trust this will not constitute an insurmountable problem. Also, this approach helps to better explain why a legal system developed in England so different from that found on the mainland, in spite of the fact that around 1100 the picture was actually quite similar.

One of the other objectives of the book is to help lawyers and legal professionals, of today and tomorrow, to develop the ability to critically assess their own professional endeavors. The book examines the law in the changing historical contexts in which it was forged. The law, in effect, mirrors cultural and intellectual trends, and is never impervious to social, economic, and political processes. But this should not lead us to forget that law also possesses great autonomy, evolves according to its own internal dynamics, and is an active agent in shaping all the aforementioned areas. The structure of most of the chapters takes into account this dual role of the law as both a reflector and agent of history.

The work pays particular attention to the sources of law: the criteria upon which judges base their decisions. In the West the most important sources of law have always been four: jurisprudence, custom, court decisions, and legislation. These four elements constitute the axes of the arguments advanced in each chapter, with jurisprudence, perhaps, being assigned a slightly predominant role. Jurisprudence – the constant work of reflection and doctrine performed by legal scholars – is one of the most characteristic features of the European legal tradition, largely responsible for the very existence of the common tradition. In addition, readers who are not legal professionals will find in jurisprudence an easier way to recognize the legal world's contributions to culture and thought. Slightly more emphasis is also placed on private law, which until the eighteenth century included criminal law, than on public or constitutional law. For a long time private law was seen as the only true, permanent expression of juridicity; public law is, indeed, more dependent on political thought and also on raw power struggles. As such, it is more volatile and unstable. However, we are confident that we have given political and institutional frameworks, and the political ideas behind them, their due.

The structure of the work itself is essentially chronological. It begins in Rome and ends in the early twentieth century. The decision to start with Rome, instead of Greece, is owing to our aim to focus on the law as a shared language. There may be memorable or remarkable cases of ancient Greek law, such as the Draconian laws, inspiring images of texts written in blood rather than ink, but, generally speaking, the ancient Greeks left no traces on the law as a common language. Only Roman law provided a shared legal vocabulary and grammar of that language. The texts upon which jurists would work for several hundreds of years, even after the collapse of the Empire, were purely Roman. It was in ancient Rome that law was first emancipated from religion, morals, and politics. Such is its enduring gift to mankind, and the basis for our own conception of what law is.

It may appear paradoxical to end this book short of the moment when law, as a shared language, seemed to receive an institutional embodiment through the founding of what was going to become the European Union in 1951. There are two reasons for this. The first is that we are all myopic. The great trends and key developments after World War II are still somewhat blurry. Yes, Europe has developed towards supranational integration, but as we write these very words the European Union is undergoing a deep identity crisis, visible in various problems, including the "Brexit," the scaling back of the Schengen Agreement, and a deep financial crisis not unconnected to the common currency and the European Central Bank. Within a few years the European Union may be viewed as but an accident of history, like the former Soviet Union. And, yes, law has extended into new fields of interest, and it will continue to do so. But the language of the law remains essentially identical, as it builds on foundations, categories, and techniques that are centuries old. No transnational organization, no new area of interest has changed this. We thought it wise to leave analysis of the legal developments after World War II to the specialists in the relevant fields. The second reason is that an account of European legal history in the second half of the twentieth century could appear geographically limited, as developments within Europe, particularly in legal thought, are increasingly influenced by non-European experiences, particularly – but not only – in the United States. Attempting to address this in a short chapter would create conflicts, in terms of consistency, not justified by the limited benefits that could be expected from such a necessarily eclectic endeavor.

We do not underestimate you, our dear readers. We are aware that we are asking a lot from you, particularly from those of you who are not immediately familiar with the outlines of a Europe-centered history. We have faced two challenges here. The first one is the book's focus on the history of the sources of the law, with a slight emphasis on jurisprudence, which sometimes makes for a highly theoretical account. We provide examples to illustrate the text, but these typically refer to the formal sources themselves, not to substantive law. It would be fascinating to compare, for example, the historical evolution of non-contractual liability in civil law systems with that of the common law of torts, or the evolution of the civil law of obligations and contracts with that of the *assumpsit* and consideration in common law, or property law, family law, criminal law … However, addressing these topics and linking them to the general discussion would require such a level of detail that it would probably alter the book's whole approach, and would hamper our communication with most of you. The second challenge was more practical. The book covers such a wide span of time, with so many different characters, concepts, and institutions, that it would take a lifetime to explain them all in detail. In the brief account that we envisioned, it was sometimes necessary to provide only the most concise information on certain concepts or characters. Footnotes are lacking too. We are aware that almost every sentence in this work is debatable, and might benefit from further refinement. Once again, though, including footnotes to introduce a nuance, or a reference to an authority, or an alternative standpoint, would hinder reading and inflate the size of the book, throwing up another barrier between its authors and the reader. We did include a select bibliography at the end of the book, with you in mind, curious reader, rather than critics or academicians. The works listed there refer you, in turn, to even more specialized books and articles.

No true teacher of the law can remain unmoved by Justinian's brief, yet warm salutation. This book is dedicated to law students: those filling law school classrooms today, those who will do so tomorrow, and also those who did so in the past. Thanks to their efforts law in the West – a cornerstone of its freedom – retains the vigor of youth, even at the ripe old age of 2,500.

1. Roman law

I. JUSTINIAN

A. The Codification Project

The main source of current knowledge of Roman law is a collection of texts collectively referred to since the fifteenth century as the *Corpus iuris civilis,* or simply the *Corpus iuris*. This collection is made up of four books: the *Digest*, *Institutiones*, *Codex* and *Novellae,* all of them drafted at the behest of Emperor Justinian (527–65) in the first half of the sixth century.

In his palace in Constantinople, the "new Rome," Justinian dreamt of restoring the glory and the unity of the Empire, ruptured by the barbarian invasions. He considered himself the direct successor of the illustrious line made up of Romulus, Caesar, Augustus and Constantine. Thanks to the recapture of Rome and the rest of Italy, he was largely successful in this endeavor. However, in Justinian's eyes the renovated Empire was in need not just of military success, but also of the solid foundations that only laws can provide. Thus, he undertook a colossal codification and legislation project.

A small commission of jurists led by the cultured and able Tribonian took on this ambitious undertaking. Their main mission was to carry out a careful selection of texts and rules based on the writings of the most renowned jurisconsults of the past centuries, as well as laws from the Roman imperial period. They were not charged with designing or drafting new legislation, for which reason they came to be called "compilers," referring to their role as textual "stackers": after excerpting from ancient legal books those materials that were still of value, in their view, they proceeded to "stack" them, by arranging the excerpted texts under new subject headings.

The *Institutiones* (commonly referred to as the *Institutes* in English) is a brief textbook intended for students beginning their legal studies; in short, an introduction to law. The work was studied at all the Empire's law schools, both because it contained the most important principles of jurisprudence, and because Justinian granted it the force of law. The source of inspiration behind it was the eponymous book by the second-century lawyer Gaius. It divides private law – the *ius* – into three parts. After a brief introduction, it addresses law governing persons and family, followed by that pertaining to things, in turn divided into law applying to property, obligations and inheritances. A final section covers civil procedural law. This tripartite distribution – persons, things and actions – would be adopted as a model for the structural arrangement of numerous legal books in the modern era. The order of the *Institutes* is still very recognizable in both the French *Code civil* (1804) and the many that it inspired, such as Spain's (1888–1889) and Italy's (1942) as well as the German Bürgerliches Gesetzbuch (BGB) (1900).

But the most ambitious work forming part of Justinian's project was, without any doubt, the *Digest* (*Digesta* in Latin; *Pandektes* in Greek, meaning "all-containing," among other possible translations). The *Digest* represents an anthology of excerpts from classical Roman legal texts. In their pursuit the compilers reported to have read over two thousand scrolls and volumes containing some three million cases, with their corresponding legal *regulae* (solutions to actual or hypothetical cases put forward by the jurisconsults). From this massive volume of material their charge was to cull what was still of value in the sixth century. In the end the compilers chose approximately 5 percent of the writings at their disposal and divided them into 50 books featuring fragments of writings from 39 jurists active from the first century BC through the third century AD. However, the commission did not limit itself to collecting and selecting; its purpose was not so much to faithfully transmit the original texts as it was to draw up a new code based on them. Thus, they did not hesitate to rework and alter some fragments in order to edit out contradictions, eliminate superfluities and repetitions, update legal terms that had fallen into disuse and, in general, adapt the texts to current circumstances. These alterations are known as "interpolations." All in all, the *Digest* is a truly monumental anthology of classical Roman jurisprudence. Justinian gave it the force of law in 533.

The third part of Justinian's codification project was the *Codex* (534), which contains fragments of laws enacted by the Roman emperors as of Hadrian (117–38). In the fourth and fifth centuries, coinciding with absolute monarchy, imperial legislation became the primary and almost exclusive source of law. The commission of compilers was called upon to discern, from amidst the huge mass of laws, those which continued to be valuable. The compilers were inspired by and drew upon previous, similar initiatives (though smaller in scope) such as the *Codex Theodosianus* (439), of Emperor Theodosius II (408–50), or the *Codex vetus* (*Old code*, 529), commissioned by Justinian himself at the beginning of his reign. As a tribute to the Law of the Twelve Tables – the initial, legendary compilation of Roman law – the new *Codex* was divided into 12 books, dealing with ecclesiastical law, sources of law, administrative law, private law, criminal law and tax law, in this order.

With the *Codex*, Justinian's project came to an end; the laws enacted after 534 were never officially compiled, although this did form part of Justinian's plans. Some of these new laws, however, for which Justinian himself and his immediate successors were responsible, were grouped into private collections known as the *Novellae constitutiones* (*New laws*) or simply *Novellae.*

B. The Historical Background of the *Digest*

The *Digest* stands out from among the books of the *Corpus iuris* as an illustration of Rome's legal genius and its unparalleled originality. Formally Roman law did not recognize jurisprudence (*iuris prudentia* or *iuris scientia*, knowledge of the law) as a legitimate source of law. The advice and opinions (*responsa*) of jurisconsults (*iuris prudentes*, "those who know the law," here referred to interchangeably as "jurists") lacked normative force, although in practice they enjoyed great influence. Recognizing this social reality, the first emperors granted the most eminent jurists the privilege to reply on their behalf to legal questions posed to them, the so-called *ius respondendi.* While the opinion of such eminent jurists officially lacked normative force, the reality is that judges to whom these opinions were presented rarely deviated from them. This is just one more example of the characteristic distinction and balance maintained in Rome in all areas between *potestas* (formally valid and binding power) and *auctoritas* (socially recognized prestige or authority). For centuries it was the jurists who, with their peculiar *auctoritas*, contributed to the thorough refinement and development of Roman law.

This unofficial status, however, was also a source of problems. Firstly, not all jurists' writings were easily accessible in an empire as vast as that of Rome. In addition, after centuries of accumulation and refinement of legal knowledge, the sheer number of writings and opinions proved excessive, significantly undermining their effective application. Finally, not all the writings and jurists agreed, clashing on many issues. In an effort to solve these problems, Emperor Theodosius II considered the possibility of carrying out a selection of those texts and writings retaining contemporary value, but the plan could not be carried out. Theodosius then enacted the *Lex citandi* (426), the Law of Citations, which stated that only the writings of five classic jurists – Papinian, Paulus, Gaius, Ulpian and Modestinus – could be invoked before the courts, and established the procedure to be adopted should the opinions of these five jurists conflict: the majority opinion was to be respected; in the event of a tie that of Papinian was to prevail; and where Papinian had issued no decision on the issue, it was up to the judge to choose between the other opinions.

In the end the Law of Citations proved to be no solution. Some writings were difficult to find, or their authenticity was questioned. Moreover, the system of numerical majority was not devoid of arbitrariness. As such, it starkly conflicted with the very essence of Romans' conception of the law: legal problems were expected to have rational, not arbitrary solutions, as was such dependence on chance majorities. However, the Law of Citations would end up having a lasting influence when Justinian set about resuming Theodosius's project of selecting those legal texts with contemporary value. It is no coincidence that the vast majority of the fragments in the *Digest* came from the writings of the five jurists recognized by the Law of Citations; the other 34 jurists cited in the *Digest* account for only a small portion of the total.

In another example of sharp conflict with the spirit of classical jurisprudence, Justinian prohibited the drafting of further comments or additional interpretations of the *Digest*. If an excerpt was found to be vague, the question was to be referred to the emperor. The objective was thereby to prevent the excessive proliferation of opinions and interpretations, so characteristic of classical times, and which had inspired the Justinian compilation in the first place. This prohibition exemplifies how the emperor presented and established himself as the sole source of law, expressing the monarch's ideological and political agenda. It also illustrates how the *Digest* marked the end of an entire era, the involuntary certification of the demise of Rome's great tradition of jurisprudence.

C. The Importance of the *Corpus Iuris*

In practice Justinian's work was of limited importance during the sixth century and those immediately following. Any possible application of the new codes proved impossible in the West when Italy fell to a group of fierce warriors dubbed Langobards or Lombards ("those with long beards"). Justinian's recovery of Rome for the Empire would prove a brilliant but ephemeral reality. The codification did not take root in the eastern part of the Empire either. To begin with, it encountered a linguistic problem: as a collection of ancient Roman excerpts, the *Digest* was written almost entirely in Latin, despite the fact that Greek was the dominant language and the number of people speaking Latin was rapidly decreasing. There were, in addition, distribution problems: copies were sent to the provincial capitals, but transcription was very expensive, placing the books out of reach for most engaged in legal tasks. Furthermore, in many places around the Empire the codes failed to supplant systems of customary law, which continued to be applied at the local level. Finally, the vastness, complex structure and casuistic nature of Justinian's work made it difficult for most law practitioners to use it.

The transcendental importance of the *Digest*, however, lay not in its having been applied to varying degrees in a particular place or moment, but in its having been adopted, as of the eleventh century, as the document wielding the greatest legal authority in Europe. Its rediscovery in the eleventh century triggered not only a completely new way of understanding law, but also lay at the very origin of the medieval university and the scholastic method, which, born of study of the *Digest*, was soon successfully applied to theology, philosophy, and all the different branches of knowledge. Justinian's project, moreover, was the first major codification of laws: its purpose was to collect all law in a manageable and understandable set of books which aspired to unity, completeness and exclusiveness – principles that inspired the codification movements of the eighteenth and nineteenth centuries. Finally, the *Corpus iuris* was the foremost historical source of law in Roman times. The *Digest* condenses ten centuries of the richest and most original jurisprudence to have ever existed. In fact, we owe our current knowledge of some Roman jurists exclusively to their incorporation in the *Digest*.

II. THE HISTORY OF ROME

A. The Archaic Period

According to legend, Rome was founded in the year 753BC on seven small hills on the shores of the Tiber. Multiple Italic peoples were involved in its inception: Latins, Sabines and Etruscans. The most important of them were the Latins, of Indo-European origin, who were organized into family clans (*gentes*) that possessed most of the land, filled the ranks of the priesthood and the army, and, in short, essentially provided Rome with its language, culture and religion. This was a society based on agriculture and livestock, and a radically patriarchal one in which the *paterfamilias* was, quite simply, the owner of his family, which included his wife, children, slaves and livestock. He also acted as a patron for a more or less numerous group of voluntary subordinates: his *clientes*. Legal capacity and the full right to act lay with him, the only party capable of acting in his own right. His wife and children depended on him legally, even after they had grown into adulthood, while slaves were equivalent to livestock or "things." This core legal structure of the archaic times would leave a long-lasting footprint on family law and property law. The Latins' form of government was based on an elective monarchy for life in which the ruler (*rex* – literally king) wielded supreme power (*imperium*), which encompassed all political, military and religious functions.

With the rise of Etruscan society in what is now Tuscany, Rome, due to its geographical position, acquired strategic value. The Etruscans made it part of their trade routes with the Carthaginian and Greek colonies in the south of the Peninsula. As the Roman economy opened up to trade, the Etruscans' power grew, and they took control of the monarchy. In 509BC the so-called "patricians" – the landowning nobility of Latin descent – rebelled and established the Republic. The term *rex* was stigmatized and would become one of the most enduring taboos in Roman politics; not even the most powerful emperors, many centuries later, would dare to call themselves *reges*, or kings.

The new constitutional order's main concern was to prevent the excessive concentration of power. *Imperium* came to be exercised by two consuls, necessarily of patrician origin, chosen for one-year periods and with mutual veto power. Later other magistracies would be added – *praetors*, *aediles*, *quaestors* – while almost always maintaining the same temporary and collegial nature. The popular assemblies were organized in a range of ways, but always assured the preponderance of the upper classes, which were charged with choosing the magistrates and voting upon their proposed laws. The plebeians, those Roman citizens who were not patricians, met separately in the plebeian council. Over all of them stood the Senate, the gathering of the *patres* (from *pater*, the Latin word for "father"), which, however, theoretically lacked *potestas*. The well-known slogan *Senatus populusque Romanus* ("the Senate and the people of Rome") summarized the various organic elements of the Roman city, stressing its unity and majesty (*maiestas*).

The first centuries of the Republic were marked by constant demands lodged with the patricians by the plebeians, who were originally excluded from all public positions. This struggle was usually resolved via specific commitments, with concessions granted providing the plebeians access to this or that magistracy, or new ones were created, such as the plebeian tribunes, which featured a special inviolability and were specifically dedicated to defending their interests, being the only magistrates with right of legislative initiative. One of these commitments spawned the Romans' first legal code: the Law of the Twelve Tables. The Twelve Tables put legal directives down in writing for all to see. Hitherto those legal directives had been discreetly transmitted and drafted in pontifical colleges, with access thereto restricted to patricians. Ultimately, the distinction between patricians and plebeians came to be all but devoid of institutional importance.

In addition to the restlessness within it, the young Republic would also face external pressures as a result of the expulsion of the Etruscan kings. Rome managed to consolidate its position of power in the center of the Italian Peninsula and gradually to expand its sphere of influence, as military victories induced peoples from central Italy to forge alliances with the city of the she-wolf. By the beginning of the third century BC Rome would control the entire Peninsula.

The era covering the Roman monarchy and the first centuries of the Republic is sometimes called the Archaic Period, and extends roughly until the outbreak of the Punic Wars – Rome's clashes with Carthage, the other great power in the Western Mediterranean – in 264BC.

B. The Republic

The expansion of Rome's area of influence into Southern and Western Europe, North Africa, the Middle East and Egypt deeply transformed Roman society and the entire ancient world. Its initially agricultural character would give way to an economy based on large-scale trade and massive financial operations. In Rome the distinction between patricians and plebeians was largely superseded by a new distinction between a proletariat and an aristocracy made up of the senatorial class and the richest of the plebeians. Power in republican politics continued to emanate from the Senate, a purely aristocratic institution composed of illustrious patricians serving for life and plebeians who had risen to become consuls, or their descendants. As the dominions expanded it became evident that republican political structures no longer responded adequately to the new needs. After the first century BC, which saw Rome suffer through a state of almost permanent civil war, and after some attempts at the personal seizure of power (by Sulla and Julius Caesar), Octavian took over in 27BC.

During this era Rome came into closer contact with Greek culture, which had a certain effect on the development of law in the Late Republic. It was not that the Greeks had developed their own jurisprudence; the importance of Greek influence on Roman law is explained more in terms of philosophy, rhetoric and logic, all fields impinging upon but not falling precisely under law. It is no coincidence that the scientific and systematic study of law began in the second century BC after the conquest of Macedonia and Greece, when the Romans began to organize and refine legal texts and to develop some abstract legal concepts, without sacrificing their typically Roman pragmatism. In summary, Hellenic influence on Roman law was limited; the essence of Rome's *ius* remained intact, true to its native genius.

Contact with other peoples and the influx into Rome of foreigners and non-citizens lay at the origin of the *ius gentium*, literally meaning the "law of peoples," a system which did not constitute international law in the sense of one governing relations between nations, but rather law created and developed by the Romans, in accordance with Roman categories, to settle disputes involving one or more foreigners. The *ius civile* (or *ius Quiritium*) could be applied only to people enjoying Roman citizenship (*cives* or *Quirites*). The *ius gentium* contained a general system of private law consisting of legal rules formulated in a general way and based on values of fairness and reason. Precisely because the *ius gentium* was based on general views of justice, succeeding jurists have often identified it with *ius naturale*, or natural law. This notion, however, already familiar to the Romans due to Greek influence, would not be developed in Rome to the extent that it would in modern Europe.

C. The Principate

Though young, when Octavian took power he already boasted experience as an administrator and general. Called "Caesar" by his adoptive father, and "Augustus" (a title with religious connotations) after winning the last civil war during the Republic, he gradually managed, with remarkable political sagacity, for the entire Republican order to revolve around him – a regime of which he was, in appearance, the restorer. Octavian took constant care to avoid being called a king (*rex*) or a dictator. Rather, he purported to be only the first among his equals, the *princeps senatus*, he who presided over the Senate, to which he belonged. Formally the Republic still stood, and there was no trace of the emperor as an institutionalized position; originally *imperator* only meant "commander in chief". Although Octavian (or Augustus, as he came to be more generally called) managed to hold sway over all of Rome's social and political life, he remained formally outside the order of the republican magistracies, content to serve as their protector, closely linking his exceptional charisma to the majesty of the Roman people. Augustus limited himself to securing his power within the republican order by assuming strategic positions within it, such as plebeian tribune, the only magistrate with legislative initiative, a capacity in which he served for life, and occasionally as consul and supreme pontiff (*pontifex maximus*). The new regime can, therefore, be considered a duopoly, with two centers of power: the emperor and the Senate. With Augustus's ascent to power the Senate had not suddenly turned into a servile institution, but remained a political factor whose opinions had to be taken into account. Important matters of state, such as the succession of the incumbent emperor, had to be negotiated and were subject to political settlements. In 27BC it was, therefore, not at all clear that Rome would be transformed into an Empire. It was Augustus's charismatic leadership and extraordinary political attributes, the solid relationship that the new order developed with public opinion, and the stunning period of peace and stability that he established, which ensured the continuity of the new regime after his death in AD14.

The Empire would continue to spread, incorporating the territories of what is today England, Romania and, for a brief period, Iraq. Men of exceptional political and military talents, such as Vespasian (69–79), Titus (79–81), Trajan (98–117), Hadrian (117–38), Antoninus Pius (138–61), Marcus Aurelius (161–80) and Septimius Severus (193–211) ably took over the helm of the Empire through a long era of peace and relative stability: the *Pax Romana*.

This period coincided with the apex of classical jurisprudence. It was during this era that emperors exalted and availed themselves of the most talented jurists, first through the concession of *ius respondendi*, and later also by appointing them to senior positions in the imperial administration.

At the beginning of the third century the Empire was immersed in a period of profound institutional crisis, sometimes bordering on anarchy, with a number of emperors being assassinated. In response Rome's rulers increasingly looked to the army as the basis of their power, at the Senate's expense. On its borders Rome was also on the defensive, and an economic crisis racked the entire Empire. With regard to jurisprudence, the death of Papinian (d. 212), one of the greatest jurists in Roman history, marked a certain decline, and with it the beginning of a transition to what has been called the post-classical era of Roman law. In 212 Caracalla (211–17), motivated by a desire to be able to levy taxes on a greater number of people, granted Roman citizenship to all free inhabitants of the Empire, making Roman law universal; this marked one of the key steps towards territorial integration and legal unity, which would accelerate during the Dominate.

D. The Dominate

After the crisis of the third century, two forceful figures – Diocletian (284–305) and Constantine (306–37) – managed to gain power and hold it firmly for a long period, though the latter would be forced to fight two civil wars to do so. Diocletian realized that he needed to limit the power of the army in order to stabilize the government. For this purpose he removed generals from key executive positions and fomented the development of a body of civil servants in each government branch. Such initiatives were complemented by the glorification and even worship of his own person; the emperor was no longer merely the *princeps* or "first citizen," but "lord over all," or *Dominus*. Diocletian employed a series of ceremonies to exalt his position, including substituting the old salutation by the prostration before the imperial purple robe, thereby illustrating the infinite distance between the emperor and his subjects. His few public appearances were orchestrated as epiphanies of an almost sacred nature. Thus ensued a period of absolute monarchy, depending upon an anonymous but effective bureaucracy, which came to be termed the Dominate.

During the Dominate the division between the Eastern Empire and Western Empire became more pronounced, and there was rarely optimal collaboration between the two. The center of power shifted towards Constantinople. In the West, Rome even lost its status as a political center when the seat of government was moved first to Milan, and then to Ravenna. With the Empire Christianized, only the Bishop of Rome remained an important political figure in the Eternal City.

Diocletian and Constantine did manage to keep the territorial integrity of the Empire essentially intact. The West, however, was devastated when in the fifth century Germanic and Asian barbarian tribes invaded in search of new territories. In 476 the last Western emperor was toppled. The eastern part of the Empire, however, managed to survive, and during the fifth century enjoyed a period of peace and relative prosperity. In the sixth century, under Justinian, it even undertook an attempt at expansion, albeit a short-lived one.

Theodosius I (379–95) was one of the last great emperors. In an attempt to shore up the crumbling unity of a politically, socially and ethnically diverse Empire he declared Christianity – already officially tolerated as of 313 and widely favored by Constantine – to be the Empire's sole and official religion. The Christianization of the Empire had consequences for private law, particularly with regard to that governing people and families, which was softened in comparison to the harsh family regime largely inherited from the Archaic Period. The legal status of slaves and women, for example, substantially improved. In other areas of law Christianity intensified a moralistic tendency and a certain disregard for form, which spread along with the classical *ius*. The growing importance of the bureaucracy tended to undermine the role of the classical jurists and their refined reasonings. Likewise, the bureaucratic vocation of post-classical jurists made them venture into areas beyond the old *ius*, such as administrative, tax, and criminal issues; the distinction between private law and public law became significant. Neither did jurisprudence escape the general crisis. Only in some schools of law, such as those at Berytus and Constantinople (modern-day Beirut and Istanbul) – both located, not coincidentally, in the eastern part of the Empire – was jurisprudence still cultivated.

III. THE EVOLUTION OF ROMAN LAW

A. Archaic Law

As with any primitive society, Roman law was initially characterized (seventh–fifth centuries BC) by a close connection between the legal and the religious spheres. Ancient Rome, however, would quite quickly draw a distinction between the two. Laws of a religious (or magical-religious) character were identified by means of the *fas–nefas* dichotomy. In order to remain in the good graces of the gods, who were also involved in and formed part of the community, society carefully assured that all human behavior was in accord with the concept of *fas*. Behavior contrary to *fas* was *nefas*: for example, high treason, the secular use of sacred sites, or the holding of a trial on any of the days on which this was forbidden. What was *nefas,* insofar as it affected the city's relationship to its gods, was capable of bringing down calamities on society as a whole, thereby threatening its very survival.

Though related in various ways, *ius* was different. *Ius*, the laws governing relationships between citizens, could be traced back to the *mos maiorum*, or customs of the elders. Behavior that somehow wronged a fellow citizen violated *ius* and, as such, constituted *iniuria*. This did not mean that these acts or behaviors lacked any connection with the divine or supernatural; for example, obligations fell under *fides* ("good faith"), an attribute and purview of Jupiter. However, it was recognized that *ius* essentially governed the sphere of relationships between individuals, without affecting the community as a whole.

The same rigidly ritualistic nature of *fas* was found in the archaic *ius*. If when dealing with *fas* it was necessary to thoroughly comply with the prescribed ritual in order to obtain the supernatural result desired (with expiatory offerings, for example), in the most ancient law it was also ritual and exact compliance with it that produced the desired effects. Thus was the case, for instance, with *mancipatio,* which was originally the only way to convey the ownership of Italic land, slaves or cattle: its legal effects proceeded not from the intention or the consent of the parties (basically irrelevant factors) but from proper execution of the corresponding ritual (seizure of the object in front of its owner, weighing a coin of copper or bronze on a scale in front of five adult witnesses, pronouncement of prescribed phrases). The same dynamic applied to civil procedure: a mistake in the pronouncement of the prescribed words – saying "vine" rather than "tree," for instance – sufficed to invalidate the action. Form and protocol would always retain considerable importance in Roman law, even in subsequent stages of its development.

The close relationship between *fas* and *ius* in the remote past is clearly evident from the fact that both were the exclusive competence – probably undifferentiated at first – of the same priestly college, that of the pontiffs (from *pontifex*, literally "bridge-builder"): sacrifices, calendars, and legal forms and models were viewed as phenomena of a similar nature. They, the pontiffs, were responsible not only for preserving and transmitting the law, but also interpreting and applying it. Thus, citizens submitted their legal questions and consultations to a pontiff who – as if he were an oracle, but without the ambiguity associated with Greek religious oracles – issued a brief and precise response. This method of questions and answers (*responsa*) constituted the method intrinsic to the *ius* and, as such, would remain intact – preserving even its peculiar "oracle-like" character, defined by its conciseness and exactness – throughout its development, even after legal knowledge grew to be a secular sphere.

The existence of a rudimentary but complete body of jurisprudential thought as early as the era of the incipient Republic would be suddenly manifest when the plebeians, in the context of their struggle with the patricians (the only citizens permitted to enter the pontifical colleges), demanded the codification and subsequent publication of the *ius*. This would take place circa 450BC via the Law of the Twelve Tables, which condensed all the secular heritage of pontifical law into a general law known by all, patricians and plebeians alike. The entire *ius* would be open to public access in the form of 12 bronze tables hanging on the walls of the Forum. It is not possible to reconstruct the content of the law exactly, as the objects were lost due to a fire in 380BC. Towards the end of the Republic, knowledge of their content was already incomplete. It is clear, however, that most of their stipulations involved private and procedural law, along with some regarding sacred, criminal and public law; in summary, the areas encompassed by the pontifical *ius*. They did not contain regulations pertaining to the organization of the state. As such, the Twelve Tables did not represent an *avant-la-lettre* constitution. In the legal tradition, the Law of the Twelve Tables would acquire legendary status. Cicero (106–43BC) recalled how as a boy he learned the Law by heart, reciting it along with other children. During the Principate the law was still the object of jurisprudential comments, despite the fact that the text was no longer available.

With the drafting and publication of the Law of the Twelve Tables, however, the pontiffs did not suddenly relinquish their legal authority. Rather, they maintained their roles as privileged legal advisors: still turned to for *responsa*, they would retain control over the development of the *ius*. Only they knew and were versed in the law's provisions and its many exceptions, the models and forms for acts and actions, and the method and style that characterized the *ius*. It would not be until during the third century BC when the pontiffs gradually lost their monopoly on knowledge of and the application of the law, sharing it first with lay patricians who took an interest in these issues, and ultimately surrendering it altogether.

As a whole, archaic Roman law played a decisive role in shaping the *ius civile*. The core of it all came about during this period. Many of the specific elements of archaic law would subsist at the heart of Roman law in all its later developments. This may be explained by the fact that Roman law was, to an extreme degree, one based on history: the new did not replace the old via repeal and replacement, as this clashed with the Roman sensibility, characterized by a deep respect for tradition. Rather, new elements were only gradually superimposed over older ones as they fell into disuse, with a number of ancient ones enduring. Examples of ancient elements were the *mancipatio* ritual to convey ownership of important goods, and the *stipulatio*, the most ancient contract with a rigid form of questions and answers between the contracting parties.

Surely the most important and lasting achievement during this era, however, was how the *ius* came to be independent of *fas*, which marked nothing less than the gradual but inexorable establishment of law as a secular order. The radical autonomy of the specifically juridical – the perpetual search for a just, prudent and rational solution for each specific case (*suum cuique tribuere*: give to every one his due – Inst. 1.1.3–4) – is, without any doubt, one of Roman law's greatest achievements. This, which would become one of hallmarks of the West's identity, was conceived and achieved during this early age.

B. The *Ius Civile*

During the third century BC, the pontiffs saw their influence upon the application and development of law reduced as the jurists and praetors came to supplant them. At the beginning the study of law formed part of a young patrician's general education, along with military training and, somewhat later, rhetorical skills. Some of these men pursued their studies in the law and managed to acquire a deep level of understanding in this area. Increasingly their fellow citizens would turn to these legal scholars for legal advice. The jurists inherited function, method and style from the priests, continuing to formulate *responsa*: concise answers to particular cases with which they were presented. As a result, except for the Law of the Twelve Tables, the *ius civile* remained eminently casuistic.

In principle the *ius civile* applied only to the law of the Romans, i.e. those who possessed Roman citizenship. As of the third century BC the *ius* featured three layers or strata: the oldest and most archaic was made up of moral and custom-based precepts which, as a class, were referred to as *mos maiorum;* the Law of the Twelve Tables constituted a second stratum; while the last was formed by the *responsa*, issued by experts.

In general legislation was not decisive in this phase of private Roman law, nor was it in the subsequent phase, the Classical Era. The Roman Republic featured different types of legislation depending upon the assembly that approved it. However, *lex* did not have much influence on *ius*; with a few exceptions the Roman *leges* had to do mainly with public law and criminal law. The exceptions included the Law of the Twelve Tables and the *Lex Aquilia* (c. 287BC), a law that addressed specific difficulties on tort law without, however, regulating it systematically.

During the Republic the figure of the praetor, a magistrate who exercised jurisdiction, that is, who administrated justice, became central. Under the Republic the praetor was the second most prestigious magistrate after the consul and, like the latter, wielded *imperium*, or the highest executive power. As with the post of consul, praetors were appointed to one-year terms. They did not, however, operate as a body. Over time there were several praetors, but without forming a council with a veto right. It was a non-remunerated post, as were all the Republican magistracies.

Originally there was only one praetor, but as the population of the city increased due to a massive influx of foreigners, in the middle of the third century BC a second praetor was instituted. One of them, the *praetor urbanus*, continued to handle the administration of justice between Roman citizens, while the other, the *praetor peregrinus*, was responsible for the administration of justice between foreigners and between foreigners and Romans. Over time the need arose for the establishment of additional praetorships.

In order to fully comprehend the praetor's role as a central element in the evolution of Roman law it is necessary to understand the peculiar structure of Roman civil procedure. Civil procedure consisted of two stages, its bipartition enduring as one of its most noteworthy characteristics until well into the imperial era. The first phase, called *in iure,* took place before the praetor. The second phase, *apud iudicem*, "before the judge" or *iudex*. The praetor was a magistrate of the Republic, while the judge was a private citizen who did not occupy any honorary post and was appointed as needed. During the first phase the praetor, in the exercise of his jurisdictional authority, processed the suit in the legally established manner: he took note of the claim and the defenses (*exceptiones*), verified whether they fell under any of the cases provided for, and granted or denied the action. If he denied it the process ended. If he granted the action, the litigants passed to the next phase, before the judge, who would hear the witnesses and lawyers, learn about the facts in detail and, finally, without departing from the strict limits determined by the praetor when granting the action, issue his ruling. The praetor actively participated, along with the parties, in the legal evaluation of the case, while the judge was confined to passively hearing the evidence and arguments before ruling in favor of one party or the other. The first phase took place in public, in the northeastern zone of the Forum, the central square of Rome and the heart of political life, or in a basilica near it, such as the *basilica Aemilia.* The praetor received the parties clad in his *toga praetexta* (an ordinary white toga with a purple stripe on the border), on a platform (*tribunal*) and sitting in a curule chair, a folding and portable ivory stool, flanked by six lictors, a class of bodyguards who on their shoulders carried the *fasces*, a bound bundle of rods from which an axe blade protruded. Such were the symbols of *imperium* (originally exclusive to the *rex*), which the praetor wielded. The second phase, *apud iudicem*, was usually held in the Forum or basilica itself at an agreed-upon place, but did not feature any symbols of *imperium,* which the judge, a common citizen, utterly lacked.

The praetors were not necessarily experts in law, but rather experienced politicians eager to successfully ascend during their year as praetors the penultimate step in the ranking of public offices before they could become consuls. Nor was it common for the citizen acting as the judge to have legal training. Therefore, each of them was advised by a group of jurists.

The praetors inherited from the pontiffs a rigid and solemn civil process, ritualized with certain gestures and words. Legal complaints were to be processed according to a limited number of remedies called *legis actiones* ("actions of the law"), which constituted a mode of litigation peculiar to the Archaic period. What could not be formulated within a *legis actio* lacked legal protection, in which case the praetor was forced to deny access to justice. Such was the praetor's main task: to determine whether the claim was compatible with the *legis actio* according to which it was to be heard.

The influx of foreigners, to whom *ius civile* was not applied, augmented the discretionary capacity of the *praetor peregrinus*. For foreigners Roman law provided for the development of a different procedure: the procedure *per formulas*, or formulary procedure, which allowed the praetor to bypass the *legis actiones* and decide with greater autonomy whether to allow or reject an action. In accordance with the new formulary procedure the praetor, after analyzing the case with the parties, condensed and noted down on a *formula* (literally, a "little form"), in what were instructions binding upon the judge, the criteria according to which he was to rule after having examined the evidence. This was still a formal procedure, but one more flexible, versatile and responsive to changing legal and economic conditions. Soon pressures grew and opened up the new formulary procedure to suits between Roman citizens as well. Gradually the archaic *legis actiones* fell into disuse, and by the end of the Republic they were almost forgotten. Formulary procedure characterized and left its peculiar mark upon classical Roman law.

The formula was a kind of guide or script for the subsequent trial phase before the judge, which it authorized at the same time as it concluded the phase before the praetor. In essence it consisted of a description of a hypothesis whose ultimate substantiation was to determine the defendant's conviction or acquittal. This logical core could be supplemented by other elements or clauses, but these did not alter the general structure of the formula. More specifically, they usually contained, among other clauses, the designation of the judge, a concise description of the essential legal elements of the claim, the defendant's possible defense, and, in short, the instructions for the judge, always expressed in contingent format: if the aforestated turns out to be, convict (always pending the payment of a sum); if not, acquit. Let us look at a simple example, cited by Gaius (Gai. IV, 41–43): "Titius, act as judge. If it be proven that the defendant owes 10,000 sesterces to the claimant, sentence him to pay that amount; if not, acquit him." Logically, the statement of the factual hypothesis could become very complicated through the addition of clauses containing other elements relevant to the case, but the structure remained invariable.

Once the wording of the formula was determined, usually with the agreement of the parties, it was recorded on tablets in an act called the *litis contestatio* (something akin to a "public certification, before witnesses, of the suit"). Following the *litis contestatio* the object of the dispute could not be changed and it was no longer possible to initiate another process based on the same claim.

During the second phase of the trial the role of the private judge was limited to verifying facts and giving his opinion (*sententia*) with regards to the question set down in the formula. Indeed, if after the presentation of the evidence – witnesses, documents – the judge believed that the facts described in the formula were true, he was obligated to convict the defendant. If he did not consider the facts proven, or if he considered the facts presented in the defense to have been proven, he was compelled to acquit him. He was also obliged to respect the legal qualification of the facts made by the praetor and the parties in the formula: if it said therein that the amount requested was pursuant to a deposit agreement, the judge could not investigate whether the contract was instead a lease. For all these reasons, the exact wording of the formula was crucial.

During the Republican period there was no possibility of appealing the judge's verdict, because, after all, a common citizen designated for the occasion did not form part of any hierarchical organization in which a superior could correct the errors of his subordinate. The possibility of appealing civil judgments would only appear with the Empire and, in particular, the development of its hierarchically structured judicial bureaucracy.

The execution of the judgment was primarily the responsibility of the parties, as there was no effective enforcement by the Roman authorities. Since, theoretically, a debtor responded with his limbs when he failed to comply with the decision, the creditor could physically apprehend him and take him before the praetor. He would be released from his creditor's hands only by complying with the judgment. The spread of personal guarantees and Rome's peculiar social structure meant that if the defendant had no assets his patron or friends would usually take care of payment.

The success of formulary litigation was related to the praetors' growing exercise of their power to issue edicts of obligatory compliance, which the praetor possessed, along with other magistrates, *aediles*, consuls and censors. Thus, every year, upon taking possession of his office, the praetor published an edict in which he announced the remedies or classes of claims he would be entertaining, something like the legal manifesto for his term in office, which he would place on the walls of the Forum, on a set of whitewashed wooden tablets. As a program this edict was valid only for the period during which the individual praetor occupied his position: one year. In theory every praetor was free to completely rewrite these edicts, but in practice they repeated the majority of the content established by predecessors, with amendments or innovations suggested by the jurists, based on their having found them necessary during the latest annual terms of the praetor's office. Thanks to the conscious adoption of preceding praetors' promulgations, by the end of the Republic a core of praetorian actions had been developed which remained, nevertheless, subject to adjustments by future praetors. In this wise balance between tradition and innovation, along with the versatility of formulary procedure, lies the secret of the extraordinary development of the law by praetors during the central centuries of Roman history.

The set of precepts contained in the edicts of the praetors was termed *ius praetorium* ("the law of the praetors") or, more generally, *ius honorarium* (as the magistracies were known as *honores*, and to include the *aediles*, lower magistrates who also issued edicts governing commerce). *Ius honorarium*, or honorary law, would ultimately make up a complete legal system. It did not, however, replace the old *ius civile*, but rather overlapped or was juxtaposed to it to supplement it. The praetors, indeed, did not alter the basic nucleus of archaic law. A profound respect for the *ius civile*, passed down from generation to generation, from time immemorial, a manifestation of Roman society's general conservatism, prevented the praetors from transforming this nucleus. Still, they could supplement and adapt it to the changing circumstances. The old *Lex Aquilia*, for example, did not contain, strictly speaking, a general precept establishing civil responsibility. Killing a slave or a piece of livestock entailed the requirement to offer compensation equivalent to its market value, as was the case with other damages. It was the creative activity of the praetors which extended the scope of the law's application and made it possible to establish analogies with other cases, without abandoning the pragmatic legal casuistry that characterized the Roman genius, wary of abstract formulations.

In the Late Republic there were already patricians expert in legal questions who were fully-fledged jurists: experts dedicated exclusively and professionally to the study of law and to the rendering of legal counsel – although never in exchange for economic remuneration, which was considered beneath their dignity. What the jurists did not do was act as lawyers or advocates, an activity that was exercised by a different set of professionals: the orators and rhetoricians. Nor did they often serve as judges, and only rarely did they aspire to executive magistracies. The primary function of the jurists or jurisconsults was to analyze legal problems and issue expert opinions to citizens, to orators, to magistrates and judges. In their capacity as advisors they formed part of the councils assisting the praetor or judge during proceedings. Their opinions, or *responsa*, did not have binding force, but were assigned great social and moral value (*auctoritas*), and served as precedents. Jurists also drafted documents and deeds for acts of sale, contracts and wills, and helped to draft the exact formula of the first phase of trial proceedings. Cicero –

who was not a jurist, but rather an orator and politician – summarized the activities of the Roman jurists as this three-fold role: *cavere* (drafting the documents of legal acts), *agere* (advising litigants and officials during suits) and *respondere* (responding to legal questions and giving advice).

Thus far we have used the term *ius civile* with different meanings, which must now be more clearly defined. In the first place, the *ius civile* (or *ius Quiritium*) stood apart from and in contrast to the *ius honorarium* (or *ius praetorium).* Its essential core, which consisted of the custom-based law of the *mos maiorum*, the Twelve Tables and the *responsa* of the pontifical college (*ius civile*), was conceived as different from the edicts and remedies granted by the praetors (*ius honorarium*). The term *ius civile* bore a different meaning when considered relative to the *ius gentium.* In this case *ius civile* was synonymous with *ius proprium civium Romanorum*, the "law peculiar to Roman citizens," designating the set of institutions and prescripts applying to holders of Roman citizenship, *ius honorarium* thus being included. The *ius gentium* was, in contrast to this meaning of *ius civile*, law that applied to foreigners and the relationships between Romans and foreigners.

C. Classical Roman Jurisprudence

During the Principate republican institutions did endure, although the emperor took over some of their functions. There were not, therefore, major changes in terms of legal sources. The different types of legislation continued to exist, and the emperor made rather sparing use of his legislative power to forge or force changes in the law or to steer policy in one direction or another. Thus, the evolution of the law continued its traditional course, though with some slight shifts.

The emperor, as any other distinguished citizen, could be asked for his views on legal matters. In theory his response was not binding, as the emperor replied based on his personal experience (and assisted by his council of jurists). In practice his prestige and charismatic authority were so great that no judge flouted the emperor's opinion. As this practice spread and the emperor no longer had time to reply in person to the many questions brought before him, he delegated this task to a small cadre of highly renowned jurists, to whom he conceded the *ius respondendi ex auctoritate principis* (or simply the *ius respondendi*), i.e. the authority to give *responsa* based on the emperor's authority while retaining their status as private jurisconsults. Through a subtle process involving the transmission and combination of the emperor's charisma and the personal authority of the most distinguished jurisconsults, the skillful handling of the *ius respondendi* by the first emperors allowed them to augment both their prestige and that of their jurists, as they discreetly controlled the development of law while drawing the finest jurists into the imperial orbit. By the second half of the second century the most eminent jurists had joined the imperial council on a permanent basis, rendering the practice of the *ius respondendi* unnecessary. Henceforth, a bureaucratic administration would be responsible for responding to countless queries submitted to the emperor from all corners of the Empire. The consultations thus dealt with on the emperor's behalf came to be called *rescripta*, as the answers to them were written down on the same documents (hence *re-scripta*) submitted by those making the requests. In principle the *rescripta* lacked legal validity, but the exceptional, charismatic authority of the person behind them meant that they were followed in most cases.

Thanks to the practices of *ius respondendi* and *rescripta*, it is hardly surprising that during the Principate jurisprudence was considered the most important source of law – more than legislation, custom-based rights, or the administration of justice. This constituted the era of classical jurisprudence, thus termed due to the extraordinary perfection of its style. During this period Roman jurisprudence reached its peak, a phenomenon reflected in the high social regard in which jurists came to be held.

A number of elements contributed to this development. Firstly, the praetors' formerly considerable power was on the wane, due in part to the institutional organization of the new imperial regime, but also because the fixed core of the *ius honorarium* reached such a point of refinement and breadth that the changes introduced to edicts by praetors became fewer and farther between, made less necessary with each passing year. Emperor Hadrian recognized this situation, in AD138 producing a final drafting of the edict, later to be dubbed the *Edictum perpetuum* (or "Perpetual Edict"). This constituted the most palpable demonstration that the praetors had ceased to be those driving the evolution of the law. Secondly, in 212 Emperor Caracalla granted Roman citizenship to all free subjects in the Empire, generating increased demand for capable jurists trained in Roman law.

The first great figure of this classical period, and one of the most important in all of Roman jurisprudence, was Labeo (Marcus Antistius Labeo, 43BC–AD20). Labeo was fully dedicated to his career as a legal scholar, alternately dedicating his time to study, authoring books, and serving as a jurisconsult. He was a creative jurist who promoted new institutions; his collection of *responsa* and Commentaries on the praetor's Edict were extremely influential. Faithful to the republican tradition, he was uneasy under the new regime of Augustus, which sometimes meant that he was at odds with Gaius Aterius Capito (30BC–AD22), a jurist with a considerable reputation who was a strong proponent of the Principate. Both Labeo and Capito acquired noteworthy followings of students.

Together with Labeo, another key figure in Roman jurisprudence was Julian (Publius Salvius Iulianus, c. AD100–170). Hailing from North Africa, he belonged to Hadrian's council, followed by those of Antoninus Pius and Marcus Aurelius. He rose to consul and was a governor in several provinces, including *Hispania Citerior*. A brilliant jurist with a powerful personality who left his mark in a number of areas, Julian was charged by Hadrian with codifying the praetor's edict, or the Perpetual Edict. Julian wrote several works, among which his *Digesta* (*Digestorum libri XQ*), which was lost.

A contemporary of Julian was Pomponius (Sextus Pomponius, second century AD). His introduction to the law, the *Enchiridion,* is unique in its adoption of a historical perspective: in it the author sought to explain how the *ius civile* had been born, grown and evolved into its present form. We owe much of our current knowledge of the *ius civile* and its evolution to Pomponius and the inclusion in Justinian's *Digest* of some key excerpts of his work.

About Gaius (c. 120–178), another prominent man of law, we know almost nothing. He never occupied important positions and must have served as a professor of law in an eastern province. He would go down in history as the author of the *Institutiones*, a textbook for students containing an elementary introduction to law, written around 160. He was not an innovative jurist, which explains why he was not cited by any contemporaries or immediate successors. His work, however, was chosen as a course book in the schools at Berytus and Constantinople, where it enjoyed great success and acclaim, perhaps because it anticipated the post-classical style. The *Institutiones* possesses great value for us as the only work from the classical stage that has come down to us almost fully intact and free of any manipulation by the Justinian compilers. The model of the *Institutiones* and the division of the law into persons, things and actions – in which Gaius deviated from previous systems, and which would be enshrined in Justinian's *Institutiones* – forms the structural basis for most of the civil codes drawn up in the eighteenth and nineteenth centuries.

Papinian (Aemilius Papinianus, 142–212) is considered the greatest jurist of the classical era. Probably born in Syria, he held high positions in the administration of Septimius Severus. In 212 he was killed in the conflict between Caracalla and his brother. Papinian's most important works are his *Quaestiones* (*Quaestionum libri XXXVII*) and *Responsa*

(*Responsorum libri XIX*), consisting of specific cases and featuring critiques of the views of ancient jurists, imperial decrees and directives from high-ranking officials in the administration. His original and well-reasoned thinking earned him recognition as one of the outstanding figures in the history of jurisprudence; his contemporaries recognized his eminence, with the Law of Citations qualifying him as preeminent among jurists.

Ulpian (Gnaeus Domitius Annius Ulpianus, c. 170–228) served as an advisor in the imperial legal secretariat headed by Papinian. After ably navigating turbulent waters in the wake of the deaths of Septimius Severus and Caracalla, he ascended to high political positions under Alexander Severus. Like his master Papinian, however, he was killed during an uprising of the Praetorian Guard in 228. His body of work is encyclopedic, though it does not approach the originality of the early classics. His most important writings were a commentary on the work of Masurius Sabinus, who in the first century had written a synthesis of the *ius civile*, and a commentary on the Perpetual Edict. Thus did Ulpian bridge the two systems of Roman law: the *ius civile* and the *ius honorarium.* He is noteworthy for having consulted many older commentaries, gathering the opinions of preceding jurists. For this reason Justinian's compilers turned mainly to the works of Ulpian in almost half of their great work.

The career of Paulus (Iulius Paulus) was similar to that of Ulpian, as he worked under the orders of Papinian at the beginning, and succeeded Ulpian when he was killed. Like Ulpian, he wrote commentaries on the *ius civile* and the Perpetual Edict, in addition to the usual collections of questions and opinions, an introduction to law, and various manuals for the imperial administration. Paulus boasted many followers and his work achieved great prestige. Like Ulpian, his importance stems, above all, from his capacity for synthesis. His prestige as a jurist earned him the honorific title of *prudentissimus* (literally, "the very learned one") granted by the emperor.

The last lawyer mentioned here, as in the Law of Citations, is Modestinus (Herennius Modestinus, around the middle of the third century), about whose life we know almost nothing. Neither are there important commentaries that may be attributed to him, but only a few shorter monographs and manuals on various aspects of the law.

Legal literature featured a range of different genres: collections of opinions and rulings, commentaries on the Perpetual Edict, others on the *ius civile*; all kinds of didactic manuals, like *Institutiones*; monographs on specific subjects, and annotations on the writings of other jurists. With the exception of some didactic textbooks, most of these writings were not notable for their logical or systematic structures. Like Roman law as a whole, Roman jurisprudence was essentially casuistic and lacking in abstract formulations.

The Romans' hostility to abstraction is also evident in their reticence towards the establishment of legal concepts; the celebrated quote by Iavolenus Priscus appearing in the *Digest* is telling: "*omnis definitio in iure civili peliculosa est; parum est enim, ut non subverti posset*" ("in the *ius civile* every definition is dangerous, since there is little that cannot be undermined" – Dig. 50.17.202). The same innate aversion to abstraction prevented the development of a jargon excessively distanced from common language – though Roman legal language was technical, to be sure. It is remarkable how Roman jurists preferred verbs of action to nouns derived from verbs, which they used very seldom; concepts such as legal capacity, nullity, contract, property, etc., are rare in Latin. This preference for the concrete does not mean, however, that leading Roman jurists were not masters of the subtleties of logical and analytical reasoning.

D. Post-classical Law

During the Dominate the influence of jurisprudence on the evolution of the law dwindled and almost disappeared. The first cause of this was a shift in the structure of the state: now an absolute monarch came to rule through imperial decrees, drafted in a pompous, imperious style totally alien to the concise elegance of the classical *ius*. The emperor became the mainspring of law. Jurisprudence fell under the emperor's exclusive control: with the Law of Citations it was he who conferred binding power upon the views of the five great jurists. The centralization of all the sources of law in the hands the emperor, assisted by an anonymous bureaucracy, limited its creativity. During the Dominate legal literature was entirely dependent upon and derivative of that produced during the Classical Era. Thus impoverished, the law came to exhibit the traits of what is known as "vulgarism," characterized by: a tendency to suppress everything that seemed too complex or useless for judicial use; a naturalist trend to approach law from the point of view of its economic or sociological effects, eschewing conceptual categories and the traditional autonomy of jurisprudence; and, finally, a moralistic tendency, which sought justice-dispensing solutions with scant regard for form, as vividly reflected in the vulgar concept of *directum* ("the straight way"). It is no coincidence that Romance languages refer to law as *derecho*, *droit*, *diritto*, *dereito*, etc.

But the Dominate was not utterly devoid of advances. The imperial constitutions were collected and became the object of commentaries. Law schools also flourished, reaching their apex during this era. While their contributions in terms of creating and driving the evolution of the law were meager, they certainly functioned to preserve the classical heritage. As early as the second century law schools had already been founded to educate and train future officials, such as the *Athenaeum* in Rome, founded by Hadrian, and the school of Berytus, known by its reputation and importance as *Nutrix Legum* ("Mother of Laws"). It was in the fourth century when, in addition to those two, law schools were also founded in Constantinople, Athens, Carthage, Alexandria and Caesarea. The didactic needs of these institutions explain the development of anthologies of the classical jurists' works. The *Pauli Sententiae* and *Epitome Ulpiani* are summaries or anthologies of older works by Paulus and Ulpian, and contributed to the preservation of their classical writings. Also well known are the law schools' contributions to Justinian's codification project.

As the role of the praetor declined in the development of law, while that of the emperor rose, there appeared a new form of litigation along with that of the formulary process: the *cognitio extra ordinem* ("outside the ordinary process"), or simply the *cognitio*. In this new civil procedure, which arose in provinces before later spreading to Rome itself, judicial officials took over the administrative handling of the whole process in all its phases, removing the figure of the private judge and, with him, the bipartition of the process. The *cognitio* system, less restricted by forms, proved to be more apt for application to the new law of imperial creation, which fused the *ius civile* and *ius honorarium*. Characteristic of the new *cognitio* system was that the lawsuit no longer needed to rely on the availability of a specific remedy, and thus became a generic way to seek justice.

The *cognitio* approach was also much more compatible with the framework of the imperial bureaucracy. As officers did not administer justice in their own name, but rather on behalf of the emperor, of whose hierarchical structure they formed part, it was natural for a party who had lost his case to wish to appeal to the emperor, who did regularly allow this, hearing the parties and, after consulting with his council, ruling via decree. At other times he limited himself to issuing a *rescriptum* so that a delegated judge could rule in his name. The administration of justice by the imperial bureaucracy required, in addition, the use of written documents, which made control and review possible.

From the time of Hadrian the concurrence of the *cognitio* with the old *ordinary* procedure (that is, the formulary process) intensified and the former eventually supplanted the latter under the Dominate; the "extra-ordinary" or special process, thus, became the new standard.

Many centuries after the fall of the Empire, with Europe devoid of any form of state bureaucracy, a succession of powerful and charismatic popes would create the first modern state: the Late Medieval Church. For its courts it would turn to the old Roman *cognitio* in the form of the so-called Romano-canonical procedure, which took root throughout the courts of Europe as the ordinary way to administer civil justice and which, with some adjustments (not radical changes) introduced in the nineteenth century, is, in essence, the civil procedure that we know today.

2. The early middle ages

I. TRADITIONAL GERMANIC LAW

A. The Germanic Invasions

Beginning in the second century BC Germanic tribes of "barbarians" became the Romans' principal adversaries. The westward emigration of the Huns – a tribe of horsemen from the sprawling Asian steppes – had gradually displaced the Germanic tribes towards the Roman Empire's borders, which, beginning in the late third century, some started to breach. It was the western sphere of the Empire that suffered the greatest invasive pressure.

It is not possible to paint an accurate picture of the Germanic tribes' movements. The Goths sought to settle Dacia (what is today Romania and Moldova). Divided into two groups, Visigoths and Ostrogoths, the former briefly passed into Italy before ultimately occupying much of *Hispania* and a vast territory in southeastern Gaul. Before the Visigoths' thrust the Vandals, who had established themselves in the Iberian Peninsula before, left just a small group in the south, while most of the tribe proceeded to North Africa, a rich and fertile region that was fully Romanized. The Visigoths soon lost their territories in Gaul at the hands of the Franks, who hailed from lands east of the Rhine, thereby leaving the Visigoths within the natural borders of Hispania.

The Italian Peninsula, meanwhile, was successively sacked by the Visigoths, the Alani, Suebi, Vandals and Huns before Odoacer, King of the Heruli, dealt the definitive blow and toppled the Roman Emperor in the west, Romulus Augustulus, leaving only the eastern portion of the Empire standing, ruled from its capital at Constantinople. This watershed event – the fall of Rome (476) – left a deep mark on psyches in the ancient world. Shortly after, Odoacer was defeated by the Ostrogoths, who, in turn, were vanquished by the Byzantine imperial army sent by Justinian. But, as we know, Justinian was unable to maintain hegemony for long, as the Lombards took the Peninsula in 568.

The Frisians, meanwhile, occupied the deltas of the Netherlands, while the British islands were invaded by the Angles, Saxons and Jutes, who, not satisfied with subjugating the native Britons, mostly of Celtic ethnicity and culture, and largely Romanized, drove them en masse from their homes, forcing them to flee to Wales, Ireland, Scotland and Brittany. The Alemanni, after a long odyssey and a series of defeats to the Franks under Clovis, among others, finally found a stable place on the banks of the Rhine, in Alsace and Switzerland. The Burgundians withdrew to the Rhône valley, in the southeastern part of Gaul, after being expelled by the Franks from the area of the River Seine.

Over the course of the sixth century the Franks, mainly established in northern France and southern Belgium, rose to become the preeminent power in Western Europe, dominating a territory extending from the Pyrenees to the Danube. Under the authority of the Frankish kings – first Merovingian, later Carolingian – there lived peoples of very diverse ethnic origins: Gallo-Romans, Franks, Burgundians, Visigoths, Alemanni, Frisians, etc. Each of these continued, in principle, to apply their own law: we already see here an allusion to the principle of the personality of law.

B. Traditional Germanic Law

These Germanic peoples shared certain elementary but deeply ingrained notions about what their community was and how it was organized. Far from any abstraction akin to a state, the Germanic peoples were basically groups of *sippes*, a kind of extended family unit made up of dozens or even hundreds of people united by a common ancestry and chief. Several *sippes* constituted a tribe. Affairs within a *sippe* were resolved by its chief; those which transcended it, affecting an entire tribe, required the convening of an assembly.

For the Germanic peoples war was an everyday event; with the barbarian invasions the Germanic word *werra* (fight, disturbance) almost entirely supplanted the Latin term for it, *bellum*. In the event of war the tribes would elect a temporary leader; *Volk* (people) and *follow* are etymologically related. The Roman term *dux* (from *ducere*, "to guide" or "to lead") more accurately expressed their nature than the term *rex* ("king") – a title which, however, they soon adopted, with its connotations of greater prestige and stability, after their contact with Rome. For the great invasions the tribes grouped into larger entities, essentially of common ethnic origin, those we refer to today as the Visigoths, Franks, Frisians, Saxons, etc. Their chiefs were, of course, from the groups of tribes who had elected them, not from this or that territory. The young people of the various tribes who personally accompanied them would come to form a standing warrior nobility.

The personal, temporary and elective nature of Germanic leadership, symbolized by the oath of allegiance taken at the start of a military campaign, would endure over time as a typically Germanic trait. It would take 500 years for the *rex Francorum* (king of the Franks) to become the *rex Franciae* (King of France).

What kind of law did these people bring with them? First and foremost, not one shared by them all, as each group was governed in accordance with its own traditions. Even if there never was a system of Germanic law, as such, their laws did share unmistakable hallmarks uniting them into a kind of family of kindred legal traditions. These common features included the law's grounding in custom, according to which law was valid because it was traditional, because similar cases had always been resolved in a certain way within a certain tribe or group of tribes. The almost total lack of writing is another of the defining characteristics of Germanic law which, based on the ancient customs of the community, was passed down orally, and in public. Contrary to what occurred in archaic Rome, with its exclusive pontifical colleges, jealous guardians of juridical formulas and solutions, disputes between the barbarians were resolved at public assemblies in which the community gathered. Its oral and public nature gave Germanic law a decidedly popular quality. There was nothing more foreign to the Germanic mentality than the idea of a jurist.

During the disputes brought before public assemblies, the king or his representative did not rule or legally contribute to the process. He was, rather, a silent figure essentially limited to presiding over and maintaining order in the assembly, which was the force which actually issued rulings. The two parties clashed on equal footing, without any interference by the presiding authority. Between this president and the assembly there was usually, in addition, an intermediate body: a small jury, its members selected based on their age, experience, and knowledge of tribal customs. This group proposed a verdict, and the president submitted it to the assembly for approval by acclamation, later seeing to it that the sentence was carried out.

Also worthy of mention are the criteria used to resolve disputes before the assemblies. When the dispute could not be easily resolved in accordance with customary criteria the parties could resort to so-called ordeals (such as that of boiling water, in which he who could keep his hand in boiling water longer won the suit, or similar tests) or to duels, the longest-standing Germanic tradition of justice.

Other traditional Germanic legal conceptions also merit consideration. The Germanic peoples exhibited, in general, a tendency to uphold the collective over the individual, totally unlike the case in the Roman world.

Germanic law, for example, featured a characteristic lack of personal responsibility: parents were responsible for their children's crimes, women for their husbands', the inhabitants of a village for the crimes committed in it (for example, when it was not possible to determine the culprit). Deeply rooted in Germanic conceptions of justice was the practice of "blood revenge" as legal reparation, the obligation to avenge the murder or serious offenses committed against a member of the *sippe*, which frequently led to spirals of violence between clans. *Wergeld* ("a man's price") had the same collective character: an entitlement for the *sippe* of the victim to claim damages against the offender's *sippe*. The clan's council was empowered to deprive irresponsible parents of care for their children, assigning them to a guardian supervised by relatives of the same clan. To the Romans, in contrast, depriving a father of his *patria potestas* would have been unthinkable. In this regard, particularly remarkable was the Germanic conception of community ownership and joint ownership; they viewed much property to be commonly held and utterly indivisible as stress upon the community prevailed here as well. Roman law, on the other hand, tended to conceive of community property as a temporary situation, divided into ideal portions even before its physical division, which any of the co-owners was entitled to prompt at any time.

The German tribes' lack of a public authority specialized in juridical tasks was evident not only in their embrace of the practice of vendetta, but also in institutions such as the "loss of peace": a verdict authorizing any member of the community to assault or kill the convict. The same may be said of their endorsement of extrajudicial repossession, allowing creditors to directly seize a debtor's assets.

Finally, typical of Germanic law was the gradation of penalties for wounds and injuries according to the part of the body affected and the victim's personal circumstances: resident or foreigner, married or single, young or old, noble, free man or servant.

II. DIVERSITY: THE PRINCIPLE OF THE PERSONALITY OF LAW

A. The Principle of the Personality of Law

A fundamental characteristic of law during the post-Roman era was the widespread application of the principle of the personality of law: the application of one or another set of legal rules based on the litigant's belonging to one *nation* or simply one ethnic group or another.

This principle was already widely present in Roman law: the Romans were accustomed to the members of each people pursuing justice and being judged in accordance with their own norms and customs. Caracalla's granting of Roman citizenship to all inhabitants of the Empire in 212 gave rise to a situation that could be described as exceptional in Antiquity. In reality this universal Roman citizenship never yielded completed legal unity. In a certain sense, the great legal and ethnic diversity which the Germanic invasions brought with them restored to law one of the aspects which traditionally defined it: the principle of the personality of law.

The different Germanic tribes wielded their military and political power over the territories they took, but they were still minorities (at times very small ones) in areas inhabited by people who were culturally Romanized, along with other defeated Germanic tribes, and others that had migrated recently. Aware of their numerical inferiority and looking inwards, the dominant Germanic castes did not seek to impose their own norms and customs on peoples whose ways and welfare mattered little to them. In the same territory there coexisted, as a result, during the centuries that preceded and followed the fall of Rome, a number of different peoples, each with its own legal customs and laws. This constitutes – we must repeat – the principle of the personality of law: each individual is to be judged in accordance with the legal rules of the group to which he belongs.

The principle of the personality of law is particularly important in private law, including criminal law, while tax obligations are also bound to respect this principle. Its application, however, raises ongoing problems, as it is not always clear to what group one belongs, or what law applies when the parties belong to different ethnic groups.

B. *Leges Romanorum*

Amidst the general chaos unleashed by the Germanic invasions and the fall of Rome, most of the books containing Justinian's compilations were lost. There remained different fragments of imperial laws and collections of legal rules, but the complete *Digest* all but vanished from history, hidden in recondite monastic libraries, plunged into virtual oblivion.

The Germanic monarchs, however, soon assumed responsibility for administering justice, not only among their people, but also among their subjects of Roman origin. In this effort they encountered the same problems which the legal system suffered during the last phase of the Empire, and which in the Eastern Empire led to Justinian's initiative: the lack of legal security and stability. Thus, by taking a page from the

Roman tradition and drawing upon the rubble of imperial legislation, in the late fifth century and early sixth centuries the Burgundian and Visigoth kings ordered the drafting of specific legislation for their subjects of Roman origin: the *leges Romanorum* ("laws of the Romans").

In the year 506 king Alaric II (484–507) promulgated the *Lex Romana Visigothorum* (literally, the "Roman Law of the Visigoths"), also known as the Breviary of Alaric. Through the issuance of the Breviary Alaric pursued, firstly, a political objective. The empire of the Visigoths, which spanned across Hispania and southwestern Gaul, was under military pressure from the Franks, led by the clever and ambitious Clovis (c. 466–511).

The Germanic peoples had become Christian early in history, but they had embraced the Arian variant of Christianity: a doctrine that rejected the equal standing of the three persons of the Holy Trinity and considered the Father to be the only true God. The doctrine was soon (in 381) declared heretical, but the Germanic peoples clung to it for a time, asserting it almost as a sign of separate identity vis-à-vis the Romans. In 498 Clovis became the first Germanic leader to boldly take the step of renouncing the Arian heresy and converting to the Catholic faith, virtually universal in the Roman population. His gesture was politically visionary, as it brought the Germanic and Roman populations together in the higher unity of a shared faith. As such, Clovis's conversion not only greatly strengthened his power in his territory, but also won him support and collaboration by the Catholic Roman subjects of the neighboring Visigoth kingdom, whose Germanic ruling elite was still Arian. Alaric sought to win over his Roman population by offering it a strong compilation of Roman law, by which they were to be governed. However, this proved insufficient, at least in the Visigothic possessions north of the Pyrenees: Alaric was defeated and said northern portion of the Visigothic territory fell under the domination of the Franks. The Visigothic kingdom would thereafter remain within the natural boundaries of the Hispanic Peninsula; within those limits, the Breviary would remain in force for the Roman population.

Owing to the speed with which the Breviary was composed, it is not a well-structured code, but rather quite a chaotic collection of texts. All its sources, however, are Roman: excerpts of imperial legislation and collections of opinions from classical jurists.

Despite its limitations, the Breviary was influential for centuries, even after its abrogation around 650: in the south of France, even in Germany and England, the *Lex Romana Visigothorum* would remain the sole source of knowledge of Roman law until the rediscovery of Justinian's texts in the eleventh century. As such, the Breviary promoted the spread of Roman juridical concepts, thus facilitating the reception of Roman law centuries later.

The *Lex Romana Burgundionum* ("Roman Law of the Burgundians") was also promulgated in the early sixth century, for the Roman population of the Burgundian Empire. The highly Romanized king Gundobad (474–516) – who was appointed *magister militum* of the Western Empire, and died a Catholic – ordered the drafting of two collections of laws: the *Lex Gundobada* or *Lex Burgundionum* for his Burgundian subjects, and the *Lex Romana Burgundionum* for his Roman ones. Structured and organized in the same way, their contents were adapted to the respective legal traditions of these peoples. Unlike the *Lex Romana Visigothorum*, it did not aspire to be a code or to supersede other prescripts. Rather, its aim was to provide a general response to important and frequent legal questions. Following the defeat of the Burgundians at the hands of the Franks the *Lex Romana Visigothorum* would come to supersede the *Lex Romana Burgundionum* as a source of Roman law.

The *Edictum Theodorici* was the third piece of German legislation based on Roman sources. Unlike the Visigothic and Burgundian laws, the *Edictum Theodorici* applied to both the Roman population in the Italian Peninsula and the ruling Ostrogothic population. Composed circa 500, it remained in force until 554, when Byzantine imperial troops destroyed the Ostrogothic kingdom and Justinian promulgated his own legislation.

The content of these legislative collections was based on legislation from the Roman emperors and Roman jurisprudence in general, albeit in a vulgarized format. They were also suffused with elements of Germanic origin. Hardly systematic, they cover, above all, criminal and procedural law, and, to a lesser extent, private law.

C. *Leges Barbarorum*

Along with legislation aimed at subjects of Roman origin, some Germanic monarchs also set about setting down precepts for those of their own Germanic ethnicity: these were the so-called *leges barbarorum.* Not based on a previous legislative or jurisprudential tradition, which did not exist, these documents simply aimed to put in writing a tradition that had hitherto been strictly oral. Thus the *Lex Burgundionum* and the *Lex Visigothorum* (also known as *Forum iudicum,* "Forum of the judges") were drafted for the Burgundian and Visigothic subjects of those kingdoms. These pieces of legislation, thus, coexisted with the *Lex Romana Burgundionum* and the *Lex Romana Visigothorum*, which had previously been issued for the Roman subjects of the respective kingdoms.

The most important of these Germanic documents was *Lex Salica*, the Salic or Salian Law, or Law of the Franks (who were also known as "Salians"). The first recording of the *Lex Salica* dates back to the time of Clovis, and was expanded and complemented over the course of the ensuing centuries. The *Lex Salica* is little more than a catalogue of fines one was to pay for offenses. As previously noted, this system of fines could be found throughout Germanic law. It set down the amount offenders were to pay victims or their heirs, in accordance with multiple criteria. Among other clauses, it included a provision whereby women were barred from inheriting ancestral lands – a provision of private law that would be employed in the fourteenth century to bar women from the French throne.

There have also come down to us *leges barbarorum* from the seventh and eighth centuries directed at the Alemanni, Bavarians, Anglo-Saxons, Frisians and Lombards.

D. The *Iudicium Parium* ("Judgement of the Peers")

The principle of the personality of law lay at the root of the coexistence of multiple legal systems within a given territory, something highly characteristic of this era. In addition to the disparity of legal prescripts applicable to only one group or another – Germanic or Roman – were the different criteria and special jurisdictions for nobles, commoners, servants, clergy, etc., each of which had the right to *iudicium parium*: to be tried by their peers. In principle clerics were to judge their fellow clerics, while nobles were to judge their fellow nobles, and so on. The term *privilegium fori* ("jurisdictional privilege"), used in particular when referred to clergy, conveys accurately the whole idea underlying the system of *iudicium parium*. As a result, extreme fragmentation, above any other quality, characterized early medieval European law.

III. UNITY: CAPITULARIES AND CANON LAW

This extreme legal fragmentation does not exclude the concurrence of unifying factors. Probably more than the often-fragile unity of political structures, there was the inevitable allure of what remained of Roman culture – unquestionably superior in many areas to the Germanic.

From that Roman culture probably the most visible feature was Christianity. During the late Roman Empire, the word "'Roman"' had become synonymous with "'Christian," and more specifically Catholic – the Trinitarian, Niceno–Constantinopolitan creed professed by the Roman population. The barbarians clung for a time to the Arian variant of Christianity, but, following Clovis's example, they all gradually converted to the Catholic faith. Religion became, henceforth, the strongest unifying factor in an otherwise utterly fragmented Europe.

However, Roman culture maintained the remains of another conspicuous peculiarity: its legal tradition, incomparably more sophisticated than any other existing at that time. A good example of the attraction exerted by Roman legal culture is the mere fact that Franks, Goths, and other Germanic nations began to put in writing – in Latin, a language that was not theirs – their oral precepts and customs, and the fact that they felt responsible for the promulgation of laws for their Roman subjects. The appeal of Rome's legal culture came to constitute a source of unity not to be underestimated.

The vast circulation throughout the continent of Isidore of Seville's (d. 636) *Etymologiae* embodies the appeal of the Roman and Christian heritage to early medieval Europe. A brief compendium about science and culture of the age, the *Etymologiae* summarizes many aspects of Roman learning, including a brief typology of law.

Two other key elements bolstered unity: an emerging royal legislation and, above all, canon law, or the law of the Church.

A. Royal Legislation

After the promulgation of the Germanic laws in the sixth century, legislation all but disappeared as a source of law. In an age featuring widespread illiteracy, including among the political leaders, few effects could be expected from putting laws into writing. During the Early Middle Ages society was governed by custom. Customary law was unwritten law that was orally transmitted from generation to generation and that obtained its normative effect based on the community-wide conviction that the norms in question ought to be obeyed because since time immemorial they had been observed by society. The orality of customary law, in a way, ensured that rules adapted to changing circumstances, but at the same time the community was not aware of these spontaneous modifications. In this way its normative force – the conviction that a norm was binding because it had been so since the beginning of time – was not affected by unconscious modifications.

During the Carolingian age, from the eighth to the tenth centuries, customary law was sometimes supplemented with initiatives to lay down the sovereign's will. These were the *capitularia*: orders issued by the king containing legal precepts applicable to all subjects in his territory. The Carolingian *capitularia* represent the best-known and most relevant examples, although other kingdoms also undertook similar initiatives. The capacity to effectively apply the directives promulgated by the king depended on his political and military power, which varied markedly from one kingdom to another. During the reign of Charlemagne (768–814) and his immediate successors, who had greatly expanded the ancient kingdom of the Franks to cover what is now a territory stretching from the Pyrenees to Jutland and from the North Sea to the Dalmatian coast, capitularies were issued in an effort to unify the administration of these extensive territories. The capitularies did not govern matters of private or criminal law, while quite a few of these capitularies were dedicated to ecclesiastical matters, something that can be explained by the fact that the Carolingian rulers and the Church dignitaries needed one another: the pope was eager for protection against military threats from the Lombards, while the Carolingians needed the clergy to administrate their empire and to provide their immense domains, and the wide variety of peoples living in them, with some internal coherence under the form of a common religion.

B. Canon Law

During the period of the great migrations the Church had remained practically the only stable organization in the West. In some places – in the city of Rome and the surrounding territory, for example – bishops, proving to be spirited leaders in times of tribulation, were called to serve in positions of political power, and even to occupy military and diplomatic posts for the protection of the flock entrusted to them. Leo the Great (440–61) oversaw the defense of Rome from the Huns and Vandals, and Gregory the Great (590–604) saved the Eternal City from being sacked by the Lombards.

In those early days the Church also played a stabilizing and unifying role. The emperors Constantine and, above all, Theodosius, understood this very well; the former tolerated and encouraged the Christian faith via the Edict of Milan (313), while the latter recognized it as the official religion in the Edict of Thessalonica (380). Theodosius even certified the death of paganism through his so-called Theodosian Decrees (389–91), full of dramatic symbolism, such as that which ordered that the eternal flame be extinguished at the Temple of Vesta in the Roman Forum.

During the fourth and fifth centuries the Church underwent institutional transformation, evolving from a more or less clandestine sect, tolerated at best, to become an organization aspiring to a universal (*katholikós*, in Greek) scope. In order to elucidate important theological questions the first ecumenical councils were convened. In the beginning the Roman emperor maintained a high degree of control, acting as an arbitrator in numerous conflicts between Christians (Arians and Catholics, for example). In the Eastern Empire (under Justinian, for instance) this would continue to be the case; in the West, where the Empire had been lost, the bishop of Rome would assume the leadership of the Church, with pontiffs featuring forceful personalities, such as the aforementioned Leo the Great and Gregory the Great, who would leave an indelible mark on the history of the Church.

The bishop of Rome, Peter's successor, had always been a figure of enormous symbolic significance to the universal Church, but his specific powers were, in practice, similar to those of the bishops of the other apostolic sees: Constantinople, Jerusalem, Alexandria, and Antioch. The facts that the Roman leader was the only one of these five found in the West during the migrations, and that a series of charismatic figures came to occupy the papal throne during the fifth and sixth centuries, would elevate the bishopric of Rome to a unique position of preeminence. Institutionally the bishop of Rome, as a political leader of central Italy, fell under the rule of the emperor in Constantinople. The alliance with Charlemagne put an end to this relationship of submission; in 1054 the political severance with Byzantium produced the East–West Schism: the religious rupture between the Latin Church in the West and Orthodox Christians in the East, with its corresponding political consequences.

Within this late medieval structure other bishops joined the Pope in playing high-level political roles in local and central administrations. Not to be overlooked is the cultural, economic, political and religious importance of the monastic orders that had spread throughout Europe, above all those following the Rule of St. Benedict (529). Despite the position of honor afforded the bishop of Rome, the structure of the Church was still notably decentralized.

The unifying power of the Church after the great migrations was, in short, of the utmost significance. With Arianism having been abandoned, virtually all Europeans shared the same faith and felt bound by a spiritual unity: *Christianitas*, Christendom – virtually a synonym for Europe.

The Church developed its own sources of law, which addressed important parts of private law, such as marriage law. Logically, the Bible – the Old and New Testaments – were indispensable sources of inspiration for the resolution of legal disputes. The texts making it up were originally written in Hebrew, Aramaic and Greek, but in the West only the Vulgate (from *vulgata editio*, or "popular edition"), the Latin translation produced by the eminent scholar St. Jerome between 382 and 405, was used. The texts adopted by the councils also contained important legal precepts, called "canons" (from the Greek *kanón*: "rule"). The councils could be ecumenical, provincial or diocesan. Great authority was afforded the works of leading theologians, some called "Fathers of the Church," such as St. Augustine of Hippo (354–430). Papal letters termed "decretals" were also of some importance in producing legal precepts, containing answers to questions submitted for the bishop of Rome's consideration. All of this heterogeneous material was compiled and transmitted in various collections, such as the *Collectio Dionysiana* (sixth century), the *Collectio Hispana* (seventh century) and the *Collectio Hadriana* (eighth century).

IV. FEUDALISM

Feudalism was the form chosen by the Carolingians to structure the administrative and military structure of their empire. The effectiveness of this arrangement varied greatly over time, and geographically, but there is no doubt that in the Carolingian heartland (roughly France and Germany) feudalism came to dominate political and social organization. It was less entrenched, though certainly played a significant role, in peripheral areas such as Spain, Italy and England. In Scandinavia and Eastern Europe, meanwhile, its impact was limited.

Feudalism is characterized by a number of institutions that combine personal and real property elements. The most important of these elements were the fief and vassalage, a solemn contract entailing rights and duties for both parties. The vassal promised to provide his lord with assistance, mostly of a military nature, in the form of a pre-established number of mounted knights, in exchange for protection. Often a real property element formed part of the agreement: the fief, a tract of land that allowed the vassal to provide the required help and assistance to his lord. The vassal could have vassals of his own, in relation to whom he occupied a position as lord. In principle the contract ended when the vassal died, and the lord could assign the fief again to another person of his liking. In practice, however, the fiefs became almost hereditary, as of the ninth and tenth centuries in France, and slightly later elsewhere.

This pyramidal structure of individual contracts, with the king or the emperor at its pinnacle, was the cornerstone of Carolingian administrative and military organization. The structure worked well only in times of military expansion, when there was much land to divide among ambitious vassals. Under such circumstances feudalism was a useful system for the concentration of power. In times of military difficulty, however, the system faltered. If the lord could not honor his obligation to offer protection, as when Vikings and Magyars raided Europe at will, or so it seemed, between the ninth and tenth centuries, the great vassals, such as dukes and counts, would choose to organize the defense of their own fiefs rather than sending a military detachment to a centrally organized army. The increasingly hereditary nature of the fiefs contributed greatly to this trend, which meant that the great vassals acted independently of their lords. In times of military pressure, then, feudalism contributed to a greater fragmentation of political power.

Feudalism as the backbone of the political structure was important until the thirteenth century in France and the fourteenth century in Germany, when administrative alternatives, based on the *ius commune*, were gradually implanted. However, it continued to have long-lasting effects in Western Europe into the eighteenth century.

3. The late middle ages

I. HISTORICAL EVOLUTION

A. Economy

In the ninth century the Earth experienced a sudden rise in temperatures. This climate change had very important consequences for the structure of society. Global warming, together with the development of new agricultural techniques, transformed the economy and made it more productive. Cultivated acreage increased; iron made it possible to till the soil more deeply; biennial rotation (alternating between a year of cultivation and another of fallow lands) was replaced by triennial cycles: a winter cereal the first year, a spring cereal the second year, followed by a fallow year. Food production swelled, even doubling, according to some estimates, which made possible a significant demographic increase. Surplus crops came to be sold at annual markets. As relatively fewer men were needed to work the land, more could dedicate themselves to trade or the nascent field of industry, which gave rise to the emergence of banking and financial activity. All this took place in cities, which witnessed a surge in their development as they came to function as the centers of Europe's burgeoning economic activity.

Compared, however, with the Greco-Byzantine and Arab-Islamic civilizations that surrounded it, Latin and Christian Europe was virtually a backwater, poor and still fundamentally rural. But its demographic and economic upturn would allow it to lay plans for expansion. On the Iberian Peninsula resistance to the Moors was ratcheted up, giving way to the *Reconquista* ("Reconquest"). And all Europe was caught up in a wave of enthusiastic fervor driving support for the Crusades to the Holy Land.

The long cycle of economic growth would come to an end in the mid-fourteenth century. At a certain point agriculture was no longer capable of producing enough to meet the demand of a growing population. For the first time in many decades much of Europe's population slipped into penury. Europe's state of malnutrition became evident when the Bubonic Plague broke out in the middle of the fourteenth century. Its deadly effects were compounded by those of the Hundred Years War, fought between France and England, but with ramifications in Germany, Flanders, Spain and Italy. Hunger, disease and war formed a lethal combination that left over one quarter of Europe's people dead. It would take Europe three centuries to regain the same population numbers it enjoyed in 1300.

B. Political Institutions

The Empire of Charlemagne, divided amongst his three sons upon his death, declined rapidly in the ninth century. At the end of the tenth century Otto I (936–73), after his victory against the Magyars at the Battle of Lechfeld (955), breathed new life into the imperial idea, heading what was expressively termed the "Holy Roman Empire." In theory this Empire encompassed all of Latin Christendom. In practice what is today Germany represented the Empire's territorial core. Until the middle of the thirteenth century the Empire constituted the essential reference point in European politics. It soon lost this hegemony, however, due to the decentralization inherent to the feudal system. As its emperors were elected, candidates were enticed to assure their election by ceding autonomy and powers to the seven prince-electors (for example, in the Golden Bull of 1356). Until the nineteenth century what is now Germany consisted of a fragmented amalgam of hundreds of autonomous territories. Though some emperors were forceful figures from the House of Habsburg, such as Maximilian of Austria (1493–1519) and his grandson Charles V (1519–56), they were unable to reverse the process of decentralization and, in fact, based their power upon their territories in Austria, Spain and the Netherlands.

France, on the other hand, evolved in the opposite direction. When Hugh Capet (987–96) ascended the throne, royal power in France was completely fragmented. Powerful feudal lords reigned as effective sovereigns over their territories, only in theory recognizing that they were vassals of the king of France, the supreme feudal lord. The king of France could only exercise his power in a minuscule area around Paris. He did, however, enjoy an advantage in comparison with the German emperor, one that would prove crucial: a clear and undisputed rule for the royal succession. The monarchy was hereditary. The French king gradually expanded the territory over which he exercised effective power, thus counteracting the centrifugal forces of the feudal order. Strong monarchs such as Philip II Augustus (1180–1223) and Philip IV the Fair (1285–1314) successfully upheld this centralizing policy. Over the course of the fourteenth and fifteenth centuries, as a result of a calculated series of marriages and the Hundred Years War, the kings continued to amass power at the expense of the feudal lords, such that by the dawn of the sixteenth century the king of France effectively exercised his power over all French territory.

For England this period was pivotal, as during it some of the essential features of its political and legal organization took shape. William I the Conqueror (1066–1087), a Norman duke, successfully intervened in a dynastic struggle on the neighboring isle, implanting the feudal system throughout the country thoroughly and in one stroke. During the Anglo-Saxon and Scandinavian dominance a certain administrative organization had been developed, a structure which William I leveraged to curb the centrifugal potential of the feudal regime. The new king declared himself to be the owner of every inch of English soil, which he then granted as fiefs to the lords of the new Norman nobility and those former Anglo-Saxon nobles pledging loyalty to him. The sheriffs, meanwhile, powerful Anglo-Saxon officials, were placed under the monarch's direct control. Though in England feudalism did not have decentralizing effects, political circumstances forced the king to take into account the interests of the clergy, the nobility and the commoners, as vividly illustrated in the historic signing of the Magna Carta (1215).

On the Iberian Peninsula the situation would unfold in a way similar to that in France, though not without its peculiarities. In the eighth century, the power held by the rulers of the Christian kingdoms lying in the valleys and mountains of the north – León and, later, also Castile, Portugal and Aragon – hardly differed from that of feudal lords. By the thirteenth century, however, advances in the *Reconquista* had significantly bolstered royal power, particularly in the most dynamic of those kingdoms: Castile. The nobility, ecclesiastical lords and the urban elite continued to wield power, with whom the monarchs had to grapple, especially in Aragon, Navarre and, to a lesser extent, in Castile.

The Italian Peninsula was a different case, with dozens of principalities and city-republics ably maneuvering to obtain maximum political gain from the ongoing struggle between popes and emperors, and acting as independent or semi-autonomous entities. In the south of the Peninsula the efficient rule of the Normans transformed the kingdom of Sicily and Naples into a regional power that dominated the Mediterranean until the middle of the thirteenth century. The Papal States were the political entity under direct sovereign control of the pope, and stretched out from Rome to Ravenna. The protection, or even expansion, of this territory lay at the heart of the popes' policies for centuries to come. Venice, Pisa, Genoa and Amalfi were important maritime city-republics, with extensive trade networks across the Mediterranean, able to chart independent courses to varying degrees for quite long periods. Other prominent city-states included Florence, Siena and Milan, which established their wealth and power based on trade and commerce. Chronically divided among themselves, as well as internally, these numerous Italian principalities and city-states increasingly attracted attention from abroad, notably from France and Aragon, making the Peninsula a tumultuous political chessboard during the Middle Ages.

C. The Church

The families of the Roman nobility considered the Seat of St. Peter to be their own fiefdom, and wrangled amongst themselves over the papal election. This often led to unsavory situations, especially when Carolingian power declined. During the tenth and eleventh centuries, in order to prevent chaos the emperors often intervened in the election of the pope. This policy of intervention in Rome brought them benefits in their German territories, as with popes favorable to their interests the emperors were capable of placing their allies in ecclesiastical positions of greater importance and wealth in the Empire, heading abbeys and bishoprics. Throughout the eleventh century opposition grew to the appointment of key church leaders by the emperor – a trend that constituted the root of Gregorian reform.

The Gregorian Reforms were thus dubbed in reference to Pope Gregory VII (1073–85), who was, however, only the most prominent of a series of pontiffs who, beginning with Leo IX (1048–54), aimed to revoke the right of secular princes – the emperor in particular – to appoint people to ecclesiastical positions. The Investiture Controversy – the legal and political debate regarding who was entitled to appoint ecclesiastical officials – forced both sides to greatly refine their legal arguments. In this clash the doctrine of the separation of the secular and spiritual spheres was advanced, an idea that would prove one of western history's most important controversies, in light of its impact on subsequent political theory. After a series of dramatic developments, such as the abolition of the oath of allegiance to the emperor, his excommunication and his subsequent Walk to Canossa, near Parma, in an act of penitence to plead for the Holy Father's forgiveness, the antagonists reached an agreement: the Concordat of Worms (1122), which did away with the secular appointment of ecclesiastical officials. With this resounding victory over the Empire the papacy's authority was enhanced, the pontiff demonstrating his possession of immense political power.

The Gregorian Reforms were directed not only towards the political establishment (against the emperor, that is) but also the clergy and internal ecclesiastical structures, where the Pope's position was firmly buttressed. The Church's claim of its right to name its ecclesiastical dignitaries arose from a wider exaltation of the clergy, which was elevated to a superior, qualitatively different plane from that of the secular, ordinary state. For the reformers this prominence also demanded especially virtuous and exemplary conduct. Thus, the obligation of celibacy was imposed, beginning in the eleventh century – in large measure to prevent the transmission of ecclesiastical posts from fathers to children.

The barring of secular leaders from appointing ecclesiastical dignitaries, along with the obligation of celibacy, reinforced Rome's control over local churches. During the Early Middle Ages the relationship between churches across Europe and Rome was relatively weak. The titanic struggle with the Empire, however, forced the papacy to mobilize all the resources at its disposal to carry out a structural reform of the Church based on the introduction of centralism and hierarchy. Canon law played an important role in this process.

The agenda of the Gregorian reformers was, moreover, a comprehensive one. By order of Rome, monks of the Cistercian Order, known for the excellence of their agricultural techniques, spread through Scandinavia, Poland, Hungary and other peripheral territories. Through the Crusades (1096–1099, 1147, 1189) the papacy exercised leadership over Europe's military, economic and demographic expansion, all of this illustrating the papacy's plans to integrate the secular world into an ecclesiastical framework, as the Church's mission was to win over and save souls through its social and institutional organizations. Christian morality, meanwhile, based on canon law, was extended to the most varied social fields.

The twelfth and thirteenth centuries marked the zenith of the papacy's political influence, which peaked under Pope Innocent III (1198–1216), a prodigious personality who intervened decisively in the election of the emperor in Germany; maintained the crown of Sicily for Frederick II (1194–1250), at that time a minor under his guardianship; acted as mediator in the feudal disputes between Philip II Augustus and John of England (1199–1216); placed a king on the throne of Bulgaria, and helped to overthrow another one in Norway. Finally, Innocent established the papacy as an agent speaking out – as a vicar of Christ, and when the good of the Church required it – on secular affairs, demonstrating the primacy of spiritual power over worldly regimes.

In the long term this political power would come back to haunt the papacy. In his disputes with the emperor the Pope had systematically recognized and supported the rights of territorial states (England, France,

Aragon, Castile …). When the Empire weakened and these states could forgo papal support, however, they turned against him. Boniface VIII (1294–1303) would actually be taken prisoner by Philip IV the Fair, and Clement V (1305–1314) was the first of a series of popes who resided in Avignon under the strict control of the king of France.

D. Science and Culture

In order to understand the evolution of the law in the Late Middle Ages it is necessary to understand and appreciate, from amidst the enormous cultural heritage which comes down to us from the era, two closely intertwined and constitutive elements: scholasticism and universities.

Scholasticism was crucial both at the theoretical and methodological level. Epistemologically, it took as a point of departure the existence of truth, revealed by God to mankind. How could one know this truth? Scholasticism was based on the idea that truth could be found in a set of texts of hallowed authority; man could come to know the truth thanks to his faith and to the study of these texts. Among these were, firstly, the Bible and the writings of the Church Fathers. After the rediscovery of the *Digest* at the end of the eleventh century, the *Corpus iuris civilis* would be added. Another discovery, that of the writings of Aristotle in the thirteenth century, further extended their scope. The scholastics also recognized that, at least in part, the truth could be glimpsed in the writings of pre-Christian authors such as Plato, Virgil, Cicero and Livy.

As these included texts from different disciplines and historical eras, there was no shortage of contradictions between them. But the scholastics' metaphysical conviction that there is but one truth, and that it is coherent, allowed them to employ very refined techniques in their interpretation of the different texts in an effort to resolve what were apparent contradictions. For the scholastics knowledge of the truth, through study and reason, was undoubtedly possible. They employed sophisticated techniques in their reasonings: *distinctio*, which established differences between situations which, at first glance, seemed to be equal; *aequiparatio*, which approached similar situations in the same way; and *divisio* (and *subdivisio*), which classified or divided a subject into categories. In all kinds of *quaestiones* (questions), *controversiae* (controversies) and *disputationes* (debates), the most common academic exercises, they examined given points of view, citing quotes from authoritative texts which seemed to support them, along with logical and reasoned rebuttals. Roman law and canon law proved to be subjects very apt for the application of the scholastic method.

The university can trace its origins back to the same period: the twelfth century. The study of theology was always the first objective of the medieval university. But in Bologna the focus was on the law and, more specifically, on Roman law and the compilation of Justinian, studied avidly from the moment when the complete text of the *Digest* was again available at the end of the eleventh century. From the law school the University of Bologna arose and developed over the course of the twelfth century, which served as a model for many universities (others, such as that in Paris, evolved from cathedral schools). To a large extent the scholastic method itself can be traced to Bologna's lectures on law.

II. THE *IUS COMMUNE*

A. The Discovery of Roman Law

The foundation of the law school in Bologna is shrouded in legend. It seems likely that in 1088 the town council of Bologna decided to establish a school to train the city's future officials. This decision came in response to an actual need, as at the time Bologna, one of the most prosperous cities in northern Italy, was seeing a rise in commerce that required legal experts capable of writing up documents, providing counsel, and litigating. Initially the school's curriculum was based on that of the cathedral schools, which centered on the teaching of the liberal arts: the *trivium* (introductory courses of grammar, rhetoric and dialectics) and the *quadrivium* (advanced courses of music, astronomy, arithmetic and geometry). In accord with its charge to educate the city's future officials, teaching of the *trivium* in Bologna placed special attention on the *ars dictaminis*: the art of drafting documents in the proper chancery style. In this context, at the end of the eleventh century there appeared in Bologna a copy of Justinian's *Digest*.

This discovery is also surrounded in legend. For a brief period in the sixth century Justinian's law books were actually used on the Italian Peninsula. In the following centuries legal texts of apparently Roman origin continued to appear and circulate – some more authentic than others – but the core of the compilation, the *Digest*, disappeared during the seventh century from Western Europe.

In the middle of the eleventh century – four centuries later – a copy of the *Digest* was reportedly found in the city-state of Amalfi. This city south of Naples was at that time a very prosperous trading center and an important rival of another other rich city-state: Pisa. The story goes that in one of their wars the forces from Pisa took as spoils from Amalfi the magnificent manuscript of the *Digest*, which came to be known as the *Littera Pisana*. In 1407 the Florentines, in turn, took the codex as war booty from Pisa to Florence, where it was redubbed the *Littera Florentina* and placed in the Medici Laurentian Library. There it has remained – down to the present – as one of its most precious treasures, jealously guarded, with restricted access even for jurists.

So goes the legend. Chronologically, however, it is impossible for the manuscript to have been taken as booty by soldiers from Pisa. The Pisans probably made up this story during the twelfth century to assert the superiority of their text over what by then had become the standard version of the *Digest*, the *Littera Bononiensis* of the rival law school of Bologna. Nonetheless, the Pisans' claim that their manuscript was superior may have actually been justified; the most recent research indicates that the *Littera Florentina* is a manuscript from the time of Justinian himself, created right in Constantinople. It may have remained there until the ninth century, when, in some way that we do not know, it was transferred to the Italian Peninsula and ended up in Pisa.

What is certain is that at the turn of the twelfth century the virtually complete text of Justinian's compilation was available in Bologna: the *Littera Bononiensis*. This text was not based directly on the *Littera Pisana*, but rather composed of several loose manuscripts and parchments that turned up in a gradual and piecemeal way. It may have been – though we do not know – Irnerius (c. 1055–1130) who was responsible for the first composition of the *Littera Bononiensis*, which would come to serve as the standard edition of Roman law during the Middle Ages, the legal Vulgate.

The Vulgate organized Justinian's work in such a way that first might seem chaotic, but this was due to the gradual discovery of its texts. There is a distinction, thus, between a *Digestum vetus* ("Old Digest," Books 1–24.2) and a *Digestum novum* ("New Digest," Books 39–50). The Digest's remaining books (24.3–38) appeared later, presented and named separately as the *Infortiatum*.

Thus did the *Corpus iuris* end up containing five volumes: the three Digests (*Vetus*, *Infortiatum*, *Novum*), plus a fourth with the first nine books of the *Codex*, and a fifth (called *Volumen parvum*, "small," due to its lesser interest) which featured the *Institutiones*, the last three books of the *Codex*, and the *Novellae*, which were considered complete and authentic, hence also called *Authenticum*. To this were added the *Libri feudorum*, a private compilation from the twelfth century containing Lombard feudal law and excerpts from the orders of German emperors.

From the beginning of the twelfth century the school at Bologna, with the esteemed Irnerius at its helm, taught only Roman law, as the *trivium* provided the grammatical and dialectical instruments with which to explain the texts. Irnerius may have been largely self-taught; his official title was that of *magister artium*, "master of arts," but not much more is known about him, save for that in 1118 he was still active educating the first generation of law students. The fame and prestige of Bologna's law school soon spread, luring students from all over Europe. In the middle of the twelfth century, some time having passed since its foundation, it had become evident that the academic study of law as a discipline faced a bright future. The self-conscious promotion of the image of the celebrated *quattuor doctores* ("four doctors") – Bulgarus, Martinus, Jacobus and Hugo – who had come to teach law in Bologna as successors to Irnerius, served to further bolster the law school's position. The four doctors also provided legal counsel to the emperor, Frederick I Barbarossa (1152–1190), who, in exchange for their services, awarded the school privileges that further buoyed its growth. In the year 1200 the University of Bologna boasted a few thousand members, between students and professors.

Bologna soon became a model: throughout Europe universities were founded which, until the nineteenth century, were normally composed of four departments: Theology, Roman Law, Canon Law, and Medicine. Following the Bolognese model, the School of Law at Orléans flourished in the thirteenth century, thanks to jurists such as Jacques de Révigny (d. 1296) and Pierre de Belleperche (d. 1308).

B. Glossators and Commentators

"Glossators" is the term applied to jurists active from Irnerius until 1263, at which point they were called "postglossators" or "commentators." The difference between glossators and commentators lies in the way in which they studied and explained legal texts to make them comprehensible to their students.

Initially, explaining the text meant doing so literally: the first objective was exegesis ("interpretation"): to clarify the constructions of phrases and evaluate their various possible meanings. To do so, the most appropriate instrument was the *glossa,* or gloss (hence the term "glossators"): notes or groups of notes in the margins of the text. Little by little the glosses went beyond explanations of the texts, relating them to other texts. If each passage of text enjoyed authority in itself, none could contradict another. For this reason the medieval jurist sought to solve, with logic and scholastic techniques, such as distinctions, comparisons, etc., what they considered only *apparent* contradictions. The glossators stuck very close to the text. Unlike modern jurisprudence, which associates the formation of the law with metatextual concepts and principles, social values, reason, functionality, etc., the glossator was primarily concerned with the text itself; it was the text from which authority emanated, as only in it could the truth be found.

"Glossing" a text was not a technique restricted to jurists. Any text, whether it was theological, philosophical, literary or scientific, could be glossed, explained and interpreted in annotations in the margin of the basic text. The glossator's work was closely related to his teaching of the law. Classes consisted of reading and explaining the individual texts, in their original order, not selected by subject. The teaching method consisted, first, of a reading of the basic text, with the mention of its various possible meanings, and the final selection. Then the different legal problems raised by the text were identified and separately analyzed. The issues could then be illustrated with the help of examples or hypothetical cases. Analogies with similar rules of other parts of the *Corpus iuris* or other authoritative texts could also be helpful to shed light on the text at hand. The last phase of the teaching method consisted of the refutation of possible arguments against the proposed solution or reading. With these sophisticated and rigorous intellectual tools the general juridical precept was derived from the concrete case or text.

Through this method of exegesis the glossators created a doctrinal architecture of internally coherent rules and concepts. Such was the mark, largely indelible, which they left on the study of law; their most enduring contribution to European jurisprudence.

Azo (d. circa 1220) and Hugolinus de Presbyteris (d. 1233) were among the most important glossators. They both had been students of the same teacher, Johannes Bassianus, and both competed intensely for intellectual supremacy. Azo and Hugolinus produced very authoritative and well-structured glosses on the basic Roman law texts, which maintained their appeal to future lawyers even after Accursius had published his standard gloss. Azo also wrote a very solid *Summa codicis*, a weighty summary of Roman law which followed the order of the *Codex*, and which met with notable success. The *Summa* represented a literary genre formally distanced from the text. Instead of side notes, it featured summaries and more extensive interpretations of excerpts. Although the focus of the *Summa* remained analytical, its emergence as a genre of legal literature indicates that the gloss had begun to be seen as too narrow and limited as a format.

The brilliant jurist Accursius (1185–1263), a pupil of Azo, consolidated the entire collection of his predecessors' glosses, selecting from the material produced over a period of 150 years those interpretations and explanations which in his opinion best captured the meaning of the texts. Contemporaries and successors realized that the selection made by Accursius was so flawless, so appropriate and complete that it could not be surpassed; the gloss had reached the apex of its development. The collection of glosses which Accursius created came to be considered definitive, the standard; hence its denomination as the *glossa ordinaria* or ordinary gloss. Thereafter Accursius's glosses would be used as a reference for the study of law, together with the Roman text.

In general it may be said that, above all, the commentators differed from the glossators in the greater latitude that the former granted themselves with respect to the text. They also paid greater attention to the application of Roman law in practice, and featured a divergence with respect to the form in which they published their research: not with notes or glosses in the margin of the text, but with more extensive commentaries on a specific subject. The differences between glossators and commentators, however, ought not be exaggerated, and it should be taken into account that the transition between the two occurred gradually and naturally. Some glosses are so broad that they can almost be considered commentaries; the commentaries, in turn, often used a text as a point of departure for the examination of a topic. As the impact of Accursius's ordinary gloss was immediate and universal, the distinction between glossators and commentators was more a classification established by subsequent observers than a reality consciously experienced by contemporaries.

Among the great number of commentators, mention is made of only two: Bartolus de Saxoferrato and Baldus degli Ubaldi, who were already considered by contemporaries to have figured among the greatest jurists of their time. Bartolus of Saxoferrato (1314–57) studied law at Perugia. One of his teachers was Cinus of Pistoia (d.1336), a friend of Dante's, praised by Petrarcha, and a meritorious poet himself. But Cinus's real passion was jurisprudence, and it was he who imbued the young Bartolus with his love for the law. After his studies at Perugia Bartolus went on to Bologna, where he earned his doctoral degree at age 20. After university he took a job as an assessor for the city council of Todi and Pisa. Academic life was too appealing, however, and Bartolus became a professor in Pisa in 1343, afterwards moving to Perugia. Bartolus's work was very far-reaching. He produced learned commentaries on all the Justinianic books except the *Institutiones*, as well as treatises on a wide variety of topics. Bartolus worked very hard: the story goes that he wrote a treatise on riparian rights while contemplating the pristine waters of the River Tiber during a break from his teaching duties. He died when he was only 43 years old, but his fame was well established: his name literally became synonymous with jurist, as evidenced by the popular phrase in his honor: *nemo iurista nisi bartolista* ("nobody is a good jurist unless he's a Bartolist").

Baldus (1327–1400) had studied under Bartolus, and started his academic career in 1351 at the University of Perugia. Universities competed fiercely with one another in order to attract the best professors, and Baldus was subsequently professor in Pisa, Florence, Padua, and Pavia, with two more intervening periods in Perugia. Throughout his entire academic career Baldus rendered many consultancy tasks for clients, which brought him fame and wealth. Baldus's output was enormous in scope; he wrote not only on Roman law, as could be expected, but also published on canon law, feudal law and all kinds of particular issues, a consequence of his many consultancy assignments. Bartolus and Baldus had a lasting influence on jurisprudence and the evolution of law in the West. The two left a diverse body of work comprising the most important legal categories.

As the biographical sketches of Bartolus and Baldus show, excellent professors of law were very much in demand during the Middle Ages, and there was stiff competition between universities to attract the most talented academicians. Given the endless and well-paid career opportunities for good lawyers outside the university, professors of law schools were always paid much better than their counterparts at schools of theology or liberal arts, sometimes up to 50 times more. The difference provoked frequent outbursts of envy and jealousy at professors of law and lawyers in general. The city of Bologna went so far as to threaten experienced professors of law, aged 50 or older, whose loyalty often had been bought with handsome salaries and other benefits, with the death penalty if they left to take on teaching positions at other universities.

By the end of the thirteenth century jurists would gradually expand the genres in which they published their research, no longer producing merely glosses or *summae*, but legal literature in a whole range of formats.

We may cite first among these genres their consultations or *consilia*: the jurist's expert opinion on a legal question posed to him. Most of the issues presented proceeded from actual cases, to which the commentators responded, with the help of Roman texts. Sometimes the consultation required some flexibility with regard to the text, such that an effort was made to adapt its meaning to contemporary legal needs. The jurists did not hesitate to employ quotes taken out of context – for example, quotes addressing private law used in the context of public law – such that they came to be understood in new ways. New legal precepts were drawn from Roman law. The positive consequence of this practice is that it tailored Roman law to contemporary needs. The negative part, for which the humanists would subsequently criticize them, is that they created a body of law that the Roman jurists themselves would scarcely recognize.

The second genre of legal literature was comprised of the massive commentaries on the entire *Corpus iuris civilis* or elements of it. Here the commentators also proceeded with greater freedom than the glossators in their approaches to the text. They were more concerned with a systematic and logical approach, preferably by subject. Rather than worrying about the precise meaning of the texts, the commentators focused on what they could mean applied to their own era. Thus, commentators also began to deal with subjects that had little or nothing to do with known Roman law, such as, for example, criminal, procedural, mercantile, maritime, corporate and feudal law, subjects on which the commentators wrote in their observations on Roman law, despite the fact that they were barely addressed by it.

Treatises constitute the third literary genre developed by the commentators. While their commentaries followed the same order of subjects appearing in the original Justinian texts, their treatises took the step of analyzing an institution or area in a complete and thorough manner. For example, Bartolus de Saxoferrato produced treatises on riparian rights (*De fluminibus seu Tyberiadis*) and heraldic law (*De insigniis et armis*).

The commentators did not limit themselves exclusively to Roman law, but also employed other sources. First among these, they turned to canon law. Most of the medieval jurists simultaneously studied both bodies of law, for which they obtained the degree *doctor utriusque iuris* ("doctor in both laws"). It is only logical that in their commentaries the jurists also used canon law, especially because it offered greater flexibility and featured new and influential positions in many fields. The commentators also drew upon other sources, such as contemporary legislation, custom-based law and jurisprudence. The ordinary gloss, of course, but also the writings of Bartolus and Baldus, were so highly regarded that they verged on functioning as sources of indisputable authority.

The glossators and commentators agreed on considering Roman law as a body of texts not written by a particular people and suitable for a particular era, but as works of universal value that bore *truth* and *reason*. Their studies transformed Roman law into a system that could respond to the needs and questions of their own time. In this way Roman law maintained its value, though it continued to be a subject of scholarly study, rather than one directly applied in the courts. This was no obstacle preventing Roman academic law from leaving its mark on European juridical culture, due to the social prestige which university jurists enjoyed and the application – conscious at times, unconscious at others – of Roman concepts and principles in custom-based law and the courts.

C. Canon Law

Unlike Roman law, which in the West largely disappeared for five centuries, canon law was continuously transmitted and developed throughout the Early Middle Ages. The writings of the Church Fathers, the Bible, the canons of councils and synods, the decretals of popes and bishops, were fairly well preserved, and many copies of them were produced.

The authenticity of each text was not, however, assured, above all if it originated in the Carolingian era. Two examples will suffice to illustrate this.

The "pseudo-Isidorian" decretals were a major compendium from the ninth century, composed, on the one hand, of genuine conciliar canons and papal letters, and, on the other, by forged decretals, the identity of their authors remaining a mystery. The apocryphal decretals, supposedly written during the earliest times of the Church, certify the authority of the bishops, and especially that of the popes. The forgers introduced, for example, a new ecclesiastical position, that of the primate, situated in the ecclesiastical hierarchy between the metropolitan bishop and the patriarch. Papal authority was reinforced, as the falsified letters suggested that the pope had headed the Church since the beginning of ecclesiastical history. They also assigned him important powers, for example, by establishing that conciliar decisions required papal ratification in order to enjoy validity. The pseudo-Isidorian decretals exerted enormous influence, and would appear in subsequent canonical collections. Without being cognizant of their falsification, the popes did not hesitate to use the pseudo-Isidorian decretals to concentrate power in Rome. It would not be demonstrated that the decretals were forgeries until the seventeenth century.

Another example is the so-called *Donatio Constantini* (the Donation of Constantine), a false document that claimed to be drafted in the fourth century, through which the Roman Emperor Constantine had supposedly ceded secular power over the city of Rome and central Italy to Pope Sylvester I (314–35). In reality it was an eighth-century falsification created in a context in which the papacy definitively severed its political bonds with Byzantium and opted for an alliance with the Carolingians. The Donation of Constantine later appeared in the *Decretum Gratiani*, where it served another function as an argument in the fight against the German emperors, wielded by the Pope to justify his claim to the highest political authority. Though during the Middle Ages the authenticity of the Donation of Constantine was already doubted, it was not until the fifteenth century that the humanist Lorenzo Valla (1407–57) proved that it was a fake.

Due to the transmission of canonical material from generation to generation and the continuous production of new materials, it became necessary to properly compile the West's enormous heritage of canon law texts.

Among the most important collections from the Early Middle Ages, apart from the aforementioned pseudo-Isidorian decretals, were those of Regino of Prüm (d. 915) and Burchard of Worms (d. 1025). The Gregorian reformers needed new collections, as they had to demonstrate that their arguments were based on canons and precepts of a respectable antiquity, and also because the fight against abuses within the Church required the promulgation of new ones. Therefore, in the second half of the eleventh century new collections came about, such as those of Anselm of Lucca (d. 1086) and Ivo of Chartres (d. 1115).

The most foundational of all medieval canon law collections was the work that came to be known as the *Decretum Gratiani*: literally, the Decree of Gratian, as from the 1160s onwards the authorship of this fantastic work was ascribed to a certain "Master Gratian." The only three things that we know with some certainty about Gratian is that he worked on a version of the *Decretum*, that he was in Venice in 1143, together with two Bolognese jurists, and that he died on an August 10th (though we do not know in what year!) as the Bishop of Chiusi. Exciting recent research has brought forward the working hypothesis that Gratian was a teacher of practical theology, possibly for a very short period at Bologna in the early 1140s. As a teacher he had started drafting the *Decretum* as a didactic tool for his classes, but had left it unfinished to take up a better-paid job in the ecclesiastical hierarchy; more specifically as Bishop of Chiusi (where he died soon afterwards, possibly in 1144 or 1145). Another author (maybe several) picked up the version of the *Decretum* where Gratian had left it and expanded it greatly. The *Decretum* would take on its final form close to 1150.

The sources of the work are both ancient and from the Early Medieval era: canons of councils and synods, patristic writings, elements of Roman law and the Carolingian *capitularia*, along with, to a lesser extent, papal letters and pontifical law. The author did not consult these sources directly, but rather made use of previous compilations, such as those of Anselm of Lucca and Ivo of Chartres. The actual title of the work, *Concordia discordantium canonum* (*A Concordance of Discordant Canons*) was every bit a declaration of intentions: the aim was not only to compile ancient and medieval canon law and transmit it to future generations, but also to offer a solution to all those apparent contradictions between materials in various places and times. To this end he incorporated his own commentaries into the text.

The *Decretum Gratiani*, a private effort undertaken towards academic teaching ends, would prove to be not just any textbook, quickly becoming an irrefutable reference work. Gratian's influence was due to the quality of his work, both in terms of its compilation – ecclesiastical precepts from antiquity and the Early Middle Ages not cited in the work henceforth lost all relevance for ecclesiastical tribunals – and for his efficacious reconciliation of apparent contradictions through scientific study. The work's success also owed, in part, to the Gregorian reform, with which it was perfectly compatible and of which it may be considered, in a way, the culmination. Spiritual power was placed above worldly power, the clergy enjoyed preeminence over the laity, and the Pope was the undisputed head of the Church. Multiple variations on these basic themes were found throughout the work, which undoubtedly serves to explain the authority of the *Decretum Gratiani*, despite the fact that it was never officially promulgated as ecclesiastical legislation.

The Gregorian reformers believed strongly in the mission they had been given: integrating the world into a religious and ecclesiastical framework. To achieve this, numerous objective measures were called for in almost all areas of social life. The most effective tools in the pursuit of this end were legislation, justice, and administration, as within the Church the pope was legislator, supreme judge, and supreme administrator.

The decretals were the standard form of pontifical legislation in the Middle Ages: a case or an issue was submitted to the pope, whose decision, published in the form of a letter, or "decretal," in principle applied only to the specific case, and was sent only to the parties involved. The papal letter, however, also contained the foundation upon which the pope had based his decision. This rationale behind the decision, duly explicated and advanced by the pontiff, was also applicable to other similar cases. Therefore, the canonists were eager to have access to the content of these decretals, as it allowed them to ascertain the most recent views of the pope, the supreme judge of the Church.

Beginning in the second half of the twelfth century there was a real need to fully compile papal law and jurisprudence. Initially the compiling of papal decretals was carried out via private initiatives, but beginning with Pope Innocent III the pontiffs came to recognize the need to promote official compilations of them. In this way the popes guaranteed the authenticity of the compilations, the security of the texts, and control over their contents.

In 1234 Pope Gregory IX (1227–41), who as a canonist understood the benefits for students and practitioners of having easy access to the text of the decretals, charged the Catalan Dominican friar Raymond of Penyafort (1180–1275) with compiling a systematic collection of decretals to be enacted as law. The result was entitled simply *Decretales Gregorii IX*, (*The Decretals of Gregory IX*), also known as the *Liber extra* (from *Liber decretalium extra decretum Gratiani vagantium*, or the *Book of the Decretals Outside the Decree of Gratian*), and it was promulgated with the force of law, thus reinforcing the universal and compulsory nature of the rationale behind papal decisions in particular cases. The *Liber extra* represents a remarkable effort to unify the law throughout the Church and place it under the pope's control. Before the Gregorian reform relations between Rome and local churches had been much more lax, and there were significant differences between the different local congregations. With the availability of a single, authentic text, the popes expected all ecclesiastical tribunals to apply the same body of law.

After Gregory IX the popes continued to draft new legislative materials, compiling collections of decretals and promulgating them as universal laws. In 1298 Boniface VIII promulgated the *Liber sextus* (the "Sixth Book," as a sequel to the five books of the *Liber extra*). Pope Clement V took the initiative for the next official collection, promulgated under the pontificate of his successor, John XXII (1316–34) in 1317, and known as the *Constitutiones clementinae*. These collections did not nullify the works that preceded them, but rather complemented them.

In summary, throughout the Christian world during the fourteenth century a number of official collections were in circulation that placed secure and homogeneous texts at the disposal of the ecclesiastical courts. However, it was not until the end of the fifteenth century that there was talk of the *Corpus iuris canonici*, after the French jurist Jean Chappuis gathered the *Decretum Gratiani*, *Liber extra*, *Liber sextus* and *Constitutiones clementinae* in a single edition and complemented them with two lesser collections, the *Extravagantes* ("lying outside") of John XXII and the *Extravagantes communes* of Sixtus IV (1471–84). In 1582 Gregory XIII (1572–85) brought together all of these writings in a single book, with which the *Corpus iuris canonici* acquired its final form. The medieval texts would remain in force until the promulgation of the *Codex iuris canonici* in 1917.

The importance of canon law transcended the sphere of the ecclesiastical organization. In a society where Christianity was the sole framework of reference for man, canon law exerted significant influence outside the strictly ecclesiastical domain. Administrative acts and commercial transactions could fall partially or entirely under the jurisdiction of canon law, and canon law was also present in some fields over which secular courts normally had jurisdiction, but which, *ratione peccati* ("due to sin," that is, to avoid mortal sin) were governed by ecclesiastical jurisprudence. Canon law frequently encompassed fields which secular law did not. Because of the importance of the family unit in Christian morality, and the sacramental nature of marriage, it was canon law that dealt with the rules related to marriage, adultery, bigamy, kinship and consanguinity, divorce, annulments and separations, and donations between spouses and between parents and children. Canon law also held sway, *ratione peccati*, in the criminal sphere with regard to perjury, violence, theft, murder and rape. And in property law it was applied to purchases, contracts, guarantees, donations and wills. The presence of canon law in society acquired such significance in the Middle Ages that it rivaled that of Roman law. It is worthy of mention, moreover, that while canon law was actually implemented and applied, Roman law remained primarily a subject of university study. In classrooms the scientific study of canon law took on the same degrees of complexity as those that characterized Roman law.

D. Decretists and Decretalists

When speaking of the medieval scholars of canon law, a distinction is usually drawn between decretists and decretalists, one entirely hinging upon the texts upon which the two groups based their work: those who focused on the *Decretum Gratiani* were called "decretists," while those who looked to the *Liber extra* and other collections of decretals were known as "decretalists." The former were active until the middle of the thirteenth century. Due to the growing importance of decretals after 1234, attention given to the *Decretum Gratiani* waned somewhat, though it was still the subject of scholarly research until the eighteenth century.

Though it is an error to view the relationship between decretists and decretalists as analogous and equivalent to that between glossators and commentators, it is true that the first generation of decretists, until Johannes Teutonicus (d. 1245), approximately, used the same method as the glossators; that is, glosses or notes on the margins explaining the text. Subsequent decretists also produced more extensive and systematic commentaries on the *Decretum*.

Immediately after the publication of its final version, around the middle of the twelfth century, the *Decretum Gratiani* attracted much scholarly attention and became the object of scientific study by the decretists. One of the most influential commentaries on the *Decretum Gratiani* was produced by Huguccio of Pisa. Born around 1150 in Pisa,

Huguccio became a professor of canon law in Bologna, a position that he used as a platform to become bishop of Ferrara in 1190. During the pontificate of Innocent III (1198–1216), who had been his student, Huguccio acted regularly as a papal judge-delegate. He died in 1210. Huguccio's *Summa Decretorum*, written at the urgings of his students, is one of the widest in scope, offering the finest in-depth analysis and breadth of knowledge. The author based his ideas on a wide variety of sources, not only, as could be expected, the writings of other canonists, church law and scripture, but also Roman law, philosophy and the works of classical authors such as Cicero, Livy, Virgil and Seneca.

Huguccio's work was one of the main sources of what would become the ordinary gloss on the *Decretum Gratiani*, drafted by the German canonist Johannes Teutonicus. Born around 1170, Johannes Teutonicus studied both laws at Bologna, probably under the famous jurist Azo. He stayed on as a professor in Bologna until around 1220, when he returned to his hometown of Halberstadt, where he enjoyed a career in the cathedral chapter. He died in 1245. Apart from the ordinary gloss on the *Decretum Gratiani*, he wrote a commentary on the decrees of the Fourth Lateran Council, and also produced a collection of papal decretals. Johannes wrote these three works between 1210 and 1218. Bartholomew of Brescia later updated the ordinary gloss and in this updated version Johannes Teutonicus' gloss became, as of 1250, the basic guide to make the great *Decretum Gratiani* accessible to students and teachers.

The *Decretum Gratiani* continued to be the object of academic study after the adoption of the ordinary gloss by the law schools. However, these later studies tended to be less line-per-line explanations of the words of Gratian's *Decretum*, evolving into rather wide-ranging and often very rich commentaries, such as the *Rosarium*, by Guido of Baysio (d. 1313), published in 1300.

The decretalists were those canon lawyers who focused their scholarly attention on the papal decretals. Until the publication of the *Liber extra* this focus was primarily directed at collecting the texts of the papal decretals themselves, such as the aforementioned work carried out by Johannes Teutonicus and Raymond of Penyafort. However, after 1234 the focus was more on the scientific explanation of the official collections. Immediately after the publication of the *Liber extra*, the decretalists limited themselves to glosses alongside the text, before later proceeding to produce systematic studies of the pontifical decretals.

Among the most noteworthy decretalists of the thirteenth and fourteenth centuries mention must be made of Sinibaldo dei Fieschi, who as Pope Innocent IV (1241–54) still found time to write a very influential and sophisticated commentary on the *Liber extra*. He had begun as a law student in Bologna, where he studied Roman law under Accursius and Azo, and canon law under Johannes Teutonicus, among others. For a brief period he taught canon law at Bologna himself, but switched to an ecclesiastical career at the Roman curia. There he befriended Cardinal Hugolino of Ostia, later Pope Gregory IX, and with the help of his mentor ascended rapidly in the church hierarchy. Even though before his election as Pope in 1241 his reputation as an able canonist was well established, it was his incisive and well-balanced commentary on the *Liber extra*, written during his very turbulent pontificate, that would bring him lasting fame as a canon lawyer.

Henricus de Segusio, better known as Hostiensis (d. 1271), had been a law student at Bologna at approximately the same time as Sinibaldo dei Fieschi. After earning his degree he also embarked first on an academic career, teaching canon law in Paris, and then switching to an ecclesiastical career, which took him to England. He was created a cardinal in 1261. His commentary on the *Liber extra* met with immediate acclaim, and is known as the *Golden Summa*, or *Summa aurea*.

Even if most canonists were ecclesiastics and aspired to careers as officials or dignitaries in the Church, there was the occasional lay canonist as well. The most famous among them was Johannes Andreae (d. 1348), who was married and had three sons and four daughters (in addition to several children outside his marriage). Johannes had been a student of Guido de Baysio and was appointed in 1301 to teach the *Decretum Gratiani* to future canonists in Bologna. In 1307 he was appointed to the chair of the Decretals at the same university. He combined his academic commitments with numerous consultancy jobs, which allowed him to amass considerable personal wealth. His extensive commentary on the *Liber extra* was entitled *Novella*, which means literally "new things" but, coincidently, was also the name of his mother and of his youngest daughter. This commentary was very successful. His gloss apparatuses on the *Liber sextus* and the *Clementina* were soon regarded as the standard glosses on these collections. Johannes died of the Plague in 1348.

Apart from global glosses and commentaries on entire collections of decretals, the canonists were also interested in particular areas of canon law, which they addressed thoroughly and systematically, particularly as of the second half of the thirteenth century. The aforementioned Johannes Andreae published, for instance, a coherent *Summa* on marriage and its problems, and William Durantis, also known as *the Speculator* (d. 1296), a French canonist who had studied at Bologna, wrote the single most important treatise on procedural law, the *Speculum iudiciale*, which would stand as the standard reference work for centuries. Gradually more and more works were produced that would systematically address individual areas of canon law.

Canonists would very soon occupy positions of leadership within the Church. What we know of the lives of Gratian, Huguccio, Johannes Teutonicus, Sinibaldo dei Fieschi and Henricus de Segusio points to a common pattern: bright, ambitious and hardworking men considered an academic career on canon law faculties as the ideal springboards to establish their reputations, after which they would ascend to better-paid and more prestigious jobs within the Church hierarchy. For those with ambitions of becoming cardinals, bishops or abbots, canon law was the most propitious course of study. Some canonists even rose to occupy the papal throne: Alexander III, Innocent III, Gregory IX, Innocent IV, Boniface VIII … Most of Peter's most powerful successors during the twelfth and thirteenth centuries were, in fact, canonists. The numerous academically trained canonists who did not end up in the ecclesiastical hierarchy would often find employment in the chanceries or judiciary organs of various church bodies; or they were retained as experts by religious communities, or by lay people and institutions.

III. *IUS COMMUNE* AND *IURA PROPRIA*

A. The Relationship between *Ius Commune* and *Ius Proprium*

Over the course of the twelfth century academic study of Roman and canon law grew and developed. Students frequently studied both subjects at the same time, obtaining an *utriusque iuris* ("both laws") degree. The line between the two fields was not always easy to draw. In both legal departments the same methodology was employed and the legal literature featured the same format: glosses, commentaries, treatises, consultations, questions. Jurists wrote commentaries on canonical issues, and canonists wrote treatises on Roman law. With great permeability, the concepts and institutions typical of one of the two systems of law seeped into the other, where they acquired new nuances and meanings, which, in turn, affected the first. The interaction between Roman law and canon law was, thus, intense and fertile. To refer to both at times the term *ius commune* was used to indicate the object of scholarly study, common throughout Europe (not to be confused with the "common law" of England, peculiar to the island). It should not be understood from this that throughout Western Europe the courts applied the same precepts of Roman and canon law. Only canon law was actually applied, and even in the ecclesiastical courts, despite the pontifical law, there were still local differences as a result of variable political circumstances. There is no doubt, however, that, from the standpoint of juridical science, Roman law and canon law formed a tandem that would determine the evolution of the law for centuries. The concepts, doctrines, systematics, techniques, and principles common to both legal systems would prove to be decisive in the history of private law.

In contrast to the term *ius commune*, the term *ius proprium* – or perhaps even better in the plural, *iura propria* ("particular laws") – refers to the multitude of specific jurisdictions and laws existing across Europe, each with its own dispositions and customs. These jurisdictions were different in both their territorial and personal scope of application. In some regions of Europe, every town, city or region had its own jurisdictional scope where precepts not necessarily identical to those of contiguous areas were applied. In addition to this territorial fragmentation, there were also personal jurisdictions grounded in the right to *iudicium parium* (judgment by equals), the principle according to which one should be judged by individuals of his same status: thus operated the ecclesiastical, feudal, seigniorial, municipal, rural, university, guild and other courts. The *iura propria*, by their very nature diverse and fragmented, were normally governed during this era by consuetudinary law; that is, by customs.

The relationship between *ius proprium* and *ius commune* is very complex, but it is fundamental to understand the evolution of private law through Western history. Normally the *ius proprium* was subject to customary law, which, due to its intrinsic limitations, did not achieve the level of sophistication of academic law. The *ius commune* was perceived as a model, a distant ideal. Its value as a common body of rules with a European and universal scope would never materialize as a tangible reality. Unlike the case with canon law, of everyday application in the ecclesiastical courts, Roman law was never applied with direct and immediate force throughout Europe – though it was applied in some specific places as suppletive law when a specific provision was lacking in local law.

In light of this fact, the question inevitably arises as to why for centuries, up to the eighteenth, the law curriculum consisted exclusively of courses in Roman law, which was not actually applied in the society of the era. Why would people devote so much time, money and effort to studying something that they later would not even directly implement in their work as judges, lawyers or royal officials? The answer to this question can only be found in the refined concepts and methods of the *ius commune*; the subtlety and depth of analysis it brought to cases and problems; the breadth of the legal, social and cultural context in which only learned law was capable of situating problems ... all these features qualified specialists in these bodies of law as highly esteemed figures, called to occupy leading positions in society. In contrast, the *ius proprium*, due to its relative poverty and fragmentation, proved incapable of spawning and transmitting a sophisticated legal culture.

Taking the above into account, it is no surprise that the Roman and canonical institutional principles, far from being locked in an ivory university tower, soon began to influence the multiple *iura propria* in various ways.

In southern Europe – Italy, Spain, southern France – Roman law was commonly accepted as *lex scripta* ("written law"); that is, law supplementing local dispositions. Thus, when local laws did not offer solutions to a concrete case, the courts looked to the learned law for answers. The reception of academic law in southern Europe came about easily and naturally, as in these regions customs were already often shaped by the vestiges of the Roman heritage. Written collections were used based on Roman law, albeit distorted, through the *Lex Romana Visigothorum*, the *Lex Romana Burgundionum* and the *Edictum Theodorici*. In Italy Justinian's compilation had even briefly been in force. To all of this was added the constant circulation of Roman texts during the Middle Ages. Without denying the presence of Germanic elements, some strongly rooted also in southern Europe, in this region the *iura propria* always bore the mark, in one way or another, of the Roman legacy.

To the north of the Loire the process of adopting the academic law was not so simple, as there had been less contact with the Roman texts during the Early Middle Ages, and because adherence to local precepts of Germanic origin was deeply rooted. As a result, the autonomy of the *iura propria* survived until later. Thus arose the distinction between *les pays de droit écrit* ("the countries of written law"), in the south, and *les pays de droit coutumier* ("customary law countries") in the north. The northern regions were not, however, unaffected by the techniques and concepts of Roman and canon law, which also made an impact there. In the north, *ius commune* did not function as *lex scripta*, as occurred in the south, but it did at least as *ratio scripta* ("written reason"). There were two particular infiltration channels in this regard: the ecclesiastical courts and the social prestige of jurists and canonists, who would soon be sought after to sit on the benches of royal chanceries throughout Europe.

Beginning in the twelfth century, canon law functioned as a precursor to the reception of Roman law, from which it borrowed concepts, principles and methods. In many regions canon law was notably present in non-ecclesiastical courts and in areas falling outside its strict scope, placing those courts and areas into contact with the techniques and concepts of learned law. In addition, in many places ecclesiastical tribunals performed functions that today we would associate with notaries. For the drafting of important documents and certification of their authenticity, only ecclesiastical courts, at first, had sufficient knowledge – often only the clergy could read and write – and the necessary authority and skill. As drafters of records and documents clergy educated in canon law occupied a key position, not only in the ecclesiastical courts and episcopal administrations, but also – and this would be of extraordinary importance – in the chanceries of secular rulers. Canon law, the ecclesiastical courts, and canonists played, in short, an important role as precursors of the absorption of the concepts, techniques and institutions of Roman law.

In their quest for greater freedom of action vis-à-vis nobles and other feudal vassals, kings greatly appreciated the capabilities of jurists trained in the *ius commune* at prestigious universities, and offered them lucrative career prospects at their royal chanceries and courts. Even though the *ius proprium* continued to be applied, in the long term the penetration of concepts and techniques from the *ius commune* was inevitable, this being especially evident in legislation, courts and customary law.

B. Legislation

The possibility of enacting laws generally depends on the strength of a state. In other words, the importance of legislation as a source of law depends on the degree to which a government has advanced in the long process of establishing itself as a structure capable of exercising public authority over a defined territory. In a public sphere based on feudal contractual relations which were, in a certain sense, private, legislative activity was feasible only when the ruler wielded power, acquired by distributing the spoils of war, riches and honors to pacify and appease the great lords of the realm. This situation occurred, for example, during the central Carolingian period, when the king amassed enough power to promulgate what were called his *capitularia.* The end of their military expansion, however, soon put a halt to the Carolingian kings' legislative activity.

The rediscovery of Roman law and the development of canon law afforded the king an added incentive: the revival of the ideal image of the monarch as the supreme legislator, a figure ever present in the Romano-canonical tradition. Justinian is the quintessential example, along with the other great Roman emperors. Embodying this ideal in the medieval era, beheld by all intelligent and ambitious kings, was the example of the pope, the Church's supreme legislator, especially after the *Decretum*

Gratiani. This model of a legislating "Caesar" would powerfully capture the imagination of twelfth-century kings in their ongoing search to centralize power.

Initially the creative and innovative potential of legislation was very limited, not going much beyond the mere confirmation of some traditions and customs, often directed at only a part of the population. Letters, or "privilege charters," are a good example. The monarch granted cities privileges via letters, which recognized mutual rights and obligations between cities and monarchs with regard to jurisdiction, administration, taxation, etc. In this respect, the *cartas pueblas* and *fueros* (municipal charters) of Spain's Castilian and Aragonese cities were peculiar in that they featured, rather than a series of pre-existent customs, a series of especially attractive conditions designed to foster their growth, privileged status designed to attract people to the perilous borderlands recently wrested from the Moors. The privileges also constitute, in general and across all Europe, evidence of participation by subjects in the promulgation of laws. That is, the monarch did not act as an authoritarian legislator who imposed his law from above. Rather, in the Late Middle Ages legislation was often the result of complex negotiations through which subjects, via various pressure groups, secured many of their aspirations – even when texts stated that laws were promulgated based on the monarch's sole authority.

Academic law was key to providing new vigor to the hitherto languid creativity of legislation. Little by little the political and creative potential of law was comprehended. The popes, with their interminable series of decretals, were the best example. Academic law, meanwhile, heir to the Roman imperial conception, rediscovered the state as an abstract, public entity transcending dynastic and private relationships. Thus did the notion spread that it was the state's responsibility to maintain law and order, and that, above any other consideration, the monarch embodied this responsibility. The strategic position occupied by jurists and canonists in the chanceries and their role in the drafting and negotiation of the texts of laws facilitated the spread of Roman and canonical concepts. Little by little legislation would come to be seen as the most direct route to introduce changes to laws, although customary law would still remain the most important source of precepts for a long time. Two early examples of the monarch as a conscious and confident legislator would come with the *Liber augustalis* (1231) of Frederick II, as King of Naples and Sicily, and the *Siete Partidas* of Alfonso X the Wise (1252–84) for the Kingdom of León and Castile.

Frederick II, Holy Roman Emperor and King of Sicily and of Jerusalem, very consciously and with full historical awareness, viewed himself as the successor of Justinian, revered in the Middle Ages as a paragon of justice. Frederick undertook the task of unifying laws in his Sicilian kingdom; the ordinances promulgated in Melfi in 1231, comprising the *Liber augustalis*, were the result of extensive and thorough work in the imperial court, the collection in itself a kind of body of public and administrative law. The code was partially based on old Norman laws, as the Normans had conquered the realm long before. To construct accurately the texts of these old Roman laws, the authors appealed to the memories of the realm's most aged elders. But it also contained new laws promulgated by Frederick II at the beginning of his reign. In its structure and inspiration the *Liber augustalis* conforms to the compilation of Justinian, revealing the influence and work of university jurists, some of them already educated at the University of Naples – founded by Frederick II himself a few years earlier, in 1224. The emperor is depicted in the work as the only party responsible before God for peace and justice in his kingdom, and that responsibility spurs him to undertake initiatives to enact laws. The code was the subject of glossing activity both in the Kingdom of Naples and outside it.

The *Siete Partidas* of Alfonso X the Wise represent the most important Spanish contribution to the history of legislation in the world, as the most ambitious and complete project of its time aimed at expediting the spread of learned law. The breadth of its subjects, technical soundness and concise prose – in Spanish, not Latin, an audaciously modern feature – make these seven books a truly exemplary legal work. Divided into seven parts (hence its name), the *Partidas* stretched beyond the strictly legal sphere to include philosophical reflections by classical thinkers such as Aristotle and Seneca, theologians such as Thomas Aquinas, as well as biblical texts, making it a veritable humanistic and doctrinal encyclopedia. During the reign of Alfonso X a commission of jurists chaired by Alfonso worked for nine years, from 1256 to 1265, on the drafting of the Code. Its legal sources can be traced back to the *ius commune*: the *Corpus iuris civilis*, the decretals, the texts of glossators and commentators, and the feudal sources of the *Libri feudorum* (which formed part of the medieval edition of the *Corpus iuris civilis*).

Alfonso X's aim in drafting the *Partidas* is not clear. Some scholars suggest that, due to its lack of specific references to the Iberian Peninsula or Castile, and its emphasis upon the *ius commune*, the document was designed to present a political agenda at a time when Alfonso X aspired to the candidacy of the imperial throne. Undermining this hypothesis is the fact that the text was written in Spanish rather than Latin. Other scholars believe that the text was driven by purely cultural aspirations, such that this legal encyclopedia represented one more work forming part of a whole range of different cultural initiatives and undertakings. In any case, Alfonso X was responsible for a serendipitous synthesis of history, law, music and literature.

The work soon acquired enormous prestige among a diversity of jurists, politicians, chroniclers and writers, and for centuries was considered required reading and a key reference work. Even though it took a long time for it to officially enter into force, its growing prestige led to the application, under the reign of Alfonso XI (1312–50), of some of the Code's laws in the courts, and in 1348 it was assigned validity as suppletive law.

C. The Administration of Justice

The fragmentation of central power over the course of the ninth century yielded a correlative fragmentation in the administration of justice. Firstly, the fragmentation was territorial: courts' jurisdiction coincided more or less with the territories (sometimes very small ones) over which feudal lords effectively wielded power. The principle of the *iudicium parium* accentuated decentralization, giving rise to a myriad of courts – seigniorial, rural, municipal, ecclesiastical – and similar institutions for guilds and universities, etc. With the strengthening of royal power, and consciousness of its public nature, beginning in the twelfth century the monarch began to exercise tighter control over the administration of justice. His strategy involved not so much trying to impose order upon the miscellany of functioning courts, but rather to offer his own justice administration in addition to those already in place.

The image of the monarch as a supreme judge came, like that of the supreme legislator, from the *ius commune*: both Justinian and the pope occupied the pinnacle of a pyramidal judicial system. But rulers would need time to realize this ideal.

For centuries, the practitioners who provided their services in rural and municipal courts lacked university training. They learned the profession via hands-on practice in the courts in question, through the application of precepts rooted in custom. Due to the growth in the number of cases presented before the monarch and his officers, it became necessary to channel jurisdictional functions towards specialized and professionalized bodies, invariably staffed by university jurists educated in the *ius commune*. For example, in the middle of the thirteenth century, Louis IX the Saint (1226–70) founded the *Parlement de Paris*, a royal court charged with hearing and deciding cases submitted to royal justice, whether via appeal or, in certain cases, in first instance. Similar institutions were established throughout Europe during the thirteenth and fourteenth centuries. In 1274 in Castile the *Tribunal de Corte* was founded – the forerunner of the *Chancillerías* and *Audiencias* (Chanceries and High Courts) – to settle cases traditionally reserved for the king. In 1286 the Crown of Aragon established the *Audiencia*, later decentralized in the fifteenth century to better serve Aragon, Catalonia and Valencia. It was through these courts that one of the most important and lasting creations of canon law would be received: Romano-canonical procedure.

Romano-canonical procedure was the litigation system that was institutionalized in the ecclesiastical courts of the Late Middle Ages. It took direct inspiration from the *cognitio extra ordinem*, Roman civil procedure from the Late Roman Empire.

Roman procedural law underwent important changes in the different stages of its development. The *Corpus iuris civilis* preserved elements of the old *legis actiones* and of the *per formulas* procedure, but the truth is that during the Justinian era and, in general, during the Dominate and later stage of the Principate, the only existing process was the *cognitio,* the most consistent with the hierarchical and bureaucratic administration of the late Empire. It should come as no surprise that the canonists of the twelfth and thirteenth centuries would adopt the *cognitio* as a model for a new way of handling cases, more suited to the new centralized organization of the Church, and which was termed *ordo iudiciarius* (the solemn judicial proceeding). Its basic features were the elimination of all non-rational elements, such as ordeals; the introduction of writing into the procedure, which entailed its division into phases or successive periods of a preclusive character; the introduction of the appeal, which was also made possible by the writing principle; and the reinforcement of the judge's procedural and evidentiary initiative.

Ordeals, of Germanic origin and widely employed during the era, were an obvious obstacle to the construction of a centralized and rational jurisdiction. The practice was based on the conviction that God himself intervened in the trials of water and fire. Judges were not to issue their opinion, but rather only to read the sentence issued by God through signs. Much has been written about the irrationality of the ordeals, though they did not lack some rudimentary elements of rationality: pre-established rules were applied which had to be respected; justice was rooted in the private sphere, but was carried out in a public forum; and in all cases a definitive decision was reached to which the community gave its full assent.

All this could work in primitive medieval European communities, but not in ecclesiastical courts made up of learned doctors with a degree in both laws. For these professionals, versed in scholastic logic and full of confidence in reason as an instrument given to man by God so that he might better know the truth, ordeals represented an intolerable pagan superstition. With tenacity and perseverance the ecclesiastical tribunals – and the royal courts which later drew inspiration from them – managed to eradicate the practice of ordeals beginning in the twelfth century. By the beginning of the thirteenth century the situation was ripe for a formal ban on the practice, which happened at the Fourth Lateran Council (1215).

One of the most important features of the Romano-canonical process was the introduction of written record-keeping. This was the external element that most clearly differentiated the Romano-canonical process from the other trial methods implemented in Europe, which tended to be completely oral. The commitment to keeping records was comprehensive, encompassing the suit, citation, response, jurisdictional issues, the *litis contestatio*, witness statements, sentence, appeals … everything was placed in writing. Moreover, documentary evidence – notarial records and deeds – took on a central position in procedure, to the detriment of that supplied by witnesses.

The principle of judicial record-keeping carried with it another essential feature that also significantly distinguished the new procedure with regard to its external forms: the division of the legal process into successive phases after which the possibility of bringing new allegations or presenting new evidence was precluded. In procedure then widespread in Europe, precisely because of its oral character, everything – allegations, evidence, decision – tended to be concentrated in a single act. The principles of orality and concentration were always closely linked, just as were the keeping of written records and the division of procedure into successive phases.

Writing guaranteed a rational and objective assessment of the facts and legal issues to be judged. In addition, written records made it possible to document that the accused's or defendant's necessary guarantees had been observed, a principle – procedural fairness through respect for forms – to which the ecclesiastical courts assigned great importance.

All this made it possible, in addition, to provide the parties with the possibility of appealing judgments before a hierarchically superior court, and, eventually, even before the pope. The appeal, a powerful tool of centralization, was conceived from the outset as a fundamental objective of the new model. Logically, it was not possible to appeal against a trial by ordeal; God's judgment was, by its very nature, indisputable. But within the system of the Church's courts it was practicable to appeal the judgments of lower courts, in theory all the way up to the pope, the sole source of jurisdictional authority. Thus, it is understandable that they spoke, when appealing to the higher body, of "devolution": the lower court returned (or devolved) jurisdictional power to the superior one, which had only delegated it. Due to geographical distances not everyone could travel to Rome to appeal a ruling. The sending of case documents, thus, was confirmed as the best option to ensure the possibility of appeal. The principles of legal records and hierarchical judicial organization were, therefore, mutually reinforcing.

Another new development was one affecting criminal matters: the inquisitorial principle. Early European medieval criminal procedure, of Germanic roots, was based on the adversarial principle: the initiation of the process, as well as the burden of proving allegations, lay with the purportedly aggrieved party. In Romano-canonical criminal proceedings the judge possessed the authority to initiate the procedure *ex officio* and to investigate and verify the truth about what happened. It should be stressed that the inquisitorial principle was reserved to the criminal sphere. Under canon law offenses were considered, above all, sins, and the salvation of the soul licensed judges to take the initiative if circumstances so required. In the civil sphere, however, the Romano-canonical process featured what we know today as the principle of party disposition, under which the parties exercise sole control over legal proceedings (*nemo iudex sine actore*: "nobody be a judge without a plaintiff") and the rule that it is the parties that bear the burden of presenting the evidence they consider most appropriate to support their allegations.

Due to their peculiar characteristics, judicial proceedings could be slow and complex. For certain types of matters, which could be resolved in a speedier and more and cost-effective way, and drawing upon the proposals of lay jurists from the Italian cities, in turn inspired by effective commercial marine jurisdiction, in 1306 Pope Clement V issued the *Saepe contingit* decretal (Clem. 5.11.2), which established a new, simplified process of summary proceedings that combined the rationality and guarantees of what was coming to be called "due process" with the advantages of orality, concentration and limited appeals.

The Romano-canonical process had an extraordinary impact on the development of modern litigation, with all its main features being copied by kings in their embryonic judicial structures: the development of a hierarchized judicial organization, the use of jurists with university educations, the elimination of ordeals, and the introduction of records and appeals. The procedures of customary law gradually either gave way to the new procedure or were imbued with its rules and principles through the permanent supervision and control of the central courts. Romano-canonical procedure would retain its essential characteristics and remain practically intact down to the present day.

The Romano-canonical procedure was also an essential tool for monarchs to increase control on local and particular jurisdictions. Even if this process of centralization would not be completed until the end of the eighteenth century, the royal courts managed to gradually streamline the administration of justice throughout the country.

This process took place based on three pillars. The first was the imposition of nullity on sentences of non-royal judges in the event of formal errors in the judicial procedure. This rescissory function was a technique first developed by ecclesiastical tribunals and later copied by monarchs, as a means to provide justice when the proper courts failed to do so. The second pillar was the broader appeal, which ruled not only as to whether or not the sentence was valid, but encompassed a full review of the case, including the possibility of resubmitting evidence. In addition to these supervisory functions, and by virtue of a firm and sustained political strategy, in some cases the monarch managed to establish his own jurisdiction of first instance. Royal judges could entertain grievances committed against residents in territories over which the king held direct, ordinary jurisdiction. He would be authorized also to hear first instance cases involving serious harm to the kingdom, such as treason, sexual assault, theft from churches or sanctuaries, setting houses on fire, and counterfeiting, as well as suits against officers of the king. Royal jurisdiction would continue to expand, to include suits brought by royal officers, widows, orphans, and the poor, regarding possession (but not property), tax-related claims, etc.

D. Customary Law

During the Late Middle Ages customary law served as the main source of private law, and would continue to do so until the late-eighteenth century.

Customary law was initially characterized by the fact that, despite not being recorded in writing, it nonetheless represented a genuine body of law, its binding force proceeding from a shared conviction that a prescript should be respected, and that its violation generated liability. This conviction was also reinforced by the opinion that a given law was good because the community's ancestors had recognized it. Customary law prescripts tended to be so deeply rooted in traditional practices that the groups employing it could not even recall or conceive of a time before their existence. As such, custom-based law was by its very nature conservative, as it was through constant and repeated use that a custom acquired binding force. Despite this anchoring in tradition, however, it did undergo a gradual, though barely perceptible, evolution. Precisely the fact that rules were not set down in writing allowed them to be gradually adapted to fit new social conditions and general notions of justice. Precepts could also disappear if they were no longer compatible with newly prevalent ideas about justice. But this did not mean that rules were not set, or that they could not vary depending on certain cases. Rather, it meant that the community's collective memory could undergo changes, which would lead to corresponding shifts in the prescripts based on them.

Customary law's non-written nature has made it difficult for legal historians to verify its contents, above all during the period between the ninth and twelfth centuries. With regard to precepts prior to the ninth century, quite a bit is known thanks to records of the *leges* (laws) of the different Germanic tribes. Beginning in the twelfth century there were official and private codifications of the then-existing customary law.

The German tribes' different *leges* (Salic Law, *Lex Gundobada*, *Lex Visigothorum* …) in reality were little more than the putting into writing of Germanic customary law: a snapshot of the configuration of Germanic law. But these laws were applicable only to German subjects; Roman or Romanized populations were subject to other laws, most often variants of Roman law. Beginning in the ninth century the application of the principle of the personality of law declined and bodies of customary law based on territory, rather than ethnicity, flourished. Due to the difficulty of travel and political fragmentation, the territories where the same laws were applied were very small, and every religious, political or administrative unit could have its own body of customary law. As Voltaire observed in the eighteenth century, when travelling from the north to the south of France the legal system changed even more frequently than one had to change horses. This said, this fragmentation was hardly absolute. Towns, cities and regions often shared a core of laws, and the closer they were to one another, the more similar those laws were. Moreover, in essentially transnational fields, such as trade, and especially with regards to maritime trade, the trend towards unity was remarkable.

From among these medieval systems of law, arising from the consuetudinary tradition, what has been called the "Law Merchant" (or *lex mercatoria*) stands out for its originality, creative force, and subsequent repercussions. The development of currency exchange and the use of credit during the era led to an expansion in mercantile relationships, giving rise to many new legal practices used by organizations of merchants, such as bills of exchange and other negotiable instruments.

The disputes arising in this field were frequently settled by and within communities of merchants. Maritime trade on the Mediterranean, for instance, was subject to its own "consular" jurisdiction in which non-jurist merchants, dubbed "consuls," served as judges and arbitrators, somewhat independent of political or religious oversight. Procedure in these mercantile courts was fast, flexible and informal. While adjudicating commercial disputes, the "consuls" developed a jurisprudence of mercantile practices and a separate legal system, the basis for the adoption, in the nineteenth century, of separate commercial codes and courts in many civil law countries.

When in a legal procedure one appealed to a consuetudinary law precept, grounded in custom, it was imperative to demonstrate that the precept actually existed; due to the non-written nature of such a law, this proof was not always easy. One also had to prove that a precept was valid and in force, which could be done only by demonstrating its constant and repeated use, something difficult when precedents stemmed back into the distant past and had been lost. Thus, during the thirteenth century techniques were developed to legally certify the existence of a custom. These techniques included, for example, qualified witnesses versed in the law, or a formal request presented before another court to state whether it had ever applied the precept cited by the party. These methods had two effects: the gradual unification of law and the introduction of written records into the process.

In order to deal with the problems inherent to customary law as a result of its lack of record-keeping, in the thirteenth century multiple private initiatives were undertaken to resolve the situation. On occasions the members of a given court decided, for their own use, to put the rules applied in it down in writing. These "custumals" were initially of a very rudimentary nature: a simple listing of rules and their precedents, lacking any apparent systematic order. In a second phase more systematic books appeared, with laws organized by subject. Once completed, these writings often took on a life of their own, their influence being felt beyond the territories in which they were written.

In this way some works contributed to a greater unification of customary law. Famous examples may be cited from the field of mercantile law: the *Llibre del Consolat de Mar* (Valencia, thirteenth–fourteenth centuries), the first work containing the maritime laws and customs of the Mediterranean. Circa 1250 the *Rolls of Oléron* comprised the mercantile law applicable to the Atlantic coast, and featured a set of judgments issued by the maritime court on the French island of Oléron on the wine trade. The *Rolls* were of decisive importance in the development of English admiralty law and, as such, their influence extends to present-day maritime law. The *Rolls* also provided the core provisions of the *Waterrecht* ("Water Law"), a collection of judgments by the Maritime Court of Damme, near Bruges, and which was also used at other Hanseatic ports, such as Lübeck and Danzig. In spite of widespread knowledge of the customary law contained in the *Rolls of Oléron*, it would not be correct to say that the entire Baltic trade was governed by a single corps of supra-territorial law; many Northern European ports continued to apply primarily their own customs and regulations, and were only loosely inspired by the *Rolls of Oléron* and its derivatives.

Prominent custumals that indirectly inspired a greater unification of customary law along territorial lines include the *Grand Coutumier de Normandie*, drafted in the thirteenth century. This was one of the earliest drafts of ancient Norman law, which was of peculiar importance because of the privileged relationships between Normandy and England. Even today this collection remains a major source of private law on the islands of Jersey, Guernsey, Alderney and Stark. This work was widely influential in Normandy and beyond, because of its jurisprudential rather than its practical approach; an example of it was the inclusion of a treatise on the law at the beginning of the work, clearly inspired by a chapter with a similar approach at the beginning of the *Decretum Gratiani*.

In Northern France the *Coutumes de Beauvaisis* (1280) were a prime example of a private initiative to record the law in a small area. It was Philippe de Beaumanoir, bailiff of Clermont, who wrote down the customary law of the county where he exercised his official duties. It is one of the most significant and original contributions of the *ius proprium*, for its comprehensiveness and clarity. Even if the author did not include express references to the legal books of the *ius commune*, his acquaintance with Roman and canon law is unmistakable.

The *Sachsenspiegel* (the *Saxon Mirror*) by Eike von Repgow (d. 1235) marked the beginning of German jurisprudence. It was comprised of customary law from Saxony, in the center of Germany, but the work would have an enormous and enduring impact on Central Europe as a whole, because of its capacity to link customary rules and practices with wider theoretical and political reflections on the origins and workings of legal custom. Although he had not enjoyed a formal training in the Italian law schools, the author had sound knowledge of canon law, and was familiar with the *Decretum Gratiani* and the papal decretals.

Further north, in Denmark, mention must be made of the laws of Scania, Zealand and Jutland. These laws were not typical medieval custumals, for two reasons. Each of these laws covered one of Denmark's main provinces, instead of only small territorial units. Moreover, they included royal legislation. However, customary law certainly was an important source of the contents of these laws, which remained the basis of Denmark's legal system until the second half of the seventeenth century, when they were replaced by a nationwide book of law. The laws include some technical terms that lead us to the conclusion that their authors must have had some kind of knowledge of Roman and, above all, canon law, as taught at foreign universities. The Jutland Law probably inspired a similar Norwegian legal code in 1275.

The growing systematization of these books containing and describing customary law revealed the growing infiltration of the *ius commune* into the *ius proprium*. This evolution can be explained by the training of their authors: the professionals who in the thirteenth century served in municipal courts were practical officials without university education. As time passed, due to the central courts' increased activity and demand for professionals, more and more university-educated jurists ended up serving in courts where customary law was applied. The growing importance of record-keeping also contributed to this development. Customary law was, by definition, oral. Over time, however, it was laid down in writing due the combined influence of private codification initiatives, evidentiary techniques, and efforts by public authorities to produce records of custom-based law. Also worthy of mention is the increasingly scientific handling which customary law was given: the style and methodology governing the study of the *ius commune* came to be applied to an ever greater extent to customary law, and by the fifteenth and sixteenth centuries one can truly speak of the scientific study of the *ius proprium*. Finally, due to the greater unification of customary law, the common core of shared precepts expanded, and fragmentation decreased accordingly.

4. The early modern age

I. A GENERAL OUTLINE OF EARLY MODERN HISTORY

When did the Middle Ages end and the Modern Era begin? Since we are dealing with conventional categories that are largely arbitrary, this question is impossible to answer. However, there are moments in history which, due to events of great importance, or simply for their symbolic significance, help us to better understand historical developments. Take, for instance, the landmark year of 1453, which saw the fall of Constantinople, the end of the Hundred Years War between France and England, and the invention of the modern printing press. The year 1492 is also rich in symbolism, with the discovery of the New World and the end of the Reconquest following the taking of Granada – the final Moorish stronghold on Spain. Neither can one overlook the year 1517, when Martin Luther brought religious unity in the West to an end. All of these dates serve to illustrate how dramatically Europe was transforming during this era. It must be said, however, that although the consequences of these events were important, history, properly seen, is more about slow, gradual evolution than abrupt, radical changes – mankind has never risen one morning to find that it has awakened in a new era.

A. Economics

The discovery of America in 1492 triggered an immediate series of important economic consequences. It should not be overlooked that the European voyages of exploration during the fifteenth century were driven by the desire to find trade routes to the Orient. On behalf of the Crown of Castile, Christopher Columbus (d. 1506) discovered a new continent rich in new food products and, above all, precious metals. Portugal would find a way to the Indies via Africa (the East Indies) and Brazil (the West Indies). In the wake of the Spanish and Portuguese discoveries, Europe would go on to dominate the world.

Over the course of the fifteenth and sixteenth centuries Europe's population gradually recovered from the demographic disaster it had suffered in the form of the Black Death in the middle of the fourteenth century, while a new era of fruitful weather ensured enough food for a growing population. By 1600 Europe's population had returned to the levels it had enjoyed in 1300. This auspicious era, however, was ephemeral, as growth was soon halted by a spiral of war, famine, and plague. The consecuences would be – yet again – devastating, and the trend would not be reversed until the second half of the eighteenth century, when, as a result of developments in the fields of medicine, agriculture, and technology, the population once again surged in Europe, this time at an unprecedented rate, increasing until the twentieth century.

Demographic growth bolstered trade and industry, which developed with great dynamism, driven by key economic centers in Italy and the Netherlands. The port city of Antwerp supplanted Bruges as the continent's leading financial center, a position it would retain until 1585. The great commercial cities of the Italian peninsula – Florence, Genoa, Milan, Venice – would thrive as centers of trade, industry and finance until their era of glory finally came to a close in the seventeenth century.

Europe's discovery of overseas territories was immediately followed by their exploitation and colonization. During the sixteenth century Spain and Portugal enjoyed a virtual monopoly on commerce with the New World. Then, beginning in the seventeenth century an ascendant and ambitious England, followed by a somewhat more tepid France, would set about colonizing the new territories. But it was above all the United Provinces (the modern-day Netherlands) that, through the highly efficient *Vereenigde Oostindische Compagnie* (East Indies Company) took the greatest advantage of transcontinental trade. Inevitably, the competition between the colonizing powers escalated in its intensity and violence. Many of the wars on the European continent were waged to increase or maintain dominant positions in the colonies, into which they often spilled over.

A growing attention by public authorities to economic prosperity characterized the modern economy since its very inception. This concern was manifested, firstly, in the colonies and transoceanic trade, but internal industry was also subject to study and control. Spurred by the astronomical expenses generated by their military ventures, the western monarchs came to perceive the need for prosperous domestic economies. Spain, where the flow of silver from its New World holdings (Mexico, Peru …) brought about catastrophic inflation and the authorities did not foster the creation of conditions adequate for the development of industry, had lost its position as a superpower by the middle of the seventeenth century. In the second half of the 1600s England, France and the United Provinces would act aggressively to bolster their national economies. The most striking example of government intervention in the economy came with France's Jean-Baptiste Colbert (1619–83) and the mercantilist policies he pursued during the reign of Louis XIV (1643–1715). Colbert's policy consisted of maintaining raw materials in the realm by levying very high export taxes on them, while at the same time blocking the access of foreign-made products to the internal market through the application of import tariffs. Colbert also moved to eliminate internal barriers to trade – taxes and tolls of all kinds – and improve infrastructures to facilitate the distribution of products throughout France. The state would even acquire a portion of the capital of some large companies.

B. Politics: The Modern State

From the ashes of the Hundred Years War the territorial state arose triumphant: in the century following 1453 France, England and Spain saw the development of states which would wield effective control over their respective territories. Even the Italian Peninsula would witness a period of internal peace (Lodi, 1454). There were many signs of growing "nationalism" – if we can call it that. Dante (1265–1321) and the humanists portrayed Italy as boasting a glorious and commonly-held past. Spain unified, both during and after the Reconquest, drawing upon the image of supposedly shared enemies: the Jews and Moors within the country and heretics outside it. France came to view itself as the country chosen by God, who intervened in human history through its *christianissimus* or *très-chrétien* ("most Christian") king, assigned miraculous powers. In England anti-papal and anti-French sentiment was widespread, sowing fertile ground for national fervor.

The idea of the nation as an object of autonomous, quasi-religious worship was not new. During the Middle Ages many believed in Christendom, extending all across Europe, as a kind of holy realm inspiring a sense of passionate belonging. The application of this idea to the territorial state, the notion of a chosen people, and the corporate, mystical connection between it and the crown would promote exaggerated forms of patriotism. Where one of these elements was missing, whether a unified territory (Italy), a crown (Burgundy), or a national sense of belonging (the Holy Roman Empire) it was difficult for the state to establish itself as an effective authority and an abstract object of veneration.

The construction of the state as a unique power structure entailed the concurrent elimination of other authorities, inside and outside, which it perceived as competitors, including the feudal nobility, autonomous cities, and the Church. The rapid evolution of military technology had a particularly decisive impact on the first two; the new applications of gunpowder came to be decisive on the battlefield; small structures, such as cities or fiefdoms, could not afford costly investments in the latest military technologies – only states could. A series of stinging defeats suffered by the French cavalry at the hands of the English infantry illustrated the obsolescence of the feudal military model. Massive, combined attacks by rifles, bows and cannons were much more effective than the old personal charge on horseback with a sword, spear and armor. The feudal cavalry would give way to mercenary infantry and artillery as medieval walls were no longer an obstacle for heavy artillery and independent cities were left vulnerable.

With nobles and the bourgeois class unable to bear the costs entailed by the new form of warfare, both would lose political relevance. The feudal nobility, as a class, would see its influence gradually undermined as it was replaced by professional bureaucrats. Cities would also see their power undercut, as a limited set of clashes would normally suffice for monarchs to neutralize the influence of their most representative institutions.

The strengthening of the state was the direct result of the suppression of domestic competition, but was also accompanied by other initiatives. The importance of the enormous sums of money needed for an aspiring power to maintain military viability – amounts which only kings were ultimately capable of amassing – cannot be overemphasized. In order to quench its increasing thirst for tax revenues an increasingly powerful bureaucratic apparatus would see to it that royal power was projected into every last corner of a state's territory. Once again, the hierarchical institutions of Roman law and the Church were the most important sources of inspiration. During the fifteenth and sixteenth centuries institutions were created or reformed, courts of first instance and appeals courts charged with applying royal law and state legislation, staffed by professional, learned jurists responsible for their effective operation. With their new hierarchies in the court system and the elimination of the feudal nobility and cities as true centers of power, monarchs would feel capable of imposing their will upon their subjects as law. It was during this era that the figure of the absolute monarch was conceived, took shape, and was imposed. The power of these rulers was not, in reality, arbitrary, nor could it ever have been so. Despite brilliant and drawn-out theories regarding royal sovereignty and the divine right of kings, advanced by authors such as Jean Bodin (1530–1596) and Robert Filmer (1588–1653), the absolute monarch was only "absolute" according to institutional theory and protocol. In practice the king had to negotiate and grapple with a whole range of established interests, and his power depended, above all, on his personal savvy and skill as a politician, and that of his closest advisers.

Spain constitutes one of the earliest examples of the state formation process. The marriage of the two princes heir to the thrones of Castile and Aragon (1469) joined the two realms. Direct conquests, first of the Moorish kingdom (1492), followed by the Christian Kingdom of Navarre (1512), brought territorial unity to the Peninsula, with the exception of Portugal – which, however, between 1580 and 1640, also fell under the Spanish monarchy. Existing institutions, such as the representative assemblies, or *Cortes*, were not completely eliminated, but were partially supplanted by new, central institutions such as the Inquisition. The four feudal military orders (Santiago, Calatrava, Alcántara, and Montesa), with their extensive domains throughout the Peninsula's kingdoms, originated during the Reconquest, were brought under the king's direct control. Even so, Spain would remain, above all, the sum of several crowns, a dynamic which periodically became apparent, such as during the Portuguese and Catalonian revolts of 1640. Administrative centralization and the elimination of the power of the *Cortes* were more evident in Castile than in Aragon, in part due to the silver brought in from Spain's New World colonies and contributions from the clergy.

Until the middle of the seventeenth century Spain would stand as the premier superpower on the European continent, thanks to its overseas territories and states associated with the crowns of Castile and Aragon in Europe: Sicily, Naples, Sardinia, Milan and the Netherlands, as well as, under the reign of Charles V, territories in the German Empire, brought under Spanish control through royal family ties, such as the Archduchy of Austria. Spain's decline would become patently manifest during the War of the Spanish Succession (1701–1714), from which the Bourbon dynasty would emerge triumphant, ultimately subject to the dictates of Paris – a momentous change in Spanish foreign policy.

England, after its ultimate defeat in the Hundred Years War, in 1453, suffered a bloody period of civil war waged between the House of Lancaster and the House of York. The Wars of the Roses concluded in 1485 with a secondary branch of the House of Lancaster, the House of Tudor, emerging victorious. The dynasty's first king, Henry VII (1485–1509), stabilized the kingdom and laid the financial foundation for a policy of centralization, one successfully continued by Henry VIII (1509–1547) and Elisabeth I (1558–1603). As from the 1530s English *common law* was applied in Wales, from whence the Tudor family hailed. Also, with the help of shrewd advisers, Parliament was transformed into a docile and manipulable instrument. In 1603 James VI of Scotland would also occupy the English throne as James I. The new dynasty, the Stuarts, would immediately endorse radical ideas about the divine right of kings, drawing it into a pamphlet war with Catholic authors such as Francisco Suárez (1548–1617), and a debate ensued, followed with great interest throughout Europe. The English monarch aspired to rule without Parliament, but the theory of the King in Parliament was so solidly established that he was unable to do so. In 1628, Charles I (1625–1649) accepted the Petition of Rights, under which he pledged not to impose new taxes and fees without Parliament's approval, or to arbitrarily deprive anyone of their personal freedom. A lack of money compelled Charles I to convene Parliament in 1640, which gave rise to a new civil war, this time between Crown and Parliament. Charles's enmity towards the democratic body, and his religious policies, which ran counter to prevailing sensibilities, brought about his downfall and execution in 1649. His overthrow precipitated the establishment of a fleeting republic, the so-called Commonwealth (1649–1660), under the leadership of Oliver Cromwell (1599–1658), followed by the restoration of the Stuarts, with Charles II (1660–1685) on the throne. The latter monarch embraced a policy of pacification, in 1679 accepting the Habeas Corpus Act and promising to refrain from arbitrary arrests and detentions. But Charles II was succeeded by his brother, James II (1685–1688), who generated hostility once again between Crown and Parliament. Suspected of harboring Catholic and French sympathies, he was toppled by the Glorious Revolution (1688), the foundation of England's parliamentary monarchy down to the present day.

The reign of William III of Orange, stadtholder of the United Provinces (1672–1702), marked the beginning of the transition from the Stuarts, who sought to concentrate power and authority in the monarch, to the Hanovers, more decided and willing to rule in collaboration with Parliament. In 1689, just after taking the throne, William accepted the Bill of Rights, a document designed to clearly and definitively stipulate the relationship between the king and Parliament. In 1707 traditional personal ties between England and Scotland were transformed into a constitutional union with the formation of the United Kingdom of Great Britain (Treaty of Union). In 1714 the German House of Hanover took the throne, its first kings acting more like German princes than kings of England, which made possible the development and consolidation of the parliamentary regime.

The territory under the control of the crown in France had relentlessly expanded during the Late Middle Ages, the construction of a central administration under the monarch's authority a process which had already been initiated during the reigns of Philip II Augustus and Philip

IV the Fair. Suddenly suspended during the Hundred Years War (1337–1453), the process was resumed with renewed vigor after the final victory in 1453. With the invasion of Burgundy in 1477 and the annexation of Brittany in 1532, the territory under the king's direct control was augmented and France's borders were almost definitively set. Louis XII (1498–1515) and Francis I (1515–1547) centralized the administration of the kingdom through the creation of effective administrative institutions, such as the *conseil privé*, central courts, and *parlements* (provincial courts), which served to provide subjects throughout the realm with access to central and professional justice administrated by university-trained jurists expert in Roman law. The feudal nobility, meanwhile, with much of its political clout having evaporated, dedicated its energies to enjoying a refined life at the court in Paris.

Religious struggles between Catholics and Huguenots (the French offshoot of Calvinism), endless civil wars, dynastic succession problems, and defeats to the powerful Spanish armies would combine to undermine the French monarchs' centralization of power during the second half of the sixteenth century. In 1589 Henry IV took the throne (1589–1610), a Protestant who had converted to Catholicism remembered for his (possibly apocryphal) phrase: "Paris is well worth a mass." Henry IV would undertake an active policy of pacification which would earn him the moniker *Le bon roi Henri* and his being remembered as one of the finest rulers France ever had. Through the Edict of Nantes (1598) he granted freedom of religion to the Huguenots and made peace with Spain. After decades of bloody conflicts French monarchs, jurists and politicians would eventually acknowledge the need to put an end to them, as they proceeded to convert the king into an object of veneration and concentrate power in his hands as a guarantor of peace. In fact, the Estates-General (*Etats généraux*) would not be convened after 1614 until the French Revolution in 1789. Cardinals Richelieu (1585–1642) and Mazarin (1602–1661) moved to both raise taxes and strengthen the Crown's control over the Church and the provincial and local authorities. In 1661 Louis XIV announced that henceforth he would rule as absolute monarch, identified with and embodying the state, a development dramatically illustrated by his purported assertion "*L' état, c'est moi*" ("I am the state"). Louis pursued an aggressive policy of expansion which expanded the boundaries of his kingdom, and installed his grandson on the Spanish throne. After ill-advised commitments by the French throne in the War of the Austrian Succession (1740–48), the Seven Years War (1756–63) and the American Revolutionary War (1778–83), France was bankrupted and the country careened into chaos, with the Revolution breaking out in 1789.

The dream of the dukes of Burgundy of gathering all the Netherland territories under their crown would never be realized, ending in fruitless frustration. Some of these territories, such as Flanders, were subject to the French crown through a feudal relationship. Others, such as the Duchy of Brabant, were vassals of the Holy Roman Emperor. Through an astute series of political marriages the Dukes of Burgundy managed to bring nearly all the territories under their authority, except for the prince-bishopric of Liege – a situation which would be inherited by Charles V. Their holdings, however, would always be based on personal unions between the different territories. Thus, the Duke of Burgundy cannot accurately be called the ruler of the Netherlands, but rather the feudal lord of the seventeen provinces: Count of Flanders, Duke of Brabant, Count of Holland, etc. Charles V, however, would take some steps to unify the Netherlands into a single state. The aforementioned personal unions were legally consolidated in 1546 when he uniformized the succession law in all the provinces: henceforth all of them would be inherited and fall under the rule of a single lord. In 1526 the Peace of Madrid had ended the feudal relationship between Flanders and the French Crown (which spared Charles V from having to swear allegiance to his archenemy Francis I of France, while also precluding the possibility of having verdicts handed down in Flanders appealed to Paris courts). The Transaction of Augsburg (1548), meanwhile, undid ties with the Holy Roman Empire, releasing the Netherlands from the jurisdiction of the *Reichskammergericht* (the "imperial chamber court") and unifying them under a single legal arrangement: the *Kreitz* of Burgundy. Administrative centralization also progressed considerably through the creation of new central institutions.

This centralizing policy generated many misgivings, sparking a revolt by the provinces' elites against Philip II (1527–98). The conflict would escalate on both sides, and in the end the northern provinces, forming the Union of Utrecht (1576), signed the *Akte van Verlatinghe* (Act of Abjuration), in which they renounced the authority of Philip II and declared their independence. The Republic of the United Provinces had been born: a confederal structure of seven states with a common foreign policy and army, and a minimum set of institutions charged with shared fiscal and administrative affairs. After a number of failed attempts to find a suitable king, a republic was declared, though a monarchical element was present in the form of the stadtholder, the army's commander in chief, always to proceed from the House of Orange.

Spain's reconquest of the southern provinces prompted mass emigration to the north. This, along with the blockade of the River Scheldt, which provided access to Antwerp, shifted power towards Amsterdam.

Boasting an extensive trading fleet and buoyed by their intelligent economic and diplomatic policies, the Dutch would rise to become a key power in seventeenth-century Europe. After the Eighty Years War the Spanish were forced to recognize Dutch independence via the Peace of Munster (1648). The southern provinces chose to remain under the authority of the Habsburgs; until 1714, the Spanish Habsburgs, and, henceforth, that of the Austrian branch of the family.

The Holy Roman Empire entered the modern age as a collection of semi-autonomous kingdoms and territories. Beginning in 1440 the imperial title was held by the Habsburgs, but this did not mean that they did not have to secure this title with each election, often paying a political price to do so. Both Maximilian of Austria and Charles V sought to put an end to this state of affairs through the establishment of a central court, the *Reichskammergericht* (1495), as well as through wars inspired by political and religious factors: against the Turks, aginst the Schmalkaldic League, (1546–55) and, above all, in the Thirty Years War (1618–48). In the end, however, the Peace of Westphalia (1648) established the German territories' autonomy and freedom from imperial authority. The emperor henceforth focused on administrating those territories which he controlled directly: Austria, Bohemia and Hungary, never managing to centrally administrate all the Empire's holdings.

C. Church and Religion

In the twelfth and thirteenth centuries the papacy had laid the foundations for a centralized and hierarchical Church – the first modern state, according to some historians – and, without any hesitation, utilized this powerful apparatus in the political struggles with the emperor, first, and, later, though with less power to exert, with the king of France. France's subordination of papal power was made manifest by the relocation of the papacy to Avignon, where the pope was accused of frequently exploiting the ecclesiastical apparatus in a manner that was, at best, ethically dubious. The reactions, both from within and outside the Church, were swift. Locating the Holy See in Avignon was considered extremely detrimental to the Church and the most illustrious Catholics of the time – Catherine of Siena, most prominently – advocated a return to the Eternal City. The result of these constant struggles was the so-called Western Schism, during which there were actually two (and even three) popes at the same time. The Council of Constance (1414–17) resolved the situation by deposing the "anti-popes" John XXIII and Benedict XIII and accepting the resignation of Gregory XII, before nominating a single pope, Martin V (1417–31), and returning the Chair of Peter to Rome. As is hardly surprising, this entire situation sparked numerous and heated controversies, among them a decisive debate as to whether a general council could be ascribed powers to depose the pope in certain cases.

After his election Martin V refused to recognize the conciliarist doctrines that had emerged from the Council of Constance, but was forced to endorse the periodic holding of councils and certain measures to reform the Church in the pursuit of greater austerity and spirituality. His Renaissance-era successors, however, did not feel bound by such commitments, and would dispense with councils, further concentrate power in Rome, and draw severe censure for their desire for glory and riches. Reformers such as Girolamo Savonarola (1452–98) and Erasmus of Rotterdam (1466–1536) openly criticized the Church's excessively worldly ambitions.

The emergence of figures such as Martin Luther (1483–1546) and John Calvin (1509–64) must be viewed in this broader context of appeals for general internal reform of the Church. The forces they would unleash would forever alter the course of European history. Indeed, what came to be called the Reformation was, in reality, nothing less than a profound and radical revolution.

An underestimation of the magnitude of Luther's social support, as well as the disastrous political backlash to his rebellion, secured the short- and long-term success of the Protestant churches. Political support for the Protestants, first in the Empire, but also in France, the Netherlands, England and Scotland, was often the result of political considerations rather than religious convictions. In England, as in other places, the temptation on the part of the Crown to confiscate extensive ecclesiastical assets explains, in large part, the foundation of the Anglican Church through the 1534 Act of Supremacy. In 1555, after a war waged by Charles V against the union of Protestant princes known as the Schmalkaldic League, the Peace of Augsburg established the principle of *cuius regio, eius religio* ("Whose realm, his religion"): the religion of each territory would be determined by its feudal lord. This policy represented a momentous recognition of the religious division which had come to split Europe. Many subsequent wars were waged under the pretext of religious motives, but this principle stood. By 1555 Protestantism, though always internally divided, was firmly established in the northern half of Europe.

It was, paradoxically, the Counter-Reformation, a movement for deep and genuine renewal which emerged victorious from the Council of Trent (1545–63), which aspired to reform the Church's morality and customs and enhance its education and organization. Driven by the fervor that followed the Tridentine Reform, the Church managed to halt Protestantism's territorial expansion and salvage some measure of Catholic unity. Even so, the popes had to make concessions to Catholic monarchs, in particular with regard to the right to appoint key officers in the Church hierarchy, and in relation to taxes and fees on the clergy and ecclesiastical assets.

The end of religious unity also had important consequences in the field of private law. Luther maintained that true faith could be found only in the Holy Scriptures, rather than in the Christian tradition and the Church that sustained it. He believed that the centralization of ecclesiastical and papal power were based on canon law, largely a product of that tradition. Well known is Luther's symbolic burning of a copy of Gregory IX's *Decretals*. In the countries which adopted Protestantism, however, the courts continued to apply canonical precepts to matters such as marriage, wills, etc., not because they acknowledged the authority of Rome or of the *Decretals*, but because they had come to constitute customary law.

D. Science and Culture

In the fifteenth century there emerged in Italy, and later throughout Europe during the sixteenth century, the cultural and scientific phenomenon known as the Renaissance, or Humanism. It is not easy to classify this movement, but it was defined by a new conception of man and the world different from that of the medieval era.

The humanists' predilection for the Greco-Roman world is often underscored. The expressive term "Renaissance," after all, coined in the nineteenth century, referred to a "rebirth" of interest in classical culture. The movement sought to recover certain values and elements of Greco-Roman culture, which Renaissance proponents saw as anthropocentric, after centuries of a mentality which they derided as theocratic, rigid and dogmatic. Renaissance artists consciously broke with medieval artistic tradition, which they contemptuously described as "Gothic," that is, typical of Goths, or "barbarians". Humanists were appalled by the medieval adaptations of the classical heritage: the alteration of texts and fallacious interpretations of them to reconcile them to medieval thought and justify medieval institutions. They believed their predecessors were guilty of manipulating the Latin language itself.

Today such judgments seem to us exaggerated and biased. First of all, the Renaissance shift was never felt or embraced by the masses. It was, rather, a minority movement, and consciously so. The very idea of "reviving" a "lost" Antiquity was erroneous, as devotion to and study of the classics had, in fact, never ceased during the Middle Ages. The ongoing study of Roman law, which was never forgotten, testifies to this. Many during the medieval age had already seen themselves as successors to the classical world, and indebted to it in every way. For them the continuity was evident; the legacy of the past was received as a living, organic, reality that permeated their entire vision of the world. In short, medieval man felt classical civilization not as something alien, but something close and dear, naturally present in their lives – not a distant ideal to preserve in all its purity, as the humanists later conceived of it.

By idealizing the ancient world the humanists revealed, however, their sense of belonging to a world different from that which they imagined. The most ambitious of them would not be satisfied with imitating that past – a bygone and, hence, unrepeatable era – but would try to adapt the best of its spirit to their time and the world in which they lived.

II. JURISPRUDENCE

A. Legal Humanism

The study of Greco-Roman antiquity as a model in itself led to renewed and strenuous efforts to uncover original texts from the era in Europe's libraries. Old manuscripts would be dusted off and many texts read for the first time since their composition centuries prior. The Greek language was also rediscovered after having been almost completely forgotten during the Middle Ages, even in formal education; the phrase *graecum est: non legitur* ("it is Greek: it isn't read"), placed in the margin of the page, appears even in the works of Cervantes and Shakespeare. But Greek would attract great interest due to the fall of Constantinople and the flight of Greek scholars to the West, along with a trend towards rapprochement between the Church of Rome and the Eastern Churches in the fifteenth century. With zeal efforts were undertaken to search for pristine Greek writings uncorrupted by Latin translations and adaptations. It was sought, in short, to study Antiquity in its own context.

The search for ancient texts was applied, first of all, to those texts endorsed and lauded by authorities in the Middle Ages (and in late Antiquity). First of all, the Bible. The version known as the Vulgate is a translation into Latin of ancient texts originally written in Hebrew, Greek and Aramaic; the humanists considered it necessary to compare the translation with the original texts. Thanks to the comparative study of texts all kinds of forgeries came to light, such as the Donation of Constantine, for one. Through a comparison of the Latin in this text to that of others in the fourth century – the period during which the

Donation supposedly took place – humanist Lorenzo Valla (d. 1457) proved that it was a fake, and was even able to date it: the mid-eighth century. As one might expect, the humanists' techniques were also applied to the *ius commune*, Roman law in particular.

A first reaction led to a censuring of the work of the glossators and commentators. Medieval jurists considered the *Corpus iuris civilis* a text of hallowed authority and unquestionable validity, which through glosses and commentaries was to be interpreted and adapted to the needs of the times in which they lived. The humanists, on the other hand, rejected the glosses and commentaries, outraged by what they considered a barbaric use of Latin by their authors. They disparaged Bartolus and Baldus and did not have one word of admiration for what they scornfully called *accursianum absynthium*, the "absinthe" of Accursius: the once venerated ordinary gloss. Chief among the humanists' concerns was stylistic elegance. Hence, they aspired to use Latin as if they were ancient experts in the art of rhetoric, with Cicero as their paragon. The bastardized Latin of the medieval jurists pained their eyes and ears (as it was still a common custom to read aloud, even when alone); medieval jurists used, for example, the word *guerra*, war, in their Latin texts, rather than the classical term *bellum*.

The expert humanists, however, did not confine themselves to discrediting medieval jurisprudence. They also made positive contributions, including, for example, their critical study of the text of the *Corpus iuris civilis*. The great shift in mentality was that, unlike the medieval jurists, the humanists no longer considered Justinian's codes as texts of timeless and universal validity. Rather, the humanists studied them as writings composed in a specific geographical and historical context. Their aspiration was to bring genuine Roman law to light, without subsequent complements, including Justinian's Byzantine additions. The fragments of classical Roman jurists featured in the *Digest* were highly valued by the humanists, though this did not prevent them from abhorring the work of the compilers, whom they accused of distorting the authentic texts of classical Roman law. In his work *Antitribonianus* French jurist François Hotman (1524–90) reproached Tribonian, the *Digest*'s main author, for having drawn upon only 5 percent of the legal material available and having contaminated the purity of the text with interpolations during the compiling work. In his view the final text of the *Corpus iuris civilis* contained too many contradictions and repetitions, and the excerpts of the jurists were presented outside of their original context, mixed together with no apparent order. Neither could the French scholar understand why jurists of clearly Roman origin, such as as Servius Sulpicius, the Catos, Manilius and Sextus Caecilius did not appear in the *Digest*, while provincial jurists like Modestinus, Iavolenus, and Ulpian occupied positions of honor. His conclusion was blunt: Tribonian was a corrupt politician who, in exchange for large sums of money, altered the texts of the *ius civile* based on individual requests.

Humanist jurisprudence took a relative and critical approach to the *Corpus iuris civilis*, which during the Middle Ages had been viewed as an absolute and universal authority. This did not mark, however, an end to the intellectual allure that the *ius commune* had always exerted. The text's authority was, without a doubt, undercut, approached as a work produced by a specific society in a specific context. It would, nevertheless, continue to be a model. The refinement and systematization of Roman law, in its purest form – that is, without Byzantine and medieval additions and interpolations – would continue to fascinate academic jurists, even growing as Roman law came to be studied in its own right, without any need to adapt it to serve the circumstances of the moment. For humanists it would be a point of reference for the development of a body of jurisprudence based on the *ius proprium*.

Renaissance jurisprudence also produced a review of content. Employing a historical-philological method, the humanists managed to mend the Roman legal texts, returning them to their original state. The *Novellae* could once again be read in Greek; the *littera bononiensis* – the standard edition of the *Corpus iuris civilis* in the Middle Ages – would be carefully compared to the *littera florentina*, but also with other texts containing elements of Roman law, such as classical literature, inscriptions, etc. Open season was declared and a genuine attack waged on medieval interpolations and additions, which would be recognized as such and deleted. Translations into Latin of terms and quotes originally in Greek would be restored to the original. In 1583 Denis Godefroy (d. 1622) published a version of the *Corpus iuris civilis* that came to supplant the vulgate version based on the *littera bononiensis*; this edition would be considered the standard edition for 300 years until superseded by that of Theodor Mommsen (d. 1903). At the same time the humanists set about reconstructing original texts with the help of a whole range of materials they found both in the Justinian collection and outside it; for example, the Law of the Twelve Tables, recomposed by Aymar de Rivail (d. 1558).

Thanks to the historical-philological method, the humanists managed to achieve an even greater refinement of legal concepts. To clarify difficult or ambiguous terms they drew up a list of what ancient jurists had said about the term in question. This list was then compared to the use of the term by poets and grammarians, such as Livy and Virgil, or with Greek terms. If the ambiguity remained, the problem was resolved by appealing to the authority of Quintilian or Cicero. An example: the word *mulier*, woman. According to Gaius *mulier* referred solely to single women, while Ulpian seemed to use it to refer to both married and unmarried women. Turning to Cicero, who used it without making distinctions with regards to marital status, the humanist jurists concluded that the term referred to women in general. In this way the humanists were able to clarify many inaccuracies.

The humanists' new historical-philological method differed dramatically from the scholastic method employed by the followers of Bartolus de Saxoferrato. Andrea Alciato (1492–1550), a scholar at Bourges in France, would begin to apply the new method to legal instruction and research, leading the new method to also be known as the *mos gallicus* (French style), to distinguish it from the *mos italicus* (Italian style) of jurists who were disciples of Bartolus. The new approach was also referred to as "elegant jurisprudence." From France the new school spread throughout Europe to England, Spain, the Netherlands and the Empire. On the Italian Peninsula Bartolus's method was more entrenched, and was also of greater practical utility. After initial clashes between the two schools and methods a rapprochement would come about which, within one or two generations of jurists, yielded a sort of fusion containing the best of both.

In addition to the aforementioned François Hotman and Denis Godefroy, worthy of note are the humanists Guillaume Budé (1467–1540), Jacques Cujas (1522–90) and Hugo Donellus (1521–97), as pioneers of the new method in France. Guillaume Budé was one of the finest hellenists of his day. He advised Francis I on cultural matters such as libraries, classical language education and printing, and was in correspondance with some of Europe's leading humanists, such as Desiderius Erasmus and Thomas More. As Master of Requests he was one of France's highest-ranking judicial and administrative officials. His major contribution to legal science consisted of his revision of the *Digest* with a view to restoring the original passages in Greek. Jacques Cujas was one of France's best-known legal humanists, who essentially led the life of a scholar at different universities in France, before finding a permanent home at the University of Bourges. His main concern was not so much a grammatical approach to the Roman law texts, such as that taken by Guillaume Budé, but rather the analysis of their legal meaning, through an effort to reconstruct the mentality, ideals and values of the ancient Roman jurists. Hugo Donellus, a professor of law at various universities across Europe, took Jacques Cujas's approach a step further. Instead of limiting himself to an internal analysis of the Roman law texts, he wanted to devise an ideal system of law. He therefore looked into the Roman law texts in search of general principles of law, and to logically derive a theoretical reconstruction of Roman law. This effort yielded his massive 28-volume *Commentaria iuris civilis* (*Commentaries on Roman Private Law*), which met with instant commercial success, especially in Germany and the Netherlands.

Their Huguenot sympathies had pushed some of these French humanists to seek refuge outside their home country, which helped to disseminate the new method in various countries. Most Western European countries also produced outstanding legal humanists of their own: Ulrich Zasius (1461–1536) in imperial territory; Antonio de Nebrija (1442–1522), in Spain; the Italian émigré Angel Poliziano (1454–94), in England; and Viglius of Aytta (1507–77), in the Netherlands.

In addition to its specifically historical and philological goals, the doctrine of humanistic inspiration assigned special importance to pedagogy. The glossators and commentators had stuck very closely to the texts upon which they worked, their glosses and comments always referring to concrete fragments of Justinian's collection. Their commentaries also included references to other places in the compilation which addressed institutions similar or identical to those dealt with in the section being analyzed. In essence, however, they continued to be commentaries on a single excerpt. The humanists, on the other hand, preferred to examine each legal institution in a coordinated and comprehensive manner, even though excerpts on them could be widely scattered throughout Justinian's collection. The humanist jurists, thus, preferred the format of the treatise to publish the conclusions of their research, one which allowed them to address and systematize the matter at their own discretion rather than having to follow the fixed order of the *Corpus iuris civilis.*

Along with this predilection for the treatise, the method would spawn other, new genres of legal literature. Not only would commentaries and manuals be produced, but also dissertations, monographs, questions and answers, lexicons, etc. The greater variety is explained, again, by differing attitudes towards the texts, which were no longer slavishly followed. Rather, authors fully conscious of the originality of their work produced their own expositions.

Other projects carried out by humanist jurists worthy of note for their relevance included the application of the historical-philological method to the texts of canon law, including editions of the Bible in the three original languages of Latin, Hebrew and Greek (including the Complutensian Polyglot Bible), and scientific editions of patristic texts, such as those of St. Augustine. From these editions it became evident, for example, that upon compiling some patristic fragments in the *Decretum Gratiani*, the texts had suffered alterations (we have already cited the falsifications of the collection of the pseudo-Isidorian decretals, and the forged Donation of Constantine). Scientific editions of old canonical collections were also produced, such as those by Ivo of Chartres. Some humanists, such as Charles Dumoulin, used these scientific editions of the original texts of the Bible, patristic texts, the decrees of councils and synods, older canonical collections, the papal decretals and, of course, Roman law, to restore the canonical texts to their original state.

Faced with the danger of the application of the historical-philological method weakening the foundations of established power – as occurred with the Donation of Constantine – Rome decided to centralize humanistic work on canon law. In 1582 the official and authentic edition of the *Corpus iuris canonici* appeared after a review of the canonical texts, verified by an official commission.

Humanistic study and the application of the historical-philological method had immediate consequences for canon law. Diachronic comparison of Roman, post-Roman, early medieval and late medieval canon law clearly revealed that it had changed profoundly over time. Medieval canonists had also detected these changes, but considered them part of the same body of law they knew and in which, conceptually, contradictions were impossible. The humanists, however, saw the changes as manifestations of the ecclesiastical and social context of a particular historical period which they viewed from a distance, no longer considering themselves part of it. Humanistic study also showed that in the past the Church had not always been the rigid and monolithic structure which the Papal decretals portrayed; ecclesiastical discipline during the early Middle Ages was certainly different from that later determined by Gregorian reform. The discovery of not only chronological, but also regional differences, prior to the development of the papal monarchy, would also have a debilitating effect on the universal and eternal value attributed to the *Corpus iuris canonici*.

The loss of this universal value, both of the *Corpus iuris civilis* and the *Corpus iuris canonici*, soon had an impact on the study of the *ius proprium*. Inevitably, it was concluded that if the *Corpus iuris civilis* represented the law of a particular people in a certain historical period – and not even an authentic version of it, at that – then the local, contemporary sets of law across Europe could also be valid objects of study and refinement. Legal humanism, in short, would provide *ius proprium* with intellectual respectability, leading to further study of it in its various facets: legislation, justice, customary law. It should be noted, however, that it was not until the eighteenth century that university teaching, which historically had trained jurists exclusively in Roman law, finally offered courses in local and national law as well.

B. The School of Salamanca

Humanism did not mark the end of the scholastic method. Its refined techniques – *distinctio*, *aequiparatio*, etc. – would prove indispensable for the study of law. Moreover, as a philosophical-theological framework, scholastics would remain attractive for the fruitful way in which they reconciled – following Thomas Aquinas (c. 1225–74) – faith and reason, the universal and the particular, morality and law.

It was in Renaissance Spain, above all, where scholastics enjoyed a new period of splendor after Francisco de Vitoria (c. 1480–1546) established Thomas Aquinas's *Summa Theologica* as the premier book for theological education in Salamanca, rather than Peter Lombard's (d. 1160) *Sententiae*. This marked a small revolution in theological education and, to no lesser extent, in legal education also. The *Summa theologica* brims over with profound reflections on the law and justice. These passages from the lofty work would be, at the same time, the object of commentaries, appearing in large numbers with ambitious titles such as *De legibus* (*On Laws*) or *De iustitia et iure* (*On Justice and Law*), with theologians and jurists from Salamanca bringing their extensive knowledge of Roman, canon, and local law to the analysis of excerpts by the "Universal Doctor." Thus was born a new type of legal commentary, which no longer followed the order or systematics of the *Corpus iuris civilis*, but rather that of Aquinas. The model was not imposed in an absolute or rigid way, and authors were at all times free to structure their work according to their personal tastes.

The Dominican friar Francisco de Vitoria would have a very profound impact on the study of law, despite the fact that he published nothing during his lifetime. His ideas have come down to us through the notes taken by its students, who revered him. The scholar's works featured painstaking and independent analysis of the many disputes which arose during an era rife with new developments, garnering him great prestige and influence, both during his life and posthumously. His reflections on the legitimacy of the Spanish conquest of the Americas, rooted in a strikingly modern conception of natural law and human dignity, would be crucial to the development of the doctrine of independent international law.

The towering figure of Vitoria presides over several generations of authors in what has been called the School of Salamanca, as its first adherents taught at that university, sharing the system and methods of this "late scholasticism." Its main authors led an eminently academic life of teaching and writing. That does not mean that they lived in an ivory tower; on the contrary, they frequently engaged the most pressing issues of their times, such as the challenges posed by the new economic realities of global trade and finance; the plight of the natives in the colonies; international relations between states; Church reform; and political theory.

Domingo de Soto (c.1494–1560), a student of Vitoria and a fellow Dominican, wrote important commentaries on the *Summa theologica* and the sections *De legibus* and *De iustitia et iure*, as well as independent treatises, including works on property law. De Soto was also involved in the organization of the famous debate of Valladolid, where another Dominican, Bartolomé de las Casas (1474–1566) denounced the brutal fate of the natives in the Spanish colonies. His adversary in the debate was the humanist Juan Ginés de Sepúlveda (1490–1573), then Europe's expert on Aristotle, who claimed that atrocities against the "savage" and "inferior" Indians were justified if they refused conversion to the Catholic faith. Las Casas, in contrast, stressed the equality of the native peoples, an idea rooted in an elementary but fundamentally democratic political theory. The Jesuit Francisco Suárez is one of the most modern figures of the Salamanca School, a father, along with Vitoria, of international law and a theorist in the areas of sovereignty and the social pact. Juan de Mariana (1536–1624), also a Jesuit, emphatically defended tyrannicide in a book that the king of France ordered to be burned. Luis de Molina (1535–1600), a professor at Coimbra and Evora, argued in his *De iustitia et iure* that legitimate power is derived from the citizenry as a set of individuals with rights, portending philosophies that would prevail in the eighteenth and nineteenth centuries. In the fields of trade and commerce the Spanish scholastics were also among the most innovative thinkers of their time. Martín de Azpilcueta (1492–1586), a prominent canonist, heralded concepts key to the modern economy and defended the free market as an instrument for the determination of fair prices. Fernando Vázquez de Menchaca (1512–69), a jurist sent by Philip II to the Council of Trent, argued that the seas could not be appropriated, anticipating Grotius by one century. Finally, Leonardo Lessius (1554–1623), a Jesuit professor at Leuven, addressed with great sagacity, in his *De iustitia et iure*, novel issues related to financial, banking and insurance law, his work seeing over 20 editions in the seventeenth century alone.

The importance of the School of Salamanca to the field of political theory and its influence on the development of a doctrine of autonomous international law have long been recognized. Its contributions to private law, however, have been largely overlooked. At most it is mentioned as a precursor of Grotius and the proponents of natural law. The works of the School's scholars, nevertheless, were fundamental to the development of basic legal concepts, such as contract and property. The late scholastic authors were unique in their synthesis of Roman law, canon law, *ius proprium*, theology, philosophy, morality and ethics, and for the extraordinary ease with which they assimilated the Bartolian and humanistic methods. They would lay down the foundations upon which subsequent natural law apologists would stand.

The Spanish scholastics were closely involved in some of the most novel, urgent and controversial legal issues of their time, which required solutions which transcended national borders, religion, and even civilizations. In their search for elements through which humanity could build an order fair for all, all of them arrived at a concept which would be the subject of legal debate for the next three centuries: natural law.

Following Thomas Aquinas, late scholastics considered natural law as one created by God, eternal and universal, common to all humanity, and, of course, transcending nationality and religion. According to their thinking, there are two ways to ascertain the precepts of natural law: divine revelation and human reason. Man is capable of knowing natural law through the use of his intellect and reason, his birthrights as a being created in God's image.

One of the first problems the Salamanca School authors addressed is that concerning the legitimacy of property. Is property an institution of natural law? If so, cannot then anyone, even if they do not know the true faith, acquire property? What right, then, has the king of Castile to seize overseas territories?

This development of independent natural law offered a key advantage: in an era that had seen the notion of absolute truth wane, natural law made it possible to keep alive the alluring and cherished ideal of a universal and eternal system of law. But all the problems were not thus solved, of course.

The political model of Francisco Suárez offers a good example of this. According to Suárez God created nature and, with it, natural law. It is a principle of natural law that man forms political communities, and it is only within them that he is capable of living in peace and order. He cannot be extracted from this situation, but he can determine the political form of the community: monarchy, republic, aristocracy, democracy. Of all these models, monarchy is the best (here Suárez follows a long tradition of Aristotelian origin). At some point in its history, in some way, the political community decided to organize itself as a monarchy. For Suárez it was clear that the monarch wielded power thanks to his subjects: the community delegates part of its political power, which belongs to it, to its government. The nature of this pact was, and is, an object of debate. According to Suárez, the pact itself proceeds from natural law, although there may be other options chosen by man. In some specific cases obedience to the monarch ceases to be compulsory and resistance is legitimate, depending on the conditions of the original contract and the requirements of natural justice, provided that one can substantiate these conditions or immemorial custom with documents. It may also happen that the monarch behaves like a tyrant and leads the community into ruin, in which case there can be no doubt: the people may rise up against their monarch. When the original transfer of political power was made to the monarch the community retained its right to defend itself, which might be invoked to throw off tyranny.

In this diagram of a contractual monarchy it is perfectly conceivable for the original contract to place legislative power on the side of the community. And yet, clearly, it may also lie on the side of the king. This transfer implies a fair possession of political power, granting the king legal and, in some respects, ethical superiority vis-à-vis the community. Thus, the monarch's will is law, and there exists the obligation to obey it. The monarch can also override customary law.

This is not to say that the monarch may exercise his power capriciously. According to the definition of Aquinas, the law is nothing more than a prescription of reason, organized to serve the "common good" and promulgated by he who is charged with overseeing the community. This concept of the common good, key in the Aristotelian-Thomistic tradition, is not equivalent to the sum of the assets of each of the community's members; it is indivisible and it is only through prudential collaboration that it can be achieved, increased, and protected. Law and political power exist only in order to serve the common good. Without it, political power is devoid of any raison d'être.

The king stands, therefore, above the law and custom, but as a source of law himself he remains linked to the law insofar as the common good forms part of it. If a king places himself above the law without organizing his policies to promote the common good, he becomes a tyrant and may be legitimately deposed. In short: the constitutional pact entails both rights and duties; or, better put, expectations of conduct and fields of action whose precise boundaries it is not possible – due to their prudential character – to define a priori.

This model does not aspire to distinguish clearly between natural law, divine law and human law. It is clear that the monarchy is not established by divine law in the sense that the king receives political power directly from God. Rather, it proceeds from natural and human law, as the submission of political power to the common good, and of the community to political power – in the way decided by man – are principles of natural law.

C. *Usus modernus pandectarum* and Roman-Dutch Law

The *usus modernus pandectarum* (roughly, "the Digest brought into line with current practice") refers to a way of conceiving jurisprudence and a group of jurists who worked mostly in the German territories of the Empire in the seventeenth century and who incorporated humanistic subjects and methodologies into a traditional "Bartolist" approach to law. In this sense the German jurists were not so different from the vast majority of their European counterparts. Humanism, in its purest form, criticized the language of medieval jurists, but it could add little to the subtle analyses and reasonings of Accursius, Bartolus, and Baldus. After an initial phase in which humanism clamored for its place in jurisprudence, the advantages of the new historical-philological method were recognized and it was integrated into the old Bartolist school, which not only endured but was, in fact, still predominant.

From the beginning the Holy Roman Empire maintained a special relationship with Roman law. During the Middle Ages the German Emperor was considered the direct successor of his Roman predecessors, to the point where Roman law was naturally considered his very own. Thus, when the *Reichskammergericht* (supreme imperial court) was created in 1495, the application of Roman law was stipulated as suppletive in cases involving a lack of provisions under local law. This "reception" of Roman law would pose the constant challenge of adapting historic Roman norms to contemporary circumstances.

The *usus modernus pandectarum* was neo-Bartolist in the sense that it turned to Roman law to solve everyday issues. Quotes and excerpts were reinterpreted outside their context in order to extract answers to current issues from them. The *usus modernus* took from legal humanism the scientific advances of the historical-philological method and the consciousness of the ahistoricism of Roman law as it was being applied.

The most important authors of this school are Samuel Stryck (d. 1710), whose *Usus modernus pandectarum* would provide the name for the whole movement, and, above all, Hermann Conring (d. 1681), who in his famous *De origine iuris germanici* (*On the Origin of German Law*) set out to qualify the widespread idea of a wholesale reception of Roman law in Germany. The collapse of the German emperor's universalist claims and the new legal humanist paradigm which posited Roman law as a legal system developed by a particular people in a particular past era severely undermined the normative universality of Roman law. According to Conring, the reception after 1495 was a historical event that could be undone. The reception had taken place as a consequence of a political decision, and a subsequent political decision or a contrary custom could reverse it.

Conring's book was an eye-opener for many German jurists, because it pointed them to their own laws, which could, and should, be incorporated into the Roman law system. The pedigree of a certain rule – whether Roman or German – no longer automatically established its validity. This opened up the *ius commune* to new areas of the law, such as commercial law, criminal law and even constitutional law. The movement of the *usus modernus* was important not only in Germany, but also in other parts of Europe such as Scandinavia or the Baltics.

In the young Dutch Republic of the seventeenth century, with its broad-minded intellectual climate and economic prosperity, a generation of legal scholars heralded what would be the landmark methodology of Conring and the *usus modernus*: a blend of Roman law with local legal concepts from the province of Holland, combining an elegant humanistic approach with a practical view to the applicability of their scholarly research. This Roman-Dutch law was implemented in several holdings of the Dutch across the planet, and still forms the core of civil law in countries such as South Africa and Indonesia. Major figures include Arnold Vinnius (d. 1657), Ulrik Huber (d. 1694), Johannes Voet (d. 1713) and Gerard Noodt (d. 1715), but the best-known of them all was Hugo Grotius (1583–1645).

Grotius was born into a regent's family in Delft, which was well connected to the political and economical elite of the province of Holland. He possessed a prodigious mind, studied at the University of Leiden, and earned the degree in both laws at the University of Orléans. As a young humanist he ended up in the entourage of Johan van Oldenbarnevelt (1547–1619), the Land's Advocate of the States of Holland and, as such, one of the main architects of the consolidation of the Dutch Republic after its independence. By 1619 Grotius became involved in a theological dispute within the Dutch Reformed Church, a dispute with important political consequences: Oldenbarnevelt, a political adversary of the Stadtholder, Maurice of Nassau, was put on trial and executed. Grotius barely escaped execution and was sentenced to prison. In 1621 he managed an amazing escape and fled to France, where he received a pension from Louis XIII. In 1634 he was appointed Swedish Ambassador to the French king, a position he held until his death in 1645.

More than any other jurist, Grotius assimilated the contributions of Humanism and Late Scholasticism. With extraordinary ease he drew upon theological, legal and historical sources, ranging from classical

Greece to his own era. His vast culture and capacity for synthesis would result in notable works on the role of the state and the law.

Grotius's *Inleidinge tot de Hollandsche rechts-geleerdheid* (*Introduction to Dutch Jurisprudence*, written in 1619 and published in 1631) is one of the first and finest summaries of a national legal system within the *ius commune*, and is, as such, a prime example of Roman-Dutch law: with scholarly underpinnings, but oriented towards practice. It describes the substantive law of the province of Holland and systematizes it according to the Roman classification of people, property and obligations. This structure, proceeding from Justinian's *Institutiones*, would become the model for similar compendia of national law and, ultimately, most civil codes.

D. International Law and Rational Natural Law

Grotius was both a humanist and a precursor of rational natural law. Without discounting the seminal figures of Vitoria and Alberico Gentili, he is also regarded as one of the founding fathers of international law.

Alberico Gentili (1552–1608), an Italian émigré to England and Regius Professor of Civil Law at the University of Oxford, in his outstanding *De iure belli* (*On the Laws of War*), advanced the position that the state, on the international scene, was perfectly justified in pursuing its own interests, just as the Romans had done when building their empire.

Grotius drew heavily from both Vitoria and Gentili. In his *Mare liberum* (*On the Freedom of the Seas*, 1609), Grotius established his reputation internationally. As a Dutchman, and writing on behalf of the Dutch East India Company, he was totally opposed to the Spanish-Portuguese monopoly on colonial trade, and argued fervently in favor of the freedom of the seas. He stated and proved that the sea was so vast that, with the exception of a few miles of territorial waters, no one could effectively control or occupy it. Unlike land, which could be occupied, the sea remained, therefore, open to common use by mankind as a whole. The influence of his argument would be extraordinary.

Grotius's most important work would be his *De iure belli ac paci libri tres* (*On What is Just in War and Peace*, 1625), in which he defended the need to establish an articulated system of international law that would transcend religious and moral divisions. The work masterfully synthesized the thinking of Spanish moral philosophers, such as Vitoria, with the pragmatism of humanists, such as Gentili. By perceiving and fully appreciating the state's new and irreversible centrality in the world, the book would be recognized through the end of the eighteenth century as the leading reference work on international law.

Grotius, indebted to the Spanish scholastics, took to their final conclusions some of the reasonings already advanced by them, and advocated for a greater independence of natural law from divine law. He would formulate the famous hypothesis that, even if God did not exist (*etiamsi daremus Deum non esse*), the prescripts of natural law would continue to be both knowable and applicable. The existence of natural law would no longer be explained with arguments and on grounds found outside of natural law, but rather within it. Parting from this premise, Grotius sought to overcome religious divisions and establish the foundations of international law common to all peoples. Though Grotius may not have been the first to formulate the hypothesis referring to the non-existence of God, thanks to it his work had unprecedented repercussions. Searching for answers in Nature was, after all, the course taken by Copernicus (1473–1543), Kepler (1571–1630), Galileo (1564–1642), Newton (1642–1727) and Leibniz (1646–1716). Thus the principles of law found their own place within natural law. It would be the jurist's task to ascertain these principles, accessible to human beings through reason and the empirical method. Natural law advocates would focus their interest on the individual. In this they were preceded, at least in part, by medieval jurists and canonists, as well as scholars of late Scholasticism, who had assigned greater importance to the individual. There is no doubt, however, that the new approach would be more radical: natural law proponents would posit the individual as the centerpiece of jurisprudence.

The great discoveries of the seventeenth century ushered in an era of absolute, unshakeable confidence in Reason. Man, it was believed, is not only capable of discovering and knowing the principles of natural law, but also, thanks to his rationality and through the scientific-mathematical method, is capacited to deduce from these principles an ideal legal system (*Vernunftrecht*, the "law of reason"). Rationalist philosophers like René Descartes (1596–1650) and Baruch Spinoza (1632–77) provided the methodological tools to combine logical deduction, inducive reasoning, empirical observation and axiomatic postulations. Advocates of natural law after Grotius were convinced that they could deduce the ideal legal system, with virtually mathematical precision, by proceeding based on the eternal principles of natural law. In this way natural law, which until Grotius featured a moral and ethical foundation, was reduced to an aseptic chain of causal relationships, which informed and inspired the Enlightenment penchant for constitutions and codes.

In his *De cive* (*On the Citizen*, 1642) Thomas Hobbes (1588–1679), who may have studied under Gentili, wrote that the state of nature consists of a struggle of man pitted against man (*homo homini lupus*: "man is a wolf to his fellow man"). But man wishes to stay alive, and seeks peace. He agrees, then, through a social contract, to form part of a political community. To keep the peace within this political community it is necessary for the community to submit itself to a supreme power: what Hobbes would call, after the Biblical monster, a "Leviathan," in his 1651 work so entitled. The order which the power imposes on the community – positive law *(positivus* is derived from *positus,* "placed" by someone) – is the only order possible within the state.

Hobbes' contractual thinking left a deep mark on European jurisprudence, even though his ideas were not outspokenly shared by everyone. The German Samuel Pufendorf (1632–1694), for instance, wrote the massive *De iure naturae et gentium* (*On the Law of Nature and Nations*, 1672), in which he produced a synthesis of the thoughts of Grotius and Hobbes. Unlike Hobbes, Pufendorf did not consider man condemned to the natural plight of a struggle with his fellow creatures. Rather, he followed Grotius by believing that humans possessed all the qualities that make community life possible. However, he did concur with the English author in his opinion that only a strong civil government was capable of maintaining the order and security that was the goal of natural law. Departing from some axioms of natural law, a system of ideal law was constructed which, though bearing hardly any relationship to the law applied in day-to-day affairs, acquired, nevertheless, significance as a model, precisely because it was mathematically deduced from natural law propositions.

Pufendorf's work was extremely influential and was taken as a starting point for research on natural law by countless enlightened natural law theorists. In the German-speaking world other natural law apologists included Gottfried Wilhelm Leibniz, Christian Thomasius (1655–1728) and Christian Wolff (1679–1754), who would all offer critiques and complementary insights to Pufendorf's ideas (Leibniz was actually very critical). In the French-speaking world and, more specifically, in Geneva, Pufendorf's main work was to be translated into French by Jean Barbeyrac (1674–1744), who would add some highly valuable comments and footnotes of his own. Jean-Jacques Burlamaqui (1694–1748) and Emer de Vattel (1714–1767) wrote masterpieces of their own on international law and political philosophy within a natural law framework, which were indebted to Pufendorf (among others), or took him as a starting point for constructive criticisms. Barbeyrac's translations into French were, in turn, translated into English, which bolstered the German' fame in the English-speaking world. John Locke and William Blackstone, in England; Gerschom Carmichael, in Scotland; and American political writers, including Thomas Jefferson, were familiar with his ideas.

Abstraction and empiricism distracted attention from Roman law. Grotius continued to cite Roman law with the utmost deference, while later champions of natural law would do so only as an example of empirical reality; they would not force reality to fit into Roman concepts, as the inheritors of the Bartolist traditions often did. Rather, they referred to Roman concepts only when they coincided with the solution which they considered correct. In conclusion, jurisprudence during the modern era, compared to that of the Middle Ages, featured a trend towards fragmentation. Along with the Bartolist approach, which continued to be followed at a good number of European universities, there appeared and existed a range of different trends and tendencies.

III. THE STATE AND LAW

A. Legislation

The strengthening of centralized political power at the expense of competing internal agents reinforced the monarch's legislating activity, which by the late Middle Ages was already intensifying, and would continue to do so during the Modern Era. In parallel, the importance of customary law as a source of law would erode.

In principle it was the monarch, and only the monarch, who enacted legislation, signing laws *car ainsi nous plaît-il* ("thus is my desire") or *Yo, el Rey* ("I, the King"). Feudal lords and powerful cities were first forbidden from promulgating general ordinances and, little by little, monarchs managed to extend their legislative authority throughout their territories. With the exception of England, representative institutions lacked legislative authorities, and in most cases did not even have the right of initiative. At most they could urge the monarch to complement reforms in one way or another, but when he refused their room to maneuver was limited.

In this process of centralization an ironic circumstance arose: the chanceries and other royal judicial structures, the former spearhead of royal law and power, for a time came to serve as a counterweight to curb possible legislative abuses committed by the monarch. The eight French *parlements*, for example, possessed the right of remonstrance. Indeed, these superior courts of justice were charged with registering new laws, transmitting them, and enforcing them among all the administrative authorities in their jurisdictions. If they so decided they could actually refuse to register a law, rendering it void in their jurisdiction. By means of *remonstrances*, France's *parlements* explained to the monarch the reasons why they had decided not to register a given law. The king could choose to insist that the law be registered, but the *parlement* could, in turn, repeat its refusal. As a last resort the monarch could appear in person before the *parlement* and impose his decision (*lit de justice*), but the nuisance which such a process represented generally sufficed to persuade the king to seriously consider the *parlements*' positions.

Over time legislative activity grew more orderly and acquired greater systematic coherence. In the sixteenth century a series of sweeping legal ordinances was established that sought to set down the terms for the regulation of multiple areas in a single text, as a kind of catch-all. Thus did the French *Ordonnance de Villers-Cotterêts* (1539) provide for reform of the state's administration: it delimited ecclesiastical and secular jurisdictions, generalized inquisitorial prosecution in criminal law, and regulated donations between the living. Culminating a process which spanned across the entire seventeenth century, Louis XIV and his Finance Minister Jean-Baptiste Colbert undertook a legislative program to reform entire areas of law and unify them across France. An indicative example of this effort is the *Ordonnance civile sur la réformation de la justice* (1667), which unified and simplified civil procedural law across France's different *parlements*. The procedural regulations established by the *Ordonnance* of 1667 would enjoy a long and fruitful life, since many parts of it were incorporated, fully intact, into the *Code de procédure civile* of 1806, which Napoleon would export to a good part of Europe. Other examples are the *Ordonnance criminelle* (1670), which unified criminal law; the *Ordonnance sur le commerce* (1673), which did the same thing for commercial law; and the *Ordonnance sur le commerce des mers* (1681), which set down maritime law. Much of the content of these sets of ordinances would also form part of the great Napoleonic codes.

In the eighteenth century important series of ordinances were also devised and enacted, especially pertaining to matters of civil law, on the initiative of Henri Daguesseau (1668–1751), Chancellor of Louis XV (1715–74), and Guillaume Joly de Fleury (1675–1756), Attorney General of the *Parlement de Paris*. The *Ordonnance sur les donations* (1731) governed donations throughout the whole kingdom, and was largely inspired by Roman law. The *Ordonnance sur les testaments* (1735) sought, unsuccessfully, to resolve the differences between the northern traditions of customary law, which favored orally transmitted wills, and the traditions of the southern regions, which favored written wills with regard to testaments and inheritances. The inheritance regime in the south remained under the influence of the Justinian Code, while in northern France a very diverse body of customary law prevailed. The dispositions established regarding wills would not reconcile the differences between north and south, and would ultimately end up recognizing the existence of two different systems, though providing for unity within each region. The civil code of 1804 literally transcribed the articles of these two sets of ordinances.

In Castile much greater legislative systematization was achieved from the outset, in large measure due to the advantage of already having the landmark work of the *Siete Partidas* (1265), and as a result of repeated entreaties by the Cortes. Thus were produced several compilations, the most important of which was the project that Philip II endorsed as law in 1567 under the title of the *Nueva Recopilación* (*New Compilation*).

The *Nueva Recopilación* consisted of 4,000 laws, systematically organized into books, and with titles that grouped the texts by subject. The fundamental objective of the compilations was to gather all current royal law into single volumes, taking into account its vastness and continuous growth. Some of the laws which were included respected the compiled text, while others altered it, for example, by summarizing all the provisions on a given topic in a single text. At the heading of each law its author and date were duly noted.

In the European context the *Nueva Recopilación* represented a very early and groundbreaking attempt to systematize national law. Criticized on more than one occasion for being full of errors and anachronisms, it nevertheless constituted a useful and effective tool. After 1567 numerous editions of the work were produced, which ended with lists and dates subsequent to the compiled laws, which, to some extent, served to complement its contents. The usefulness of the compiling method proved undeniable, and the *Compilation of the Laws of the Indies* (1680), for example, would draw upon the same method.

Other examples of compilatory efforts to arrange national forms of legislation include the Danish Code (*Danske Lov*) of 1683, which unified the law in a country until then governed by the regional laws of Scania, Zealand and Jutland. In the process it consolidated previously existing laws, but did not attempt to reform them. As such it is more a compilatory systematization than an actual code of law. The Danish Code was used as the basis for the 1687 Norwegian Code, Norway being under the same dynastic rule as Denmark until the beginning of the nineteenth century.

B. The Administration of Justice

The establishment of a complete, hierarchical and centralized court system was an objective harbored by kings throughout the Modern Era.

During the final centuries of the Middle Ages contact with the Romano-canonical procedure had inspired monarchs to establish, outside and above the multiplicity of local or feudal courts, their own judicial apparatuses. In this regard reference has been made to the *Parlement de Paris* (c. 1250) and other similar institutions in Spain's kingdoms, the Netherlands, and the Empire.

Via the strengthening of this system of royal courts the monarchs achieved, directly or indirectly, control over the administration of justice. Local or feudal courts would remain, but would see power wrested from them by the royal courts – a logical development if one considers the spreading of the right to appeal the sentences of other kinds of courts to the royal level. The organization of justice systems had already begun to take on the homogeneous forms we know and expect from them today. However, the coexistence of local and royal courts would linger until the end of the eighteenth century, and in some countries well into the nineteenth century, when it was generally accepted that the monarch – i.e., the state – was solely responsible for the administration of justice.

Royal justice was also reinforced by an erosion in the ecclesiastical courts' purviews and authority, to which the king now laid claim. From the outset the Church assumed jurisdiction over certain types of people. These people were not only clergymen, but also so-called *miserabiles personae*: widows and orphans, and the destitute. The mere participation of these classes of people in a lawsuit sufficed for the ecclesiastical courts to assert their jurisdiction over the matter. Also, with regard to matters of a certain nature, the Church's courts argued that its knowledge of the affairs in question justified its handling of them, i.e. in matters of faith and the sacraments, such as marriage, and in cases related to pious donations, which involved many wills, and church property. The Church's holdings were considerable in a rural economy where at least 30 percent of production lay in the hands of ecclesiastical bodies. In short, the Church boasted jurisdiction over all cases that might affect the state and the destiny of souls. The Church also asserted its right to authority over issues involving sacred sites. Since Roman times it had dealt with the right of asylum; it was the ecclesiastical courts that were charged with judging criminals arrested in churches – especially if they had physically placed themselves under the protection of the altar – regardless of the cause. These jurisdictional aspirations were, however, never fully honored and applied. Considered too broad, they always ran into resistance of the most varied kinds.

At first – until the thirteenth century – the ecclesiastical courts were very popular among those who sought justice and were fleeing the ineffective and often biased and inequitable feudal and local courts. The introduction of the royal courts, however, which represented an effective secular judicial authority; the general tendency towards the elimination of the central power's internal competitors; and the negative reputation which the ecclesiastical courts gradually acquired, would lead to their progressive loss of jurisdictional authority, beginning in the fifteenth century. Thus, with regard to competencies over persons, the term "clergyman" would be very strictly interpreted, and the handling of cases involving widows, orphans, and other unfortunate persons would be taken over by the king. As for jurisdictional competencies over certain matters, the ecclesiastical courts would lose many of them; marriage law was separated from marital property regimes, which were administered by secular justice, and by the eighteenth century the authority to deal with wills would lie almost entirely in secular hands. The right to asylum itself would be significantly undercut, as offenders apprehended in sacred places were to be immediately transferred to the secular authorities. The permission to take them into custody requested of the bishop was reduced to a mere formality, a gesture of institutional respect.

During the modern era religion was one of the most important issues with which the state had to grapple. Political debates did not center so much on religious beliefs – there were theologians for that – but rather the presence of the Church in the political, economic, social, cultural, and educational fields. We must not forget the fact that until the late-eighteenth century it was almost exclusively the clergy that created and ran schools and hospitals, and aided the poor and needy through almshouses, orphanages, etc. Ecclesiastical bodies also wielded significant economic clout. As a result, the clergy played a crucial role in fostering and maintaining social harmony. Thus, freedom of worship and conscience was for many years conceptually impossible. After the reign of Henry IV the Huguenots systematically lost their privileges in France, before Louis XIV took the drastic step of banishing them. In the Holy Roman Empire about one-third of the population died as a direct or indirect result of the Thirty Years War, a calamitous conflict pervaded with religious considerations. England was witness to continuous tensions between Anglicans, Puritans, Calvinists and Catholics, which sparked civil wars and prompted waves of emigration to Britain's colonies in North America. On the Iberian Peninsula Jews and Moors would have to opt between converting to Catholicism or going into exile, and in the Netherlands religious differences would also produce both a civil war and a war against Spain. In the United Provinces a policy of a certain tolerance was adopted; while religious freedom was not declared, the Protestant authorities left the Catholics – who accounted for almost half of the population – in peace in exchange for considerable financial contributions, provided that they worshiped in private.

In short, religion was a matter of state and, as such, dealing with and keeping the ecclesiastical authorities in check represented a major concern of the authorities, whether they were Catholic, Lutheran, Calvinist, Anglican, etc. Protestant churches, of a markedly national nature from their very inception, usually had little trouble adapting to this situation. The Catholic states had to grapple with Rome, from which they demanded greater autonomy over internal ecclesiastical matters. By the eighteenth century a certain ecclesiastical nationalization was evident, even in the Catholic countries.

C. Customary Law

During the dawn of early modern Europe, custom constituted the most important source of law, particularly with regard to private law. With their grip growing ever tighter over the development of the law, monarchs ended up placing customary law under their control as well. To achieve this objective the most effective approach was to put customs down in writing. Documentation made it possible to verify the existence of a given prescript, while also serving to fix and put an end to customary law's natural evolution. During the fifteenth and sixteenth centuries in France some 350 customary law systems were written up, along with another 700 in the Netherlands.

Eastern Europe was characterized by the persistence of traditional customary law resting along feudal lines, more so than in Western Europe. There were several reasons for this. The first was the almost complete lack of a network of highly developed cities. The number of cities was relatively small, and a sophisticated network of roads or navigable rivers was lacking. Vast areas continued in a predominantly rural state of affairs, favoring the preeminence of customary law. Moreover, the lack of an urban elite, and the scarcity of institutions of higher learning, yielded a limited number of jurists. There were, of course, young students from Poland, Bohemia and Hungary at Western universities, but their number was not enough to shape the development of the law. The legal order in Eastern Europe was, therefore, largely medieval in character until well into the nineteenth century.

D. The Scientific Study of National Law

We have seen how the evolution of jurisprudence during the Modern Age resulted in a more scientific cultivation of national law. The relativization of sources of law hitherto considered universal and eternal sparked interest in the *ius proprium*; if Roman law was the law of the Roman people at a given time of its existence, people felt licensed to study, systematize and improve their own legal systems also.

It was the French jurists who first promoted this practice, striving to bring order to customary law and drafting elaborate academic commentaries on the matter. Charles Dumoulin (1500–66), in particular, believed in the existence of a kind of autochthonous national French law, which should be purged of any Roman or canonical influences. As such he thoroughly studied the customary law of Paris, which he considered a sound basis for the further legal unification in France.

As the importance of legislation and the administration of justice also grew as sources of national law, authors undertook the task of creating orderly collections of the decisions issued and laws established. Etienne Pasquier (1529–1615) wrote *Recherches de la France*, a historical narrative of the culture and customs of France, which he deemed at least as glorious as Roman history; Pierre Pithou (1539–96) produced a scientific edition of some Carolingian *capitularia*; Guy Coquille (1523–1603) provided a synthesis of French law in his *Institution au droit des françois*, and Charondas (1534–1613) published *Pandectes, ou Digestes du droit François*, a proposal for the unification of French law on the basis of its comparative analysis with Roman law. All these positive assessments of French law in the sixteenth and seventeenth centuries coincided with the glorification and aggrandizement of the French monarchy, with the monarch and French law upheld as the only bulwarks against injustice and civil war.

But the growing predilection for national law reached its scientific apex with Hugo Grotius and his aforementioned *Inleidinge tot de Hollandsche rechts-geleerdheid.* With its structure based on persons, property and obligations, the work came to serve as a model for similar works inside and outside the United Provinces, its influence being felt in Scandinavia, Scotland, and the Holy Roman Empire.

In Spain, the doctrine would mainly yield commentaries on the successive legislative compilations, such as the *Nueva Recopilación* (1567). Authors all but forgotten today, but of enormous influence in the Europe of their time, included Juan de Solórzano Pereira (d. 1655), with his impressive *On the Law of the Indians*, a commentary on Spain's regulations for its overseas colonies (1629), and the brilliant Diego de Covarruvias (1512–77), whose works on practical legal issues were cited across the Continent until the eighteenth century.

Natural law and its quest for an ideal system rooted in rational principles was founded not only on the principles of the *ius commune* –

to which it ascribed a certain rationality – but also on national law. Jean Domat's (d. 1695) *Loix civiles dans leur ordre naturel* (*The Civil Laws in Their Natural Order*) drew upon both sources to set forth a logical and rational system for the structuring of French law – not through deduction from axiomatic ideals, but rather from precepts of Roman law, identified as natural law principles. Domat's book marked the beginning of a trend in which national law would be studied only in so far as it corresponded to natural rationality; such would be the basis on which Enlightenment thought and a new codification movement would have to rest.

5. The bourgeois age

I. HISTORICAL EVOLUTION

We can define the Bourgeois Age as the period spanning the eighteenth and nineteenth centuries. As historical bookmarks demarcating the beginning and end of this era we can cite the War of the Spanish Succession (concluding in 1713 with the Treaty of Utrecht, in which Spain lost its European possessions), and the Great War, or World War I, waged from 1914 to 1918, which devastated and utterly mangled the social, political, economic and military structure of Europe. Traditional historiography has tended to identify the French Revolution as the end of the Early Modern Age, which is also a valid criterion, given its enormous symbolic value. The most important thing to recognize is the profound continuity between the eighteenth and nineteenth centuries.

A. Economy

The changes which occurred in the West during this period were profound and far-reaching, as an essentially rural economy developed into an industrial one. Three factors contributed to this fundamental shift: a surplus of agricultural production, the existence of sufficient capital, and major technological advances.

Over the course of the eighteenth century key improvements were made in agricultural production. The surface area cultivated was expanded, and new crops, such as corn and potatoes, offered an alternative when cereal crops failed. Technological breakthroughs and innovations were applied: new tools, crop rotation, and specialization, which together made possible a surplus in agricultural production.

Overseas territories also contributed to the general prosperity. English colonies in North America and Australia, and Spain's *Virreinato del Río de la Plata* (basically today's Argentina, Paraguay and Uruguay) featured sprawling agrarian holdings that were soon able to supply markets with an abundance of products. A recurring phenomenon which had haunted Europe throughout its history was finally coming to an end: hunger.

The surplus of foodstuffs, along with advances in medical science, allowed Europe's population to grow exponentially. It is estimated that in 1700 Europe's population stood at approximately 118 million. By 1800 it had risen to some 187 million, and by 1900 it was up to 400 million. The population spike led to a greater number of workers engaged in trade and industry, where James Watt's (1736–1818) improvements to the steam engine sparked a genuine revolution. Steam engines, followed by electricity and the internal combustion engine, supplied necessary quantities of energy, while the population increase provided cheap labor. Mass-produced products were manufactured and launched onto the European markets. European powers also found vast markets for their manufactured products in their colonies. It is no wonder that the English, buoyed by their huge seafaring fleet, were those most capable of trading large numbers of products, followed by France, Germany, Belgium and the Netherlands. Massive investments in railways in the nineteenth century assured sustained economic growth, while technologies such as the telegraph drove another revolution in communications. These interrelated trends towards industrialization, mass production, and the internationalization of commerce came to constitute what was dubbed the Industrial Revolution.

Without capital, of course, neither industry nor trade would have been possible. In pre-eighteenth century Europe the circulation of capital was very limited, as land was still the main asset. This situation changed over the course of the eighteenth century, when the foundations of the monetary economy were laid down and the accumulation of capital became essential for investments in large factories equipped with machines and the assumption of massive economic risks. The foundation of central banks was key to this process, with the Bank of England (1694) leading the way.

The economic revolution, of course, also entailed a whole series of social consequences. The surplus labor in the countryside precipitated massive immigration into cities, where populations skyrocketed. The clergy and the nobility, whose essential wealth was rooted in the possession of land, were economically undercut and superseded by the rising bourgeoisie, which, capable of amassing colossal fortunes, began to dictate economic policy. Private property and free enterprise would be the essential principles upon which the bourgeois economy rested.

With industrialization it would be not only the bourgeois classes, however, which drove social changes; little by little, the proletariat laboring in the factories also came to the fore. This low-skilled working class, inhabiting industrialized urban areas, languished amidst miserable living conditions – though often no worse than the bleak situations they had left behind in the countryside. The concentration of so many people in confined spaces, masses torn from their traditional ways and tossed into an entirely new social and cultural context, would make conflicts inevitable. It was in this context that the work of Karl Marx (1818–83) appeared.

B. Politics

Faith in Reason called into question the idea of traditional and absolute monarchy. Enlightenment philosophers such as John Locke (1632–1704), Montesquieu (1689–1755), Voltaire (1694–1778), and Jean-Jacques Rousseau (1712–78) protested against the privileges of the nobility and clergy, along with the entire feudal system. Such figures called for the rational organization of the state and society, based on the ideals of liberty, equality, and popular sovereignty. Upholding these ideas, they advocated for the separation of powers (the *trias politica*) and the explicit recognition of fundamental rights and freedoms. Thus did the political model of absolute monarchy begin to collapse, though in some cases – France being the most noteworthy – the concentration of central power, accumulated over centuries, would not be relinquished overnight. England would take the first steps in this regard, while in Prussia and Austria it would be monarchy itself which took the initiative to organize society in what they deemed to be a more rational way.

Frederick II of Prussia (1740–86), Maria Theresa of Austria (1740–80), Joseph II (1765–90), and Catherine II of Russia (1762–96) all set down foundations for more rational and efficient military organization. Instead of armies of mercenaries they established standing armies recruited from amongst their populations. Soldiers could no longer be neglected, and started receiving regular pay, food and medical care, with the wounded to be cared for by the state. Armies, thus, encouraged the organization of government administrations capable of effectively collecting taxes, providing education and supplies, and providing for soldiers' care. In this way the state took over control of certain functions hitherto performed by the Church: medical attention and education. And these new services were not simply at the disposal of armies. Because armies were permanent, the state could extend its health care and education systems to local populations – a trend that accelerated later on, at the end of the nineteenth and the beginnings of the twentieth century. This step would prove crucial in completing the process that would concentrate power in the hands of the states, as it enabled them to reach levels of social presence and control that could hardly have been imagined in previous centuries. The rational organization of these functions and tasks carried with it the provisioning of services regardless of one's faith or social status. In response to public pressure, religious tolerance would be instituted and serfs and slaves liberated (though in Russia not until the second half of the nineteenth century). Thinkers such as Adam Smith (1723–90) would hold public authorities responsible for the creation of conditions propitious for economic growth – though from a *laissez-faire* perspective. Great works of infrastructure – canals, roads, works of drainage, etc. – contributed to boosting agricultural production and trade.

Despite all this, enlightened and rational reform met growing resistance. Reforms not only undermined the interests of the nobility and the clergy, but were also a way to fortify the power of monarchs, wary of new political theories. Enlightened despots, therefore, would not fully succeed in promoting progress, which gave rise to whole series of rebellions.

In the European nations' overseas territories reactions of another kind came about: their colonists called for rational government, both in the colonies and in the mother countries, and would demand the right to take part in it. This trend took shape for the first time in England's colonies in North America, and by the beginning of the nineteenth century Spain's territories in the Americas would also commence processes for their independence. These movements for rational and effective government also featured distinctly Romantic and nationalistic components.

On July 4, 1776 the thirteen American colonies declared their independence from Great Britain, arguing, among other things, that they could not be forced to pay taxes when they were not represented in Parliament. To organize a common defense against British military expeditions a confederation was established, though lacking in authority (Articles of Confederation, 1776). With the support of the French and Spanish the Americans eventually won the War of Independence against England, recognized in the Peace of Paris, signed in 1783. The structure of a confederation of states ended up failing, and in 1787 a new arrangement was devised, assigning the central government greater powers, set forth in the Constitution of the United States of America, ratified by the states in 1789. The new nation's historic charter was immediately amended via a Bill of Rights, which ensured a series of fundamental freedoms about which Americans harbored concerns in light of the augmented authority of the nation's new federal government and its Executive. America's founding texts reflected Enlightenment and liberal thought, and were designed to strike a balance between the government's three branches, as well as between the central government and those of the states.

The war against Napoleon left Spain exhausted, unable to cope with movements for independence in Latin America supported by the local bourgeoisie of Spanish descent and headed up by military leaders such as Simón Bolívar (1783–1830) and José de San Martín (1778–1850). As stated, these struggles were driven by Enlightenment principles as well as Romantic and nationalistic ideas.

Radical revolution, which would break out in France, would constitute a third and final channel for the expansion of Enlightenment thought.

The tensions affecting eighteenth-century France had grown progressively more dire, as the struggle between a rich and dynamic bourgeoisie, on one side, and the privileged classes, represented by the clergy and the nobility, on the other, continued to rage and intensify. Even amongst the clergy and nobility there existed rivalries and confrontations. These social strains would come to light in all their harshness when in the 1780s it became apparent that the nation had been bankrupted by its wars against the English: the Seven Years War (1756–63) and the American Revolutionary War (1776–83). In the former conflict France definitively lost its holdings in Canada, and its control of the seas to an ascendant England. Their victory against the British in the American War of Independence was little consolation, as it failed to reap any benefits at all for the French. In fact, ironically, the fledgling American Republic proceeded to put into practice many of the radical political ideas which the French government was refusing to, making its position all the more tenuous.

Thus, when in 1789 the Estates-General convened for the first time since the seventeenth century, the representatives of the so-called Third Estate – mostly members of the intermediate and high bourgeoisie – gathered in a National Assembly, assumed constituent powers, and proceeded to demolish the Ancien Régime. In the summer of 1789 the privileges and prerogatives of the clergy were eliminated; in 1791 the Church was placed under the control of the state and its assets were nationalized; and in 1793 the feudal regime was done away with. At an ever faster rate more and more constitutions and declarations of fundamental rights were written up in an effort to realize the aspirations of the Enlightenment and parliamentary monarchy: liberty, equality, popular sovereignty, the division of powers, the rights of man and the citizen. Initially Louis XVI (1774–92) seemed willing to adapt to the circumstances, but a failed attempt to escape provided extremists with the pretext to dethrone him, decapitate him, and proclaim a republic. Immediate consequences of this radicalization included, within France, bloody power struggles – the Terror (1792–94) and Directory (1794–99) – and, outside it, clashes with a coalition of European allies, headed up by Great Britain. War became inevitable: not only because the European monarchs feared for their own heads and thrones, and stood aghast at the prospect of an influential France standing as a republic, but also because the radical ideas coming out of France, especially those advanced by the key figure of Robespierre (1758–94), featured universal, expansionist aspirations.

This set of internal conflicts and wars abroad paved the way for a military dictatorship (the Consulate, which in 1804 was succeeded by the Empire) headed by Napoleon Bonaparte (1769–1821). Napoleon, a military, political and administrative genius, would continue the war and place under his control – his grip varying in its intensity – nearly all of Europe: the southern Netherlands, the United Provinces, the Italian Peninsula including the Papal States, the German empire, Austria, Prussia, Spain, Portugal, Poland, and even Russia. In his domestic policies Napoleon dispensed with some revolutionary initiatives: a monarchical form of government was adopted once again when he crowned himself emperor in 1804, he reached an agreement with the Church (1801), and eliminated the revolutionary calendar (1806).

After Napoleon's fall in 1815 a great peace conference was convened in Vienna in order to determine the new map of Europe. Its objective was clear: to revert to the situation before 1789. Monarchy was restored in France; the papacy recovered its possessions, and kings, in general, were placed back on their thrones. But not all the ideals of what was termed the "Restoration" were realized. The Holy Roman Empire, eliminated by Napoleon in 1806 and replaced by the weak structure of the Confederation of the Rhein, was not re-established. Rather, some 40 states, Prussia among them, came to form the German Confederation. Austria, established as the sole imperial center, came to control most of the states of the Italian Peninsula (Tuscany, Lombardy, Veneto, Parma and Modena). Finally, the United Kingdom of the Netherlands replaced the Republic of the United Provinces, absorbing the southern Netherlands and the Prince-Bishopric of Liège.

The Restoration would ultimately prove unworkable. A return to the Ancien Régime was out of the question due to the irreversible seizure of power by the bourgeoisie at the expense of the clergy and the nobility. In some areas privileges and prerogatives were restored, as well as monarchical and absolutist regimes, but in the end the political and economic pressure to apply the principles of the liberal state throughout Western Europe was too intense, and everywhere there appeared new constitutional models, sometimes in the form of fundamental laws or charters conceded by the monarch. The political ideas of the Enlightenment, soon reinforced by nationalistic trends, had sunk too deep into the social structure, precluding a return to the Old Order.

The idea of a chosen people is as old as Judeo-Christian civilization itself, but over the course of the eighteenth century the idea would be secularized, giving rise to nationalism. While the existence of a shared human nature was recognized, nationalists underscored the existence of differences between peoples arising from their particular geographical, climatic, gastronomic, cultural, linguistic, and ethnic conditions. Friedrich Hegel (1770–1831) considered history the process of the fulfillment and realization of *Volksgeist*: the spirit of the people. Nationalism exalted the nation and its people, upholding national welfare and glory as key ideals, with the state as the nation's visible embodiment. Enlightenment ideas on popular sovereignty would contribute to this idea. A vivid example of this occurred in France, with the creation of a people's revolutionary army – in contrast to a professional one – and general conscription; the *levée en masse* (general military constription) was a novel yet highly successful innovation. France's conquest of much of Europe also promoted nationalism amongst the conquered peoples, which proceeded to organize themselves – politically, militarily and ideologically – to oppose and overcome the French invader.

Finally, nationalism would have a life of its own, often realized via *Realpolitik*. Revolutions in Greece (1821–29), Belgium (1830), Italy (1860–66), and Germany (1866–70) were driven by principally political and economic motivations. Nationalist dreams would lead to the Franco-Prussian War of 1870, among others, and eventually plunge Europe into the two global cataclysms of the twentieth century: World War I (1914–18) and World War II (1939–45).

C. Church and Religion

During the eighteenth century debates regarding the role of the Church became increasingly frequent in Europe's Catholic countries as Enlightenment-based policies called for the revocation of the clergy's longstanding positions of privilege. In a dynamic industrial and commercial economy it no longer seemed acceptable for up to a third of the land to remain in the hands of ecclesiastical bodies. The Church's dominant position in the creation and maintenance of schools and hospitals would also be challenged. Years before the French Revolution the governments of the Catholic states had targeted the Jesuits – considered staunch defenders of the Pope and insubordinate to the biddings of secular rulers – in a series of relentless campaigns against them. The King of Portugal expelled them from his territories in both hemispheres in 1759, thus doing away with, among other things, the network of socially and economically flourishing enclaves of indigenous peoples, the famous "reductions," which the Jesuits had established in South America. They were banished from France in 1763 for justifying, in the tradition of the School of Salamanca, the doctrine of tyrannicide. Spain followed in 1767. In the same year the Jesuits were also driven from the Kingdom of Naples, and a few months later, in 1768, from the Duchy of Parma. The pressure was so intense and relentless that the pope himself was forced to dissolve the order in 1773. After its restoration 40 years later (1813) the Society of Jesus would only partially recover its peculiar charisma. In many cases the expulsion of the Jesuits did harm to national interests. A prime example was in Spain, whose most important scientists and humanists were Jesuits, and where more than a hundred schools and numerous university chairs were left without teachers. Its overseas territories, meanwhile, were deprived of an important source of social and cultural cohesion with the mother country, which ultimately facilitated movements for independence. Other countries benefited, such as Prussia under Frederick II, which welcomed the banished Jesuits at its academies and universities.

The campaign against the Jesuits exemplifies the new attitude of Catholic governments towards the Church: their aim was now to bring the various national churches under state power, as Protestant regimes had done two centuries earlier. France, Portugal, Venice, Tuscany, Austria and the southern Netherlands offer good examples. Joseph II of Austria abolished the monasteries of the contemplative orders and fiercely promoted state education at the expense of Church education. The acceptance and regulation of civil marriage was further evidence that the state no longer accepted the Church's monopoly over certain affairs. Political and economic motives drove these policies; genuine convictions that society should be secularized, which during the eighteenth century were harbored by only a small minority, do not suffice to explain them.

During the French Revolution churches suffered enormously, as Revolutionary propaganda alleged that many of the evils inherent to the Ancien Régime stemmed from the close alliance between the throne and the altar. In Spain, home to a strong current of anticlericalism, a process of disentailment wrested from the Church its territorial wealth. Later the Church would be assigned, in exchange, an annual allocation, charged to the state. The Church's struggle with liberalism would shape its policies and activities through the mid-nineteenth century, a situation perhaps best illustrated by the conflict between the nascent kingdom of Italy and the Holy See, which would ultimately see its territory dramatically reduced. Subsequently, religious freedom would come to be recognized as a fundamental human right, with the separation of the Church and state representing a basic political principle, especially in France and the

United States. The two forces, in spite of this, would continue to clash until the twentieth century.

II. LAW AND JURISPRUDENCE DURING THE ENLIGHTENMENT

A. The Enlightenment

The term "Enlightenment" (*Lumières, Aufklärung, Ilustración, Illuminismo*) came to describe a philosophical, scientific, and artistic movement which sought to apply rational principles and methods to all areas of knowledge. One corollary of this school of thought was that God became ever less relevant. Here lies the main difference with the proponents of natural law: both currents believed that nature could provide the answers to their questions, but while natural law advocates respectfully considered nature to be a divine creation sustained by God, most Enlightenment philosophers severed this link and embraced deism, claiming that after creating the world the Creator essentially left it to its own devices. Their conclusion, nevertheless, would be similar to that of the natural law thinkers: answers must be rationally, almost mathematically, deduced from certain logical principles. They put limitless faith in man's goodness and rationality, to the extent that the goddess Reason would be the object of public worship during the French Revolution.

Like natural law thinkers, Enlightenment advocates also perceived differences and discrepancies between the world derived from their rational models and the real world. In their view, however, their model was far superior to reality, plagued as it was by irrationality. Enlightenment thinkers did not accept that there were things that could not be understood, nor did they acquiesce in the face of tradition. Reality was to be the subject of a systematic purge. There was a profound paradigm shift at work: whereas previously social ills had been attributed to the fall of man, his corrupted nature and his innate inclination to sin, now philosophers tended to see man as good by nature. Thus, the cause of social problems had to be sought outside the individual: in the reactionary forces and institutions of superstition and privilege which corrupted man's innate goodness. The *philosophes* believed that everything should be reformed, top to bottom, wiping clean the slate of history – which in their view was marred by darkness, ignorance and superstition – to build a perfect society based on a rational model.

Champions of the Enlightenment believed it possible to gather and compile all human knowledge. This belief gave rise to all-embracing efforts such as the *Encyclopédie* of Diderot and d'Alembert (1751–72). They were also convinced that the universe and nature could hold no secrets from the human mind, which was capable of understanding everything. There were no mysteries or miracles for them, only ignorance and a backward lack of scientific thinking. Thanks to the use of rational techniques and the infinite progress to which humanity is destined, sooner than later everything was to be rationally explained.

B. Law and Society According to the Enlightenment Philosophers

Among the enlightened philosophers' favorite subjects were law and the organization of the state. In their view both fields, as they stood during their time, were an arbitrary and chaotic jumble, the product of Europe's dark, feudal and superstitious past, and, above all, the result of tradition – which they considered utterly irrational because it was not the product of any kind of coherent plan or design. In response to society and its law thus constituted, Enlightenment thinkers advanced a divergent set of ideas upholding popular sovereignty, according to which political power is nothing but the consequence of each individual's cession of part of that sovereignty inherent to him as a citizen; this was the theory of the "social contract." As power does not proceed from God, in no case – they argued – could its placement in the hands of one person be justified. Moreover, the concentration of power may easily lead to abuses; to prevent them, the most effective solution is the distribution of power between several institutions that check one another, thus maintaining a political balance.

A few names must be mentioned here. In his *Two Treatises of Government* John Locke set forth his ideas to limit state power and protect citizens' rights. The foundation of political power is the social contract, into which men enter for the precise object of better protecting and enjoying their rights, to which they are naturally and innately entitled. The influence of Locke, considered the father of liberalism, would be momentous: the Constitution of the United States of America was directly inspired by his philosophy. Charles Louis de Secondat, Baron de Montesquieu, advocated the separation of powers in his famous *Esprit des lois* ("The Spirit of the Laws," 1748). Jean-Jacques Rousseau, meanwhile, considered the social contract to be the basis of every political community, direct democracy the best model of political organization, and believed in a "general will," to which every citizen ought to submit. His ideas would have a major influence as precursors of the collectivist theories which spread in the nineteenth century.

Enlightenment thinkers took a special interest in criminal law, where they called for the abolition of the death penalty, torture, and corporal punishment; proportionality between offences and sentences; and the application of the principle of *nullum crimen, nulla poena sine lege* ("There may be no crime nor punishment without a previous law thereto appertaining"). The most significant work on this point was that of the Italian Cesare Beccaria (1738–94): *Dei delitti e delle pene* (*On Crimes and Punishments*), published in 1764, which argued that no free individual in his right mind would enter into a social contract to establish a government with the power to kill him.

The inevitable divergences between reality and these visionary, theoretical models only intensified the philosophers' zeal for reform. And the most effective instruments for reforming those institutions was, according to the enlightened despotism of the time, legislation – considered the embodiment and expression of the people's bidding; this was Rousseau's "general will." In all cases the law was considered to be the optimal guarantor of citizens' equality. Reformers called for an end to the traditional and arbitrary fragmentation inherent to customary law. Every citizen was to be assured that he would be treated the same as any other before the law, which meant that privileges and immunity for certain groups – the clergy and the nobility in particular – had to be quashed, and the feudal system overturned.

C. Codification Projects in Central Europe

The conviction that all law could be amassed in a single book – and all human knowledge in encyclopedias – was a concept key to Enlightenment thought. Along with this belief came a determination to reform the law as a whole in order to bring about the new society conceived of and designed by the philosophers.

The first example of a complete code was the *Allgemeines Landrecht für die preußischen Staaten* (*General Laws for the Prussian States*), enacted in 1794 by Frederick William II of Prussia (1786–97). Containing all Prussian law, both private and public, its structure was inspired by the works of Samuel Pufendorf and Christian Wolff, for which it has been characterized as a work shaped by natural law doctrines. Academic commentaries on the code were banned, as was judicial interpretation. Any ambiguities were to be brought before and settled by a legislative commission. The code remained in force in Prussia until the year 1900.

The history of the *Allgemeines Landrecht* goes back to 1714, when Frederick William I (1714–40) supported an effort to uniformize private law throughout his domain (Prussia, Brandenburg, Halberstadt, Magdeburg, Westphalia, and Western Pomerania). To this end he ordered the law school at Halle, and in particular Christian Thomasius, to compile and draw up a code of laws. Frederick II ordered the publication of the draft version in order to gather commentaries from all over Europe. Everything was integrated into the final version of the code, produced under the supervision of Carl Gotlieb Svarez (d. 1796).

In Bavaria codes were also drafted. On the initiative of Maximilian III Joseph, Elector of Bavaria (1745–77), in 1751 a code of criminal law was enacted; in 1753, a code of procedural law; and, finally, in 1756, a code of civil law. This code bore the unmistakable stamp of natural law's influence in its division of the subject based on the model of the *Institutiones* (people, property, inheritances, obligations). Unlike other codes it was not intended to suppress existing law and reform it, but rather only to provide a shared body of suppletive law.

The most important legal code in Central Europe during this era was Austria's *Allgemeines Bürgerliches Gesetzbuch* (*General Civil Code*) of 1811. Much clearer than its Prussian counterpart, in it customary law was suppressed as a source of law. Empress Maria Theresa (1740–80) ordered the drafting of new codes in 1753 in an effort to unify the law in territories as diverse as Austria, Tyrol, Bohemia, Silesia, and the southern Netherlands. The first result would be a criminal law code enacted in 1768. At the same time a code of civil law was undertaken, but several versions were rejected due to their excessive complexity. In 1786 Joseph II enacted part of what would became a historic code of civil law: the *Josephine Code*. Baron Martini (d. 1800), meanwhile, was responsible for the drafting of procedural and criminal procedural law codes in Lombardy and the southern Netherlands (1786–89). He also worked on the drafting of the *Allgemeines bürgerliches Gesetzbuch*, which would not, however, be completed until after his death, under the direction of jurist Franz von Zeiller (d. 1828). The Austrian code was inspired by the principles of natural law, and returned to the structure of the *Institutiones*. It would enter into force, with some modifications, in the most important territories under imperial domain: Austria, the Czech Republic, Slovakia, Slovenia, Croatia, Liechtenstein, and, for a time, also in Hungary.

III. NAPOLEONIC CODIFICATION

A. The Dream of Legal Unification in France

Louis XIV's legislative projects embodied the dream of unifying law throughout France and gathering it into a single code of laws. These plans, however, were only partially realized.

Worth mentioning, first and foremost, is the sway and appeal held by the customary law of Paris. Despite the great fragmentation of customary law in France, that of Paris enjoyed considerable influence. In accordance with the evolution of jurisprudence, the study of national law became increasingly prevalent, and the customary law of Paris maintained a privileged position in this sphere. The study of Paris law produced by Charles Dumoulin, who in the sixteenth century advocated for a reduction in legal fragmentation, proved to be very influential on subsequent generations. Jean Domat, following the tenets of rationalist natural law, developed a complete system in his *Loix civiles dans leur ordre naturel* (1694), a groundbreaking work offering for the first time the perspective of a single body of law for all France. The commentaries on Parisian customary law, the jurisprudence of the *Parlement de Paris*, the great ordinances of the seventeenth century, and Domat's systematics all served to promote the development of a single, clear and rational French legal system, which began to take shape.

The intellectual basis for the subsequent *Code civil* was the work of two eighteenth-century authors. In 1747 François Bourjon (d. 1751) penned the remarkable *Le droit commun de la France et la coutume de Paris réduit en principes* (*The Common Law of France and the Customs of Paris Summarized in Principles*), a highly significant title. It was structured in the following way: introduction, people, property, and ways of acquiring property. The jurist with the most direct and decisive influence on France's Civil Code was, however, Robert Joseph Pothier (1699–1772), who authored a commentary on the customary law of Orléans (1740) and a synthesis of Roman law (1748), which does not approach the issue according to the traditional order of the *Digest*, but rather according to its own systematization, deemed more natural by its author. Pothier is known, above all, for his 1760 *Traité des obligations* (*Treatise on Obligations*), which came to constitute a model for its handling of law governing obligations, and for his writings on various fields of civil law: sale, marriage, possession and property, etc. Pothier was not interested in the great philosophical treatises. Rather, he was a pragmatic jurist interested in specific problems. His language was clear, his structure transparent, and his solutions sensible and practical. Many of Pothier's texts ended up in the Code itself.

B. Revolutionary Projects

One of the revolutionaries' most pressing concerns after the events of 1789 would be the drafting of a code – the instrument of choice to reform existing law. Its authors proceeded based on the convictions that a single code of laws would be the most expedient means to achieve the ideal of equality, which required that the same legal criteria be applied in every case. In the new code an effort was made to employ language that everyone could understand.

In 1791 a criminal law code and a criminal procedural law code were enacted. In 1795, with the change of regime, Philippe Merlin (d. 1838) drafted a new criminal law code, a systematic and dogmatic work packed with definitions and distinctions. With regard to civil law there was less progress. Bills were submitted to a commission headed by Jean-Jacques Régis de Cambacérès (d. 1824). In 1793, an initial draft was rejected as too long, too complex, and not revolutionary enough. In 1795 another proposal was rejected for just the opposite reasons: too short and too radical. A third document, drafted in 1796, did not receive sufficient political support. In 1799 Jean Jacqueminot (d. 1813) took a draft to the first consul, though it was incomplete.

C. The *Code Civil*

When he rose to power Napoleon brought Cambacérès with him as second consul, and in 1800 formed a four-member commission which he charged with drafting a series of civil law bills.

All four members of the commission were eminent jurists. François Tronchet (1726–1806), a specialist in customary and procedural law, was a man of the *Ancien Régime*, though this did not keep him from serving as president of the Court of Cassation, the new regime's most important tribunal. Jean Portalis (1746–1807) was the commission's intellectual, wrote most of the code's articles, and was charged with drafting its preamble. Félix Bigot-Préameneu (1747–1823) had been a lawyer at the *Parlement de Paris* and later a government delegate at the Court of Cassation. Finally, Jacques de Maleville (1741–1824), a magistrate at the Court of Cassation, served as the commission's secretary. The personal and professional careers of these four eminent jurists are altogether relevant: Portalis and Maleville, both from southern France, favored the *pays de droit écrit*, or Roman law system, while Tronchet endorsed a wide application of Parisian customary law.

In just a few months the commission completed a first draft. Each of the four wrote a part, which was then debated by the commission formed. Cambacérès and Bonaparte himself often actively participated in the discussions. Cambacérès, for example, endorsed incorporating as few definitions as possible in the pursuit of a code in which practical considerations would prevail over abstract or academic ones.

The draft was submitted for examination by the Council of State, the Court of Cassation, and the courts of appeal before being presented to the Legislative Assembly. For political reasons, however, it floundered and was rejected. Some months later, following an electoral purge of the Assembly, it was proposed once again, this time in the form of 36 different bills, each one a part of the Code. On 5 March 1804 the first bill was voted on and approved, and by 21 March all of them had been passed. A law of 21 March placed the 36 laws into a sole document entitled the *Code civil des Français*, which contained 2,281 consecutively enumerated articles, and all ancient laws, systems, customs, statutes, regulations and Roman law lost legal force.

The structure of the *Code* is simple: the first book dealt with law pertaining to individuals, including marriage and custody law; the second covered property and limited real rights; and the third addressed the different aspects related to the acquisition of property, including successions and obligations. This arrangement was inspired by the *Institutiones*, but with an Enlightenment twist; procedural law was removed from it, to be placed in another code.

When in 1804 the French Empire was established, the *Code civil* was adapted to the new institutions. The terms "Republic," "Nation," and "First Consul" were replaced by "Empire," "State," and "Emperor." From that moment on, the work became known as the *Code Napoléon* – a single code for a unified Europe. With the Restoration in 1814 the former terms would be readopted; between 1852 and 1870 the term "Napoleonic Code" would be reapplied, devoid of substantial modifications.

D. The Other Napoleonic Codes

Napoleon enacted other codes in addition to the *Code civil*. A Civil Procedure Code (1806) had become necessary after the institutional reforms of the revolutionary era, which saw the elimination of some courts and the establishment of new ones; the *Ordonnance* of 1667 was no longer adequate for the situation. Civil processes also demanded greater responsiveness and lower costs. However, many elements of the 1667 legal regime would remain totally intact; the Civil Procedure Code is surely the most traditional and least innovative of the Napoleonic legal codes. The Code of Commerce (1807), meanwhile, was the work of a joint committee composed of merchants and jurists. Bonaparte and Cambacérès actively participated in its composition, convinced that adequate legislation would save many from bankruptcy. Its content was to a great extent inspired by the dispositions of Colbert with regard to commerce (1673) and maritime law (1681), as well as a book, *Le parfait négoçiant* (*The Perfect Merchant*), written by Jacques Savary in the seventeenth century. The Criminal Code (1810) and the Criminal Procedure Code (1808) were not the first codes of criminal law and criminal procedure law in France, although the restoration of the public prosecutor's office in 1801 would require that they be updated. Differences of opinion about the functions of the jury would delay passage of the bill.

E. The Expansion of the French Codes

The French introduced their codes in those territories which came under their domain: Belgium, Luxembourg, the Netherlands, Northern Italy, the Rhineland, Geneva, Spain, etc. Its satellite states also implemented most of the French codes: Westphalia, Hanover, Poland, Naples, and the Swiss cantons. After Napoleon's defeat in many places aversion to the French and their law intensified. But many also had to concede that the codification technique did offer advantages. In many cases the repeal of the French codes was followed by the drafting of codes in the respective countries, which frequently ended up drawing upon the French models. Such was the case in the Netherlands (1838), Italy (1865), Romania (1865), Portugal (1867), and Spain (1889). Napoleonic codes were also established in the French colonies: Morocco, Algeria, Tunisia, Egypt, Syria, Lebanon, and Indochina, often adapted to local customs. French law also had a great impact in Latin America: in Haiti, the Dominican Republic, Bolivia, Uruguay, and Argentina. Through Belgian colonization it also exerted great influence in Central Africa. Louisiana, which Napoleon had sold to the United States in 1803, introduced the French Civil Code in 1825. Finally, its presence was also felt in "New France," or Quebec.

Two examples, Italy and Spain, suffice to illustrate this process by which the Napoleonic Codes were adapted.

Soon after the French withdrawal, the Italians began work drafting their own legal codes. In 1819 the Kingdom of Naples and Sicily enacted a code containing civil law, criminal law, civil procedure law, criminal procedure law, and commercial law. In the Papal States civil procedure law was codified in 1817; commercial law, in 1821; and criminal and criminal procedure law, in 1831 and 1832. The *Corpus iuris canonici* continued to govern the remaining areas. In Northern Italy – Lombardy and Veneto – Austria's *Allgemeines Bürgerliches Gesetzbuch* was introduced. The independent Duchy of Parma would maintain the French *Code civil* until the drafting of its own in 1820, which was based on French and Roman law. Parma also enacted codes of procedural law, both civil and criminal, and a criminal code in 1820 and 1821. The independent Duchy of Modena and Reggio implemented its own codes, governing civil law and procedural law in 1852, and criminal law and criminal procedure law in 1855. In 1853 the Grand Duchy of Tuscany introduced a very liberal body of criminal law, being the first country to abolish the death penalty, in 1786. In the Kingdom of Sardinia – which had its capital in Turin and then encompassed Piedmont, Genoa, and the island of Sardinia – the following codes were enacted: civil (1837), commercial (1842), criminal (1843, replaced in 1859), criminal procedure (1847, replaced in 1859) and civil procedure (1848, replaced in 1854).

The unification of Italy, accompanied by the cultural and political movement known as the *Risorgimento*, was legally carried out by the Kingdom of Sardinia annexing the other Italian regions. In each of the territories incorporated the old legal structures were dismantled and those from Piedmont were introduced, in a process termed *piemontesizzazione*. This approach triggered protests when other regions considered their codes superior to those of Piedmont, hastily drafted in 1859 to facilitate unification. The result: in general, pre-unification private law – civil and commercial codes – was maintained in the annexed territories, while Piedmont's codes governing criminal law and criminal procedure were extended to apply to Italian territory, save for the important exception of Tuscany, which kept its peculiar and rermarkably progressive criminal law.

Following Italian unification, it was in the field of private law that the greatest diversity remained. As a result, the state's new authorities assigned priority to unification in this field. Various plans were drawn up for a new national civil code. Between 1859 and 1860 the project basically consisted of a revision of the Piedmontese Code. Between 1860 and 1863 plans were produced based on a revision of the French code in combination with the Neapolitan version of the French model. The following codification project began in 1863, making use of the previous work and consulting five committees of jurists in Turin, Milan, Florence, Naples and Palermo. Ultimately Parliament granted the government the necessary special legislative powers, and in 1865 the *Codice civile* was enacted – dubbed the *Codice Pisanelli* after Justice Minister Giuseppe Pisanelli, who had championed it. That same year more codes, governing additional spheres of law, were unified: civil procedure, commercial, maritime, criminal procedure, and criminal, almost always based on Sardinian codes. By 1865 the law was unified in Italy – again with the exception of the old, liberal Tuscan criminal code (1853); Tuscany had eliminated the death penalty, but the rest of Italy had not. As in 1865 the unification technique basically consisted of adopting Piedmont's codes, except for the *Codice civile*, Italian legislators still dreamt of new codifications. In 1877 a new code of maritime law was enacted, in 1882 a new code of commercial law, and in 1889 a famous criminal code (*Codice Zanardelli*), which finally unified criminal law and extended the abolition of the death penalty to all Italy. In 1913 a new code of criminal procedure law was introduced.

At the turn of the century the legal tradition in Italy still exhibited a pronounced French influence. But the methodology of the German "pandectists" was becoming ever more evident, especially after the promulgation of the BGB. After World War I, in which Italy crossed over to the Allied side, the Italians once again embraced the French legal tradition. Plans were even drawn up for a common law of obligations that would apply to France and Italy (1927), an updated version of the law of obligations existing in the *Codice civile.* These plans would end up going nowhere due to their insufficient innovation and the confluence of two events: the rise to power of Benito Mussolini (1922–45) and the commencement of plans for a new comprehensive civil code. During the era of fascism Italian jurists continued to develop codes. A new criminal code was passed in 1930 (*Codice Rocco*) along with another covering criminal procedure. While these contained some unequivocally fascist aspects, in general they continued to reflect traditional jurisprudence and would remain in force after World War II. Other documents developed between 1925 and 1931 to reform commercial, maritime, and civil procedural law were characterized by the almost total absence of elements that could be associated with the fascist ideology; *Il Duce* displayed little interest in private law. The new *Codice civile* barely contained any vestiges of fascist ideology, which allowed it to survive the Mussolini regime. The new civil code's preparatory committees were made up of both traditional and liberal jurists. The drafts were widely studied by experts, professors, judges, and, to a lesser extent, by regime ideologues. The preparatory commissions had also aimed to draft a code that would be drawn up based on solid, technical and politically neutral criteria. When in 1942 the final draft was brought before the government, it realized that fascist ideology was missing from the code. As a result, some articles influenced by fascism were added, but they were insufficient in both number and importance to qualify the new *Codice civile* as a fascist piece of legislation. After World War II there was discussion about whether to keep the *Codice civil*, before it was generally accepted that, with the removal of some items and phrases (*ripulitura*, or "cleanup") the 1942 code could be maintained. For example, Article 147, which stated that parents were to educate their children in fascist ideology, was altered to dictate that parents should educate their children taking into account their natural abilities and tendencies. Much has been written about the possible German influence on the new *Codice civile*. It is true that at the beginning of the twentieth century, shortly after the German civil code's publication, German jurisprudence attracted genuine admiration for its conceptual clarity and terminological precision. In addition, the German code may have been influenced by the *Codice civile* of 1865, which facilitated the German code's reception in Italy. The 1942 *Codice civile* is, in short, based on the French model but drafted by jurists who had studied in Germany.

In Spain the Constitution of Cádiz of 1812 mandated that "the civil, criminal and commercial codes shall be the same for the entire monarchy." It would take years for these plans to come to fruition, as the *Código civil* would not be adopted until 1889. In the interim several drafts were produced, both partial and complete, which political circumstances kept from being implemented. The most important of these was that carried out under Isabel II, written in 1851 by the great jurist Florencio García Goyena (1783–1855), characterized by its centralist liberalism (which entailed an opposition to special legal regimes for some Spanish regions) and hostile attitude towards the Church, which was even denied the capacity to acquire assets. Based on France's *Code civil*, however, it maintained essential Spanish traditions with regard to numerous principles and institutions. Although the document was of a great technical perfection it failed to be enacted, for the political reasons alluded to above. The failure of the *Código* prompted the publication of special laws, which did not admit further delay: the Mortgage Law (1861), which created the position of the land property registrar; the Law of Notaries (1862), the Water Law (1866), the Civil Marriage Law (1870), and the Civil Registration Law (1870).

In 1880, once the Bourbon Restoration was secure, efforts at codification were undertaken by the justice minister and preeminent Spanish jurist of his time, Manuel Alonso Martínez (1827–91). In 1881 the Civil Procedure Law – very akin to the old Romano-canonical procedure – was phased in, and in 1882 came the Criminal Procedure Law. Also passed in 1881 was a first framework law setting down the foundations for the drafting of a civil code, which failed because once again it proposed the elimination of special legal regimes, or *fueros*, for certain Spanish regions. A new framework law (1889) sacrificed full legal unity in favor of political pragmatism, making it possible finally to produce a civil code for Spain. The documents drawn up under Isabel II provided two-thirds of the final draft.

Spain's *Código civil* reflects the restrained liberalism and tempered individualism typical of the time. It was French in its form and structure, yet there were entire areas, such as family and inheritance law, in which national institutions survived almost completely intact. With regards to property law, the code rejected French consensual transmission and maintained the classical Spanish system – common throughout Europe before the Napoleonic code – of the transmission of property through the combination of *titulus* and *modus*, in other words by means of both a binding agreement establishing the asset transfer (*titulus*) and *traditio* or actual delivery of possession (*modus*), neither by itself being sufficient. A set of appendices contained the *instituciones forales*, special legal dispositions governing some Spanish regions, which it was deemed expedient to maintain, in relation to which the Code operated as suppletive law.

There were two versions of the Spanish commercial code: that of 1829 and that of 1885. With regard to criminal law the Constitution of Cádiz established the individual nature of punishments, and proscribed hanging, confiscation or flogging. The return of Fernando VII brought about the repeal of the document drafted in Cádiz and its dictates, but in 1822 the same monarch ordered the composition of a criminal code based on Enlightenment doctrines. Other criminal codes followed: an authoritarian one in 1848, followed by a liberal one in 1870.

F. An Assessment of the *Code Civil*

The *Code civil* constituted a legislative enterprise of extraordinary significance. The worldwide attraction and influence it exerted cannot be explained exclusively by France's military and colonial supremacy during the Napoleonic era. The Code's intrinsic quality also contributed to its success. A well-advised balance between the legal achievements of the *Ancien Régime* and the contributions of the Revolution – a balance which Portalis masterfully sets forth in his preliminary discourse to the Code – would ensure its lasting influence.

The disputes between Portalis and Tronchet over whether to turn to Roman law or the customs of Paris show that the sources of the *Code civil* were the same as those drawn upon during the *Ancien Régime*, of special note being some of the *ordonnances* of Colbert and Daguesseau. The works of Domat, Bourjon and Pothier, who had studied pre-Revolutionary law, based on Englightenment postulates, were also taken closely into account. In general, it is fair to say that law governing the economic arrangements pertaining to marriage and inheritance was based on customary law, while that governing obligations came from Roman law. Canon law also exerted some influence, especially with regard to procedural law; it has already been noted that the Civil Procedure Code featured a great attachment to the old Romano-canonical procedure.

This traditional acquis was complemented by the contributions of the revolutionary ideals of liberty and equality, which would lead to the abolition of the feudal regime and the privileges and prerogatives formerly enjoyed by clergy and nobility, the consequent liberalization of real estate ownership, and a profound reform of succession law. The new value placed on individual freedom also gave rise to full freedom of contract, and the ability to transfer property by mere consent, without the need for it to actually change hands. The principle of equality, as well as the Jacobin ideals of national unity and the indivisibility of the nation, impacted the centralization of private law: for the first time in centuries the same private law was applied not only throughout French territory, but also across large regions of the European continent, rather than the fragmented custom-based law which had long prevailed. These elements – equality before the law and freedom of contract – would constitute the fundamental pillars of nineteenth-century society. As a result of the sudden realization of the liberal ideal, hereinafter relations between citizens would be governed by the state, and legislation would wield a virtual monopoly on the capacity to produce law.

The transparent structure, rationality of material prescripts, and wise balance alluded to above furnished the Code with a consistency that the contemporary codes of Prussia and Austria lacked. Such benefits were only complemented by its clear and simple style. The Romantic novelist Stendhal (d. 1842) reportedly told his colleague Balzac (d. 1850) that each morning, before sitting down to write, he read two or three pages of the *Civil code* to "catch the tone." Let us give Napoleon the last word: looking back at his life, on the island of Santa Elena, he stated: "*Ma vraie gloire n'est pas d'avoir gagné quarante batailles … Ce que rien n'effacera, ce qui vivra eternellement, c'est mon Code civil*" ("My true glory is not to have won forty battles … what will not be erased, what will live forever, is my civil code").

IV. JURISPRUDENCE

A. The Exegetic School

With the enactment of the Napoleonic codes a new way of understanding jurisprudence was born in France, dubbed the *école de l'exégèse*, or the Exegetic School. This group's representatives focused their attention on legislation as the sole source of new law. This legal positivism resulted, in part, from the coherent implementation of the idea of the separation of powers and the predominance given to the legislature in the French tradition. According to this line of thought the Legislative branch is the only power responsible for and authorized to enact laws; the Executive must govern and administer according to the law; and the Judiciary's role is to apply it correctly. The judicial power, according to this view, was not to play any role in the creation of law. In fact, its functions did not even extend to the interpretation of law, the judge to be nothing more than "the mouth which pronounces the words of the law," in Montesquieu's famous phrase. With full confidence placed in the codes – which, in theory, contained the law in its entirety – problems of interpretation had been rendered a thing of the past, or so it was naively believed.

Unlike in Prussia, in France there existed no ban on publishing commentaries on the Napoleonic codes. These commentaries, however, would be strictly limited to explaining and setting forth the letter of the law, word by word and article by article: *exegesis*, a term implying explanation and interpretation, especially of the Holy Scriptures. In this light its application to the Napoleonic texts by the proponents of the Exegetical School is a telling indication of the reverence with which they regarded them. A quote by Jean Joseph Bugnet (d. 1866) went down in history: "I don't know civil law; I teach nothing but the Napoleonic Code." This would be the approach followed by the first generation of jurists after Napoleon; the previous generation still belonged to the old judicial nobility and had been educated in the venerable tradition of Dumoulin, Domat, and Pothier. For the jurists of the new school, legislation was the law and the law was legislation; case law and customary law lacked validity; comparative law and legal history were expendable; and the social aspects underlying legal prescripts were irrelevant. The representatives of this school included, in addition to the aforementioned Bugnet, Charles Toullier (d. 1835) and Alexandre Duranton (d. 1866), as well as the Belgian François Laurent (d. 1887), who between 1869 and 1879 published no fewer than 33 volumes, with his line-by-line commentaries on the articles of the *Code civil.*

In both France and Belgium, along with other countries featuring civil codes inspired by the French model, in time criticism of legal exegeticism intensified. What came to be known as the "Scientific School," for example, viewed the law as a dynamic reality which must take into account economic and sociological aspects. Its defenders argued that jurists must be free to present their conceptions of law in a systematic way without being constricted by the order of the articles in the civil code. The leading representatives of this school of thought, headed by Francois Geny (1861–1959), also objected to the radical insistence upon legislation as the sole source of law, and were open to considering other sources of law, such as case law and customary law.

B. The Historical School

The postulates of the Enlightenment were, in and of themselves, ahistorical. According to the enlightened thinkers it is possible to construct a legal, rational, ideal, and atemporal legal model based solely on logical principles. Questioning whether the model meets the needs of a given time was permissible only as a secondary issue, subordinate to the effective construction of the system. The *Code civil* was for them the embodiment of a complete and timeless model.

In Germany there was a general reaction against Enlightenment thinking in jurisprudence, particularly against the *Code civil.* This reaction was framed in the context of Classicism and Romanticism, trends which had taken very deep root in Germany, as reflected in the works of philosophers such as Immanuel Kant (1724–1804) and Friedrich Hegel, writers such as Friedrich Schiller (1759–1805) and Johann Wolfgang Goethe (1749–1832), and academic classicists such as Johann Joachim Winckelmann (1717–68).

The jurists of the Historical School, headed up by Friedrich Carl von Savigny (1779–1861), saw the law as an expression of the *Volksgeist*, or spirit of the people. As such it was a product of organic evolution over the course of history. Jurisprudence, in their view, then, had everything to do with history, of which they embraced a very particular conception. Upon the basis of historical materials it was incumbent upon jurists to build an entire legal system that was orderly, logical, and coherent. The law was, thus, in their view, a kind of a model kit. The paradox is that in order to fit these historical materials into the system it was necessary to extract them from their original context, in such a way that, strictly speaking, they were no longer historical. The enduring influence of Enlightenment thought was thus manifested, with the difference that the system would be constructed here not upon rational premises, but upon historical material.

As stated, the jurists of the Historical School believed that law developed in a natural, organic way, and could not be imposed top-down. The law of a people, they argued, like its history and language, develops organically as an expression of its *Volksgeist.* As such, customary and case law are legitimate expressions and sources of the law, but legislation, imposed from above, is not. Law is a *popular* creation, not a *political* one; the jurists of this school identify with the people and function as interpreters of its legal sensibilities, this forming the whole and exclusive object of jurisprudence.

The Historical School may be divided into two subgroups: Romanists and Germanists. The former believed that the German legal system should be built on the basis of Roman law. At first glance it may seem strange to hold up Roman law as the manifestation of the spirit of the German people, but this view was not entirely unfounded. In Rome law was developed by expert jurists and the jurisprudence of the praetor, while legislation had played only a marginal role. Moreover, Roman law had been received in Germany in a particularly intense way, as part of the political justification for the Holy Roman Empire lay in the theoretical succession of imperial power going back to ancient Rome. In addition, in a territory as vast and fragmented as the Holy Roman Empire, Roman law had been declared to be suppletive, and was applied directly in the *Reichskammergericht*, the imperial supreme court. And in Germany, as was the case throughout Europe, Roman law was essentially an academic discipline, which gave Romanist jurists, interpreters of that tradition, a key position in the Empire's social and political structure. The Romanist variant of the Historical School was further bolstered by the passion for all things classical which swept the German bourgeoisie in the early nineteenth century. Enlightenment jurist Anton Friedrich Justus Thibaut (d. 1840) was a precursor of this school, his work *The System of the Law of Pandects* (1803) of special note.

The Germanists, on the other hand, imbued with the ideas of Romanticism – which also spread throughout nineteenth-century Germany – were supporters of the study of the German people's particular laws and their transformation into a coherent whole. Among the Germanists Karl Friedrich Eichhorn (d. 1854) stands out, who produced a summary of German law in 1808: *German State and Legal History*. Eichhorn argued for the construction of a system of German private law encompassing the different German states, similar to the *ius commune* in Europe's past. The taking of the first step towards the realization of this ideal is found in his *Introduction to German Private Law* (1823). Carl Friedrich von Gerber (d. 1891) then perfected it in his *The Scientific Principle of Common German Private Law* (1846). Jacob Grimm (d. 1863), in addition to his activities as a writer of fairy tales and works in linguistics, literature and anthropology, dealt with German law, paying special attention to the role of the law in the history of Teutonic culture. Finally, Georg Beseler (d. 1888) also sought to develop an internally consistent system based on Germanic historical material in his *System of German Common Private Law* (1847–55). Typical of Beseler and other Germanists was a rejection of Roman law and its legacy; the official reception of Roman law in the sixteenth century was, in their opinion, a national disaster which deprived the people of one of the most authentic expressions of their identity: their own body of law.

C. Pandectism

The Romanists built their system – a key catchword during the era – on the basis of Roman legal texts. They thereby embraced the rationalist constructivism for which they had reproached natural-law and enlightened jurists, turning to the same logical and deductive methods. The difference is that they would not work with axioms or principles, but with Roman materials.

The founder of the Historical School, in both its Germanist and Romanist versions, was Friedrich Carl von Savigny. In his *Das Recht des Besitzes* (*The Law of Possession*, 1803), Savigny takes a legal institution from the Roman material – possession – and presents it as an organic and coherent unit. He did not undertake a historical study in the sense of reconstructing the evolution of possession over the course of history. On the contrary, he considered it a fixed and unchanging concept, whose essence was the intention to possess. But historical evolution was necessary to manifest and lay down this unitary concept. In this lay, for Savigny, the jurist's function: deducing from historical material, which he considered a set of empirically observable data, general principles and institutions. This creative work of the jurist made him the linchpin sustaining and the engine driving juridical evolution. He rejected the role of legislation and, with it, efforts at codification. Thibaut, after ridding the German territories of French soldiers in 1814, had argued for a single German code in his *On the Need for a General Civil Law for Germany*. Savigny responded that same year with his famous *On the Vocation of Our Age for Legislation and Jurisprudence*. In Savigny's view the jurist, not the legislator, was the interpreter of the people's legal spirit. Savigny also championed the figure of the jurist in his *History of Roman Law in the Middle Ages* (1815–31), which featured the biographies of glossators and commentators and demonstrated the continuity between ancient Roman and medieval law.

Savigny also followed Thibaut's lead by integrating all Roman law into a single system: *System of The Modern Roman Law* (1840–49), in which he built an ahistorical scientific system based on historical material. Roman law, in its classic version, was not systematic, but rather quite piecemeal; Savigny took its casuistic material and sought to structure it in a system which could also be applied to contemporary Germany. This was the genesis of Pandectism.

Savigny did not achieve his objective, but his successors would. The methodology of conceptual and systematic thinking (*Begriffsjurisprudenz*, or *Jurisprudence of Concepts*) would be applied to Roman law, which would eventually completely overshadow the historic material which constituted its foundation.

Friedrich Puchta (d. 1846) was a student of Savigny's, but his *Lehrbuch der Pandekten* would end up making a considerable impact on his teacher's system. Puchta, even more than Savigny, proposed the construction of a logical and internally coherent conceptual system. Puchta's successors included the outstanding Bernhard Windscheid (1817–92), whose textbook of Roman law, *Pandekten* (1862–91), constitutes the most complete expression of the great project undertaken by Puchta and Savigny.

The pandectists' critics included Rudolph von Jhering (1818–92), who had begun his career as a pandectist before ultimately abandoning his belief in a logical and systematic approach to the law. In his *The Spirit of Roman Law in the Various Phases of Its Development* (1852), he presented with great originality the moral and sociological aspects which had influenced and motivated the ancient Romans, with particular attention to the archaic and preclassical periods, in which he located its authentic "spirit." Law serves certain ends, which must be pursued if one is to study it and make legal decisions. According to Jhering, law is, in reality, something that is kept alive by constant individual action, as he expressed in his booklet *Das Kampf um's Recht* (*The Struggle for Law*, 1872), a genuine juridical bestseller.

Also rejecting the excesses of the pandectists was Nobel Prize recipient Theodor Mommsen, the author of the masterful and monumental *Römische Geschichte* (*Roman History*, 1854–56) and other historical treatises on Roman public law, and Roman criminal law, in addition to his editions of the *Codex Theodosianus* (1901) and the *Corpus iuris civilis* (1868–70), the standard edition even today.

Classicism and Romanticism did not shield Germany from the positivist thinking which spread throughout nineteenth-century Europe. However, the form positivism took in Germany differed notably from that advanced by the Exegetic School, with its radical adherence to legislation as the sole source of law. In Germany what could be called "dogmatic formalism" spread, according to which principles and concepts were deduced from the system itself and political, economic, sociological, religious, moral, and scientific considerations were dispensed with, precisely because they fell outside the system. Thus, the legal positivism of nineteenth-century Germany was based not on legislation, but on the system itself. According to this line of thinking, all that was necessary to find the correct solution to a particular problem was the logical operation of placing a hypothetical judgment within a systematic set of principles and concepts.

This extreme legal formalism had its roots in the thoughts of Kant, whose influence Savigny himself acknowledged. Kant believed that the function of the law was to protect subjective rights. According to the philosopher the individual is capable of complete moral development provided that this does not infringe the rights of others. It is the role of law to protect these areas where the individual acts and develops. The moral end which objective law serves is achieved not by converting moral precepts into legal mandates, but rather by creating and protecting the domain in which the individual can live and realize his potential. The law has an existence independent of moral and social conditions. It may, therefore, be the object of autonomous, formal elaboration – which was precisely the ambitious task at which Savigny and his pandectist disciples endeavored.

V. PANDECTIST CODIFICATION

A. The *Bürgerliches Gesetzbuch* (BGB)

Though the Historical School opposed codification, paradoxically, it was creating the ideal conditions for it. With their mastery of systematic methodology, the pandectists were ideal candidates to revise and draft codes. Savigny was responsible for the revision of the Prussian *Allgemeines Landrecht* of 1794, while Windscheid formed part of the first commission charged with writing the BGB. They did not perceive any contradiction at all in this. On the contrary, they considered this participation the best proof of the jurist's central position in the creation of law, just as it had been in Roman times.

The decision to draft a civil code for unified Germany was based on the same political and social factors which had yielded the *Code civil* in France and the *Codice civile* in Italy: the unifying force of a unique code which would unequivocally establish the three pillars of liberal society: equality before the law, private property, and freedom of contract.

Following the Peace of Westphalia in 1648, the Holy Roman Empire was composed of some 335 small, independent states. Napoleon attempted to put an end to this territorial organization, dissolving the Holy Roman Empire and establishing the Confederation of the Rhine (*Rheinbund*), an alliance of 16 satellite states beholden to France that was disbanded in 1813. After Napoleon's fall in 1815 the German states forged a Germanic Confederation (*Deutscher Bund*), a union of 38 independent states controlled by Austria and Prussia. In 1866, after the Austro-Prussian War, Austria was excluded from the confederation and forced to recognize the North German Confederation (*Norddeutscher Bund*), dominated by Prussia. Under the chairmanship of Otto von Bismarck (1815–98) the *Bund* federalized, unified passports and customs agencies, and established a single Parliament (*Reichstag*). In 1871, after victory over the French in the Franco-Prussian War, the new nation state was transformed into the German Empire (*Deutsches Reich*), which stood until 1918.

The only field of private law in which the *Norddeutscher Bund*, and later the *Deutsches Reich*, could legislate was obligation-related law. In 1873 a law was passed granting the German Parliament the authority to legislate also in the other fields of private law. A civil code project was then launched. In 1873 a first commission was instituted under the direction of Windscheid. A first draft was turned out in 1887, notable for its technical perfection and systematic coherence. The document, however, sparked a wave of protests. In accordance with pandectist postulates that assigned a central role to the jurist in the creation of law, there had been almost no negotiations or consultations with representatives from other spheres of society. In addition, unlike the *Code civil*, written in a plain and understandable style for the public, the document was written in a technical language comprehensible only to jurists. Reading it was also complicated by its frequent cross-references, included in order to produce an internally coherent system. In general the code was considered too conceptual, too dogmatic, and not sufficiently practical. Its content was also criticized, with Otto von Gierke (d. 1921), a staunch defender of the role of associations within society, blasting the pronounced individualism inspiring the document.

A second commission was formed in 1890. Windscheid's code was adopted as a point of departure, so that it was not necessary to start from scratch. Rudolph Sohm (1841–1917), an eminent expert in the history of canon law, was one of the commission's most notable members. The panel addressed, at least in part, social issues formerly overlooked, but the text was still plagued by opacity, abstraction, and and excessive number of cross-references. The new commission, however, did conduct consultations and negotiations with important interest groups, resulting in more muted protests. With some minimal changes the version was completed. On 18 August 1896 the *Bürgerliches Gesetzbuch* (BGB) was completed, and entered into force on 1 January 1900.

B. Characteristics and Intellectual Context

The BGB is made up of five books, organized in a manner almost opposite that followed in the *Code civil*. The first book is the famous "general part," followed by books dedicated to the law of obligations, property law, family law and succession law.

Both in its form and content, the BGB was a product of its time and the context in which it arose. It represented a coherent, solid, and consistent system based on Roman law, with the exception of the fourth and fifth books (family and succession law). Its style – objective, scientific, somewhat ponderous, perhaps – stands out for its precise formulations, unambiguous terminology, and the scrupulous care taken with the grammatical construction of each phrase.

Faithful to their systematic ideal, the pandectists strove, given the large number of existing prescripts, to extract and distill general principles from them. These principles were formulated in the first general part. In the composition of the other books the same approach was followed, proceeding from the general and abstract to the concrete. The method was not without drawbacks; regulations regarding the contract of sale appear in various sections of the BGB: in the general part, in the general precepts on obligations, in the general precepts regarding contractual obligations, and, finally, in the part dedicated strictly to sale contracts. This type of structure made it necessary to constantly include cross-references in the text, which made for a tiring read.

The BGB is also characterized by the inclusion of *Generalklauseln*, or general clauses, guiding principles aimed at judges: for example, good faith (*Trau und Glauben*) and equity (*Billigkeit*), which appealed to morality and the judge's sense of responsibility. Here the BGB follows the example of the Roman praetor: the judge may rule according to the *bona fides*. It was these general clauses and their great plasticity which enabled the BGB to respond to Germany's dynamic and difficult circumstances in the twentieth century. However, some very serious risks should not be overlooked: the breadth of the judge's scope of discretion opened the door to ideological and social pressures, and even to the judge's personal opinions.

The BGB was the crown jewel of a society on the verge of radical transformation under the pressure of different collectivist and totalitarian ideologies. Unlike the *Code civil,* which expressed the ideals of a bourgeoisie that had just acquired power, the BGB arose when the golden age of the bourgeoisie seemed to be coming to an end. Just half a century and millions of deaths later, the optimism and faith in freedom and progress so typical of the nineteenth century would have all but vanished. The BGB and the *Code civil* stood as silent witnesses to the collapse of a civilization.

C. The Second Pandectist Code: Switzerland

After a civil war in 1848, the Swiss Confederation was transformed into a modern state with a more robust central government. As in other countries, the combination of Enlightenment ideas, Romantic and nationalist sentiments, and political liberalism and centralism gave rise to calls for a national civil code. Cantonal fragmentation in the sphere of private law was extreme; some cantons, such as Zurich, had promulgated their own civil code (1855); some followed the *Code civil*; others observed the Austrian *Allgemeines Bürgerliches Gesetzbuch*. In the second half of the nineteenth century the movement to unify private law gathered steam. In 1874 a constitutional amendment granted the Confederation the authority to set down law governing obligations. Ten years later the project was completed, and the new law of obligations was a good example of progress in pandectist principles. This success encouraged the Swiss to develop a complete civil code. Eugen Huber (1849–1923) was commissioned to carry out a comparative study of the different systems of private law employed in the Swiss cantons. The study, entitled *System and History of Swiss Private Law* (1886–93), was characteristic of pandectist jurisprudence. The work so impressed the Swiss Government that it commissioned its author for the partial drafting of a civil code. The first texts governing marriage and succession appeared in the 1890s. At the beginning of the twentieth century the Confederation obtained the necessary competencies to legislate in all areas of private law, and Huber's various texts, plus others regarding the law of obligations, were consolidated into a single work. After being put to a public referendum, with some criticisms considered and included, the text was enacted as law in 1907. A revised version of the "code of obligations" – which removed the distinction between the civil and commercial laws of obligations and contracts in favour of a unified regime – was added in 1911.

The pandectist roots of the Swiss code are evident in its incorporacion of *Generalklauseln* ("general clauses") which, however, did not comprise a "general part" such as that in the BGB. The language, clear and consistent, could be understood not only by lawyers, but also by the general public. The Swiss are rightly proud of their civil code, probably one of the best in the world.

D. The Expansion of the Pandectist Codes

The BGB had a significant influence on the states which formed part of the Austro-Hungarian Empire, then on its way towards fragmentation.

Austria (1904) took it very much into account when revising its own civil code in 1904, and Poland's law of obligations of 1927 was also influenced by it. Much can be said of the preparations for a civil code in Yugoslavia. We already know that Pandectism deeply influenced Italian jurisprudence; the conceptual clarity of the BGB was a source of inspiration for the *Codice civile* of 1942, though this did not mark an end to the traditional French influence on Italy.

Outside Europe the BGB had a great impact on the civil code of Brazil (1916), and, through this, that of Peru (1936). The initial draft of the BGB even influenced the civil codes of Japan (1898), Siam (Thailand, 1925) and China (1929).

After World War II the BGB's influence waned somewhat, though it and Windscheid's *Pandekten* would have a major impact on the civil codes of Greece (1946) and Hungary (1959).

The Swiss Civil Code also proved very successful. In 1927 it was adopted outright, with just a few minor amendments, by Turkey, where Atatürk (President of Turkey from 1923 until his death in 1938) sought to westernize and secularize his country. Its influence and inspiration, particularly its decision to unify the civil and commercial law of obligations, can generally be detected in most civil code reforms of the twentieth century, such as that of the Dutch *Burgerlijk Wetboek* in 1992.

6. Common law

It is safe to say that, until the eighteenth century, English common law did not have any particular influence on the evolution of the law on the Continent. This started to change, however, beginning in the nineteenth century as the British Empire, with its overseas dominions and colonies, became the world's dominant economic power and came to wield increasing political, cultural and intellectual influence. The United States of America, another common-law country, would succeed the UK and assume this role in the twentieth century.

Conversely, both the English and the Americans have historically been very proud of their legal systems, and have traditionally denied the influence of Roman law on their legal traditions. Even though, as we will see, recent historical research has revealed that civil law ideas, forms and principles did have an influence on English law, a profound divide between the civil and common law systems must be acknowledged, most visibly embodied in the different role of courts in the creation of law, and the lack of all-encompassing codes of law in the common law tradition.

It is intriguing to note that, until the beginning of the twelfth century, the legal systems in England and on the European mainland were roughly the same in outlook. The dominant source of law was unwritten custom, which was imposed by locally organized courts. There was no unified, nationwide law, and there was no centrally organized court system. There were no jurists, as such, and legislation was all but absent. How is it, then, that from the twelfth century onwards two different traditions started to evolve?

I. THE ORIGINS OF ENGLISH COMMON LAW

A. The Anglo-Saxon Period

Following the withdrawal of Roman legions in the early fifth century, numerous hordes of Jutes, Angles and Saxons from north of modern-day Germany reached Britain. The new peoples brought with them their Germanic legal traditions, and the Romano-British civilization, including its legal system, collapsed. In the ninth century, Britain, like the rest of

Europe, suffered the invasions of Viking tribes – above all Danish, and, to a lesser extent, Norwegian – who settled in a large swathe of what is today northeastern England, which they dubbed the “Danelaw.” Also termed “Danelaw” was the set of rules and legal provisions that the leaders of both peoples agreed upon to govern their coexistence. The word “law” actually comes from the Old Norwegian *lagu* (measure), which replaced the corresponding Anglo-Saxon term *gesetnes*, from the German *Gesetz* (law).

The presence of different tribes triggered territorial fragmentation into different realms. In the late ninth century King Alfred of Wessex (d. 899) managed to impose his authority on a single kingdom, England, and to establish an effective and uniform territorial structure. The kingdom was divided into counties, or shires. A representative body made up of notables of diverse origins, which boasted legislative, executive and judicial functions, managed each of the shires. To this institution subjects could turn in search of justice (*riht*). At the same time, the shires were divided into “hundreds,” under the responsibility of the hundredman; and the hundreds were divided, in turn, into tithings, in theory formed by a group of ten families, under the responsibility of the tithingman. Other local divisions were the borough, the manor and the village. All these assemblies, which were not necessarily hierarchically organized, led to the development of an equal number of sets of customary laws. This fragmentation, however, would not result in decentralization; the English kings were able largely to maintain a centralized government through their royal officials, notably their *sheriffs* (shire reeves), who were, at least in theory, to visit each of the hundreds of their shires twice yearly.

B. The Norman Conquest

The Battle of Hastings (1066) led to the conquest of England by William the Conqueror (1028–87) and his Norman armies. The Normans were a people of Viking origin long established in modern-day Normandy, where they had adopted the language of northern France. In England the Normans found an effective and quite centralized government which they would manage to reinforce through the introduction, in 1066, of a sudden and radical feudalism: William distributed most of England’s territories to his followers in exchange for military and financial support, and made the notion that every parcel of land belonged to the king a reality. Feudalism, in addition to becoming the cornerstone of the political system, would be of special importance with regard to private law, particularly in the area of property. In order to make possible efficient fiscal and feudal management William commissioned a comprehensive description and registration of every plot of land in England: the *Domesday Book* (1086). The efficient management of land kept the centrifugal forces of feudalism under control.

C. The Introduction of Royal Justice

In parallel to the jurisdictional bodies linked to the Anglo-Saxon division of the territory, the Normans introduced their own system of royal justice. The origin of and the justification for this system are not entirely clear, but coincided with the trend throughout Europe during the era according to which monarchs endowed themselves with justice-dispensing powers. During the rule of King Stephen (1135–54) a civil war broke out; during the process of pacification, under Henry II (1154–89), royal justice grew in importance, especially in cases involving the possession of landed property. Indeed, land law would always be considered the exclusive domain of royal jurisdiction and lies at the very heart of all common law. It is no coincidence that the advent of common law is normally associated with the reign of Henry II.

Royal justice – the working language of which was French, that of the Norman Crown – was far more effective than the local courts. To this was added the advantage that royal justice offered definitive decisions of cases, in contrast to those handled by local jurisdictions, which could be taken up again by royal courts.

The organization of royal justice featured two main prongs: itinerant justices and, on occasion, appeals to the king himself. At the end of the twelfth century the king sent his judges throughout England, their main mission to ensure compliance with royal legislation. This institution came to be known as the "general eyre." For this purpose the country was divided into six circuits. The itinerant commission of royal judges, with their sizable retinue of assistants and secretaries, periodically visited each county, there fully representing the royal government, its purview transcending the mere administration of justice. On behalf of the king they investigated crimes, ruled regarding tax and feudal disputes, and settled conflicts between individuals. The general eyre also explicitly oversaw local government. Errors and abuses committed by the sheriffs could be brought before the commission, such that it often functioned as a check and counterweight against their dominant positions. It was not uncommon for judges to act with great severity. As a tangible manifestation of royal power, this rigor would contribute notably to the establishment of a genuinely national system of law, unique in Europe.

In the political life of each county the convocation of the general eyre represented an event of the greatest importance. In theory all the people of the county were to be present during the commission's sessions, though this entailed considerable practical difficulties. There were growing protests due to the excessive frequency of the general eyre's visits. At times entire groups of the population fled into the forests, there were pay-offs to prevent their celebration, and there are even accounts of murdered judges. Over the course of the thirteenth century it became clear that the institution lacked the necessary flexibility, and at the beginning of the fourteenth it disappeared.

Individuals in search of justice were understandably upset about having to wait until the next visit of the general eyre to present their grievances. They did have the right to appeal to the king in person. In practice, however, this right was difficult to exercise, as the monarch still had no fixed place of residence and traveled continuously throughout his territory. In the twelfth century individuals could turn to the *curia regis*, a consultative body consisting of experts and courtiers who assisted the king in the determination of general policies. From amongst them were elected the judges who formed part of the general eyre. Over time the monarch would come to delegate the judicial function. The judges, who began to boast increasingly professional and technical profiles rather than political ones, ceased to follow the monarch in his travels, and a permanent court was established for them at Westminster: the Bench. By the end of the thirteenth century a central royal justice body had been established at a fixed site.

Despite the development of a central judicial authority, individuals seeking justice continued to encounter serious difficulties. It was not always possible for everyone involved in a case to travel to Westminster. Hence an institutional initiative resuscitated the old itinerant justice system, on a complementary basis, which featured similarities and also differences compared to the general eyre. Itinerant justices, charged with various functions, were also organized into six circuits. The institution in this form would continue to thrive for several centuries.

In criminal matters the itinerant justices possessed original jurisdiction. With a commission of gaol delivery (*deliverare*, to free-up gaols by either releasing or trying the prisoners), they judged cases of serious offenses that constituted clear violations of the king's peace. Commissions of oyer and terminer were given to judges to hear (*oyer*) and resolve (*terminer*) criminal cases. In civil affairs, mostly related to the possession of land, Henry II decided in 1166 that a jury of 12 citizens (*assize*) would be summoned to the royal court. Given the harsh conditions of the journey, this was not always possible. Thus, judges were sent to receive the jury's verdict and take it back to Westminster. In fact, the trial process was conducted locally, before justices of assize, and only the final sentence was pronounced at Westminster. This was known as the *nisi prius* system: jurors were summoned to appear at the royal courts at Westminster, unless prior (*nisi prius*) to the summons arriving there appeared itinerant justices in their county, which was usually arranged for. The itinerant justices boasted different functions: at times as commissioners of gaol delivery, at other times as justices of assizes, etc.

The institution of the jury, having deep Germanic roots, would be one of the pillars of common law. In this regard a distinction should be drawn between a grand jury and a petty jury, or assize. The first of these was composed of a large number of people, initially composed of the group of townsfolk who presented crimes to the itinerant justices allegedly committed during their absence. Hence the filter function in prosecution which it acquired over time: the grand jury did not issue any definitive rulings, but was limited to determining whether or not there was sufficient evidence to proceed against the accused. If there was, a petty jury was then formed consisting of 12 people, who heard the evidence and pronounced its verdict. The grand jury and the petty jury survived until 1933 in England, and still exist in the United States.

It was in the royal, central and itinerant courts, with or without juries, where common law was formed and developed. As law that was the same throughout the entire kingdom, it was termed "common" to distinguish it from local customary law, which varied from one place to another. The latter, proceeding from the Anglo-Saxon period, was destined to disappear, as royal justice was much more efficient in every way. Some Anglo-Saxon institutions, however, such as the borough and the manor, would remain in place, in certain cases until as late as 1971.

II. THE CENTRAL COURTS OF COMMON LAW

A. The Development of the Central Courts

The idea of the monarch as *fons iustitiae*, the source of justice, was widespread throughout Europe during the Middle Ages. In principle every individual seeking justice could submit his case to the monarch, who only acted personally as a judge – advised by his council of experts and courtiers: the *curia regis* – when the case was of special significance. Such was royal justice in its original context. Until the end of the Middle Ages the monarch would regularly travel throughout his kingdom – which until 1204 consisted of two spheres, divided by the English Channel – rather than maintaining a fixed seat of government. Those beseeching royal justice could end up pursuing the court for years until they were finally received.

As the monarch's judicial functions increased, along with his other political and administrative tasks, he was obligated to entrust the resolution of cases in a range of different areas to advisors specialized in each.

The first function thus separated was assigned to the treasury department, or Exchequer, so named for the place where accounts were monitored and administered. This was also the first department which, due to the obvious dangers posed by a traveling treasury, ceased to accompany the monarch and was fixed permanently at Westminster.

Towards the end of the twelfth century the permanent court of central and royal justice, the Bench, was also established at Westminster. The Bench operated without the monarch's presence. The Magna Carta had determined that there should be a permanent rather than an itinerant court for the handling of common pleas. In this way the Bench was divided into the Common Bench, or Court of Common Pleas, fixed permanently at Westminster in 1230, and the King's Bench, which heard cases in which the monarch had an interest, and which by its own nature had to follow the king if he was away.

The Court of Common Pleas, established under the terms of the Magna Carta, had exclusive jurisdiction over common pleas; that is, matters that did not directly involve the king and his interests. Most civil matters were handled through it. Medieval common law would be forged, above all, in this Court of Common Pleas.

The establishment of the Court of Common Pleas would not preclude the king and his *curia regis* from continuing to take note of the affairs in which the king had an interest, or which were of a special nature: the "pleas of the Crown." The cases in question were, above all, criminal matters, but there were also civil cases involving public order. Beginning in the fourteenth century this function would also be entrusted to a group of experts, separate from the *curia regis*, and which would also operate permanently from Westminster: the Court of the King's Bench. During the Middle Ages the activity of the King's Bench was of scant significance, due to the system of itinerant justices and the fact that the Court of Common Pleas retained residual jurisdiction over cases falling under the purview of the King's Bench, but which, for whatever reason, were ultimately not handled by it. Over the course of the fifteenth century the King's Bench became increasingly active, especially due to the application of the bill procedure, much cheaper and more flexible than the procedure by writ employed by the Court of Common Pleas. Apart from the procedure by bill, the King's Bench would also develop and apply "actions on the case." These new methods greatly bolstered the popularity of the King's Bench in the sixteenth century, which saw an increase in its workload. The court would also end up hearing cases of an ordinary nature.

In order to keep from violating the terms of the Magna Carta, it would be necessary to maintain certain fictions. According to the Magna Carta the King's Bench had no jurisdiction over cases related to contracts or torts. But the bill procedure changed this situation, as the King's Bench was able to emit a bill to initiate processes against people already in prison, in which case the Magna Carta no longer applied. The plaintiff could then have his debtor arrested (debtors' prisons would exist in England until 1869, and they still exist in various forms in the United States) by virtue of a writ of trespass, and then recover the amount owed him by the debtor through a bill before the King's Bench. The initial trespass action could then be discreetly abandoned.

The oldest of the common law courts was the last to become a permanent court: the Exchequer of Pleas. At first this court's jurisdiction was limited to tax matters. The court, however, boasted some advantages, offered by the fact that it could issue its own writs and bills. In general terms it functioned in a much more flexible way, which was only logical, as it wielded the instruments with which the king was to obtain revenue. In the sixteenth century the jurisdiction of the Exchequer was extended to civil cases, a development justified by means of a specious argument: that the plaintiff needed the amount his debtor owed him in order to pay his taxes to the Treasury (writ of *quominus*).

B. Uniformity and the Abolition of Common Law Courts

At the end of the seventeenth century there were three courts operating in London whose purviews overlapped. While employing different procedures, they could each hear virtually the same types of cases. In addition, the workload borne by the assize commissions was distributed between the three courts quite evenly. Following harsh critiques by reformers such as Jeremy Bentham (1748–1832), the Judicature Act (1873) was introduced to abolish the three central courts and transfer their competencies to a single High Court. Two years later a Supreme Court of Judicature was instituted, which came to function as a Court of Appeal and a High Court of Justice.

III. WRITS

A. Remedies Precede Rights

In Continental law, with its Roman roots, substantive law is more important than procedural. Law – substantive law – is conceived as a more or less systematic set of abstract rules that may be applied to specific situations. The application of substantive law is verified essentially through a single, general procedural channel: Romano-canonical procedure, whose purpose is precisely to allow for the application of the different prescripts of substantive law. Common law functioned in a different way and was, at least from the thirteenth through the nineteenth century, dominated by procedural formalities. As in classical Roman law, with its *actiones,* one could sue only if there existed a specific remedy for the situation in question. There was no notion of law or right outside the different legal remedies (what we would call "substantive law"), or of a procedure separate from the remedies themselves (what we would call "procedural law"). The remedy incorporated the right and the procedure at the same time. This was the principle of "remedies precede rights," or *ubi remedium, ibi ius* ("where there is a remedy, there is a right").

B. Writs Until 1258

A litigant initiated a procedure before royal courts by means of a writ, a fragment of sealed parchment that had to be purchased at the Chancery. It was this parchment which opened the court's doors to him. It should be noted that the royal courts were originally considered courts of exception with respect to local courts; access to them was, thus, formally considered a privilege, a special concession for which a price was to be paid. The writ specified the claim which had been paid for, and an order for a court or relevant official to rule one way or the other depending upon whether certain facts had been demonstrated.

Originating as an extraordinary procedure, the writ soon became the standard instrument for litigation. Many different types of writ developed: the writ of debt and the writ of covenant for cases of debts and contracts; the writ of detinue (*detinue sur bailment* or *detinue sur trover*) to demand things held by others; the writ of *certiorari* to appeal to a higher court; the writ of *habeas corpus* to prevent indefinite imprisonment by forcing the release of a detainee if criminal charges were not brought immediately. In theory a new writ could feature a new formula. In the interest of legal security, however, from the outset fixed formulas were employed, and it was practically impossible to issue a writ which lacked precedents.

It should be underscored that without a writ a plaintiff could do nothing to initiate a procedure before the Benches, as the choice of the writ determined the procedure and the evidence which could be used in a given case, to the exclusion of others.

The rapid proliferation of new writs (from 36 in the twelfth century to 120 in the thirteenth) triggered a reaction by the traditional local courts. Each new writ marked an additional encroachment by the royal courts upon the powers of traditional ones, which meant a considerable loss of revenue for the latter. In 1258, it was established that the Chancery could only issue already existing writs.

C. Writs after 1258

Operating based only on the writs set down in 1258 turned out to be impracticable. One example involved the concept of "trespassing," at first a general term indicating any wrongful conduct. Writs of trespass comprised a broad category of writs with a common feature: the granting of damages, i.e. an indemnification. Over the course of the thirteenth century it was established that writs of trespass could be issued only when in the commission of the wrongful conduct weapons or violence (*vi et armis*) had been used, or when public order had been disturbed (*contra pacem regis* – against the King's peace). Only in these cases were the royal courts to have jurisdiction, while ordinary conflicts would be settled by local courts.

But the trend towards litigation in the royal courts was too strong to be stopped by the strict casuistry of the writ system and the rigidity of common law in general. For example, local courts could not hear cases involving claims for more than 40 shillings. A flaw thus appeared: who was to hear cases for amounts in excess of this sum, but which were not of a violent nature? Initially a solution was sought through a forced interpretation of the *vi et armis* clause. For example, a case involving damage to a horse due to a blacksmith's placement of a horseshoe with nails and hammers was admitted as a violent act involving weapons. In 1350 a new writ was born inspired by the writs of trespass, and even with the same name, but without the *vi et armis* clause. In the new writ the plaintiff initiated the procedure "upon his special case," for his specific case, and according to his own claims and evidence. The category of "writs of trespass on the case" allowed access to royal justice for actions involving negligence, breach of contract, fraud in sales, damages caused by animals, etc.

During the fifteenth and sixteenth centuries new writs on the case were introduced, the writ of *assumpsit* being the most important of them. The writ of *assumpsit* forms the basis of English contract law, together with the older writ of debt and writ of covenant. The writ of *assumpsit* is a writ on the case in which it is noted that the plaintiff has suffered damages due to a breach of obligations which a debtor had undertaken (*assumpsit*). New writs tended to ensure the effective application of others: the writ of attachment, to guarantee or enforce judgments; the writ of *ne exeat republic*, to prevent a debtor from fleeing, etc.

IV. THE RISE OF EQUITY

A. The Rigidity of Common Law

Despite the introduction of actions on the case and a limited number of new writs, as well as the possibility of the bill procedure before the King's Bench, the common law always suffered from a certain degree of rigidity. In some cases, due to its strict formalism and its limited number of writs, common law was incapable of responding to new social circumstances.

For example, at law (that is, according to the common law) a claimant could only seek and obtain damages, i.e. an indemnification. Not allowed were orders for the specific performance of the contract. Another example: a debtor gave a creditor a sealed document expressly recognizing his debt when contracting it, but forgot to ask his creditor to return it upon settlement of his debt. In such a case the debtor could not evade payment if his creditor unfairly demanded it, as the sealed statement was still valid and irrefutable. Nor were solutions available in cases of verbal agreements requiring written proof. And principles of great social importance in England, such as "use" and "trust," were not protected at law. The medieval custom of "use," which would evolve into "trust," consisted of someone (feoffor) transmitting a property right to another person (feoffee), who thus obtained the legal estate and acquired the obligation to maintain and manage the property right for the benefit of the feoffor or a third party (*cestui que use*). If the feoffee performed acts damaging to the interests of the feoffor or the *cestui que use*, the latter lacked remedies at law because the feoffee held the legal estate.

B. Chancery

Common law was too rigid to allow the king to take additional measures or create new institutions to address such problems. The Magna Carta had stated that no one could be deprived of his freedom, his life or his property without due process, and to ensure this a procedure before common law courts was established. Over the centuries it came to be understood that the common law courts, despite originally being based on a cession of royal jurisdiction, functioned independently from the monarch. At the beginning of the seventeenth century the courts made it clear to James I that he was not to meddle with their jurisdiction. The monarch was permitted, however, to retain a sort of residual judicial authority. Thus, outside the regular system, the king maintained a certain degree of responsibility for the correct administration of justice, provided that life, liberty and property were not involved. On the basis of this residual authority "equity" was born to supplement common law without modifying it. The most important institution to which the king turned for this purpose was the Court of Chancery.

The Lord Chancellor, head of the Court of Chancery, became one of the most prominent members of the *curia regis*, and frequently acted as Prime Minister. He was also responsible for the conservation of the great seal, and with it, public faith. In this function the department which he headed, the Chancery, was responsible for the issuance of official documents, such as writs. The Chancery had been able to issue new writs when existing ones did not provide a suitable solution for the particular problem presented, but the limitation on the number of writs introduced in the middle of the thirteenth century greatly curtailed this possibility. From then on it was almost impossible to issue new writs if they were not approved by the king and Parliament. Such a procedure was too complex for most cases not covered by existing writs. Thus, as of the fifteenth century the Chancellor was authorized to issue, in his own name, decrees which would be applicable only to the specific case in question. These decrees contained orders to perform an act which at common law was not permitted, or, conversely, to prohibit a conduct permitted by the common law. In this way, returning to the example cited of a debt settlement certification not returned at the time of payment, if the debtor was then sued at law he could ask the chancellor to issue a decree to obviate the abusive claim for double payment.

The chancellor's judicial powers were originally to be considered exceptional. The chancellor did not stand in opposition to the common law, but rather supplemented and perfected it: equity followed the law, as did statutory law.

Initially, it lay at the chancellor's discretion whether to emit the requested decree or not, ruling according to the specific circumstances of the case and based exclusively on his own conscience. His jurisdiction was a "court of conscience." Beginning in the fifteenth century the chancellor's jurisdiction had become so popular that a need was perceived for it to possess its own court: the Court of Chancery. It is not difficult to explain the reasons for its success: new remedies, more flexible procedures via decree and bill instead of the rigid writs, the absence of juries, investigation and judgment carried out by the judge himself, and greater attention to the facts and circumstances of the case.

Along with this success, however, there came complaints regarding the unpredictable, arbitrary, and excessively personal manner (*divers men, divers consciences*) in which the Chancellor exercised his powers. Protests against the Court of Chancery were also driven by political motives, as Parliament wielded the common law as a weapon in their fight against the king's absolute power. Equity, in the hands of a Chancellor who tended to be the king's right-hand man, was seen as a tool in the hands of absolute political power, especially following James I's decision to place it above common law in the event of conflicts between the two ("equity shall prevail").

All this made it untenable for the decisions of the Court of Chancery to continue to depend only on the individual chancellor's judgment. The court would have to decide in accordance with general principles and issue similar decrees in similar cases. Consequently, equity developed until forming a body of coherent standards and principles separate from the common law and juxtaposed to it. Originally highly adaptable, equity grew progressively more rigid, particularly at the close of the seventeenth century, before becoming a separate legal system; *rigor aequitatis* had set in, and equity lost the dynamism necessary to incorporate new doctrines and concepts.

The Court of Chancery was also criticized for being too expensive and too slow. Its procedure – heavily influenced by the Romano-canonical procedure, as the Lord Chancellor was, initially, almost always a cleric or bishop – was very costly, especially due to the widespread and accepted habit of offering perquisites and gifts to accelerate procedures. Its slowness was a problem inherent to the system, as the Chancellor tended to supervise the court's entire workload.

During the nineteenth century the coexistence of two legal systems was considered an anomaly and a set of reforms from 1873 to 1875 (Supreme Court of Judicature Acts) led to the fusion of the courts of common law and equity into a single judicial structure. This did not mean, however, the merger of the two legal systems: the plaintiff, now always appearing before the same court, chose whether to pursue his case "at law" or "in equity."

V. OTHER COURTS

After the separation of the common law courts and the Court of Chancery, the judicial competencies of the *curia regis* were curbed, but did not disappear, with some transferred to new institutions, such as the Star Chamber and the Court of Admiralty.

The Star Chamber (so named for the decorative patterns which adorned the ceiling of Westminster where the court's sessions were held) gained importance in 1487 when the Star Chamber Act charged the body with oversight of law and order. Competent to hear civil matters, with some limitations, the Star Chamber was best known for its criminal jurisdiction. In the first half of the seventeenth century its reputation suffered greatly due to abuse of it by absolutist kings who exploited it as an instrument to persecute their political opponents. It was abolished in 1641, an important step towards the consolidation of the political ideal of the rule of law.

The Court of the Lord High Admiral of England, or High Court of Admiralty, was responsible for all cases related to navigation on the high seas. As there were many merchants seeking recourse to this court, it was perceived as a threat to the common law, and Parliament intervened several times to curtail its purview. Its procedure followed Romano-canonical patterns, and the law applied was largely based on rules shared with the Continental merchant community, with roots extending as far back as the *Rolls of Oléron*. This caused misgivings among common law judges. In the seventeenth century its purview was limited to collisions on the high seas and disputes regarding booty seized from the capture of enemy vessels.

The ecclesiastical courts and the *Corpus iuris canonici* they applied, of extraordinary importance on the Continent, were also relevant in England, especially during the Middle Ages. As a Christian kingdom England belonged to the same politico-religious unit as the rest of medieval Europe. Canon law, a supranational legal order reflecting the common heritage of Christian values, would thus be applied throughout English territory. In fact, it would have a considerable influence on the development of common law.

Some conflicts between secular monarchs and Church dignitaries (such as that which led to the murder of the Archbishop of Canterbury, Thomas

Beckett, in 1170, the result of a dispute with Henry II) contributed to a clear delimitation of the boundaries between ecclesiastical jurisdiction and common law. The ecclesiastical courts would be competent to judge matrimonial matters and those involving children born out of wedlock, inheritance law in relation to personal property, and with regard to a range of sins, such as adultery. Theft and murder fell exclusively under common law, as did contracts. Disputes over land in the hands of the Church were reserved for the ecclesiastical courts only if they were free of liens.

The shift to Anglicanism would mean that appeals against the decisions of the ecclesiastical courts would no longer be sent to Rome, but otherwise canon law continued to be applied without major changes, except when conflicting with common law. In the sixteenth century the possibility of fusing the ecclesiastical courts with the common law courts was considered, but the operation proved too technically complex, leaving the ecclesiastical courts functioning separately until the nineteenth century.

VI. PECULIAR FEATURES OF COMMON LAW

A. Lawmaking

One of the most interesting aspects of common law is the way in which it generates law. Does the judge make the law, or does he find it? Prior to the nineteenth century English jurists were convinced that their law was an invariable set of legal prescripts perfectly adapted to the needs of the English people. Court rulings were not sources of law but rather only explicit clarifications of it, at least according to the declaratory theory of common law. Changes in jurisprudence only responded to new, more refined nuances of legal prescripts which underwent no essential variations. The judge's function was *ius dicere* ("to pronounce the law") and not *ius dare* ("to give the law").

Declarative theory, however, was largely a myth accepted and cultivated as such by English judges and lawyers. Law, of course, changes, and judges issue sentences which deviate from established legal practices. It is true, however, that they always do so within the framework of techniques, concepts and principles found in the system itself. In general we can say that common law developed in response to both the need for legal certainty and coherence and the need to address the specific circumstances of individual cases.

The doctrine of precedent was an important factor in the development of common law, although the medieval notion of precedent was certainly different from the modern one. The registration of a ruling did not follow the same pattern as in more recent times, and there was no instrument to record the arguments put forward in suits. In the Middle Ages, certainly, judges did not diverge from generally accepted criteria, and when they did the change only came to serve as a precedent if other judges at Westminster supported the new criterion. Alterations or removals resulting from the natural evolution of the common law were, in this way, shared by the judiciary as a whole.

Beginning in the sixteenth century the influence of positivism spawned two changes: on the one hand the theory of "binding precedent" was developed, while the theory of *stare decisis* ("standing by decisions") also gained traction. Binding precedent meant that judges were bound to respect a preceding decision provided that its *ratio decidendi* was the same. The distinction between *ratio decidendi* (the "reason for the decision," the decisive argument of the judgment) and *obiter dictum* or *obiter dicta* (remarks from the judge said in passing which did not directly impinge on his decision) thus grew increasingly germane. Hence, modern era common law would cease to be blindly bound by medieval precedent – whose records were, in any case, incomplete.

The distinction between *ratio decidendi* and *obiter dicta* served to reinforce the *stare decisis* principle. The identification of the *ratio decidendi* of a similar, earlier case naturally entailed the application of the same criteria to the judicial decision. However, in the seventeenth century there was still recognition that a precedent could be erroneous, that judges could make mistakes in their decisions, which succeeding judges dealing with similar cases ought not to repeat. The extreme rigidity of the *stare decisis* principle, which became almost a kind of dogma, proceeds strictly from the nineteenth century. The possibility of overruling a precedent was never discarded, nor was the essential case law technique of distinguishing between the facts upon which a precedent was founded and the facts of the case forming the object of analysis, which, as not entirely analogous, preclude the application of the precedent.

B. Jurisprudence

The common law was born and essentially grew case by case through the decisions of judges; its characterization as "judge-made law" is very accurate. In the words of the American Oliver Wendell Holmes, Jr. (d. 1894), a judge himself: "the life of the law has not been logic, it has been experience." It is, therefore, not surprising that medieval and early-modern jurisprudence is based, above all, upon practical cases: compilations of writs, formulas, collections of cases, etc. It was mainly these materials which were transmitted in the learning of common law, which did not take place in universities or via the scholastic method, but rather at the four major inns of court (Inner Temple, Middle Temple, Gray's Inn and Lincoln's Inn), where apprentices were taught the details of judiciary practice by experienced attorneys.

Ranulf of Glanvill, Chief Justiciar from 1180 to 1189, produced a landmark compilation of writs featuring a brief description of their corresponding procedures: the *Tractatus de legibus et consuetudinibus regni Angliae* ("Treatise on the Laws and Customs of the Kingdom of England"). The fact that this text, which does not contain any references to royal legislation or local customary law, became (together with the work by Bracton) the fundamental cornerstone of common law jurisprudence gives one an idea of the writ's central position in the English legal system.

In the middle of the thirteenth century there circulated several manuscripts of the *De legibus et consuetudinibus Angliae* ("On the Laws and Customs of England"), attributed to Henry of Bracton (d. 1268), a judge at one of the royal courts. The Bracton text features a great stress upon writs. Like Glanvill's *Tractatus*, the work only addressed common law. However, Bracton introduced some commentaries that were clearly inspired by canon law and Roman law. He seems to have been familiar, in particular, with the writings of the jurist Azo of Bologna.

After Bracton, systematic works on common law would not be undertaken for a long time. Efforts were limited to modest attempts at the systematization of isolated parts. A work of great interest on real property law was the introduction to the subject by Thomas Littleton (d. 1481), directed at future lawyers. John Fortescue (d. 1479), Chief Justice of the King's Bench, wrote, among other works, the *De laudibus legum Angliae* ("Commendation of the Laws of England"), in which he set forth a very influential constitutional account of the Crown of England and, in this context, compared English common law with the law in France, reaching the conclusion that the English common law was superior. Fortescue's influence was noticeable in the treatise *Doctor and Student* written by Christopher St. Germain (d. 1540), an interesting dialogue between a doctor of Theology and a law student on the relationships between law and morals.

This relative lack of systematic works corresponded to the way future lawyers were trained. Universities such as Oxford and Cambridge offered undergraduate courses in Roman law, but for centuries the future serjeants-at-law, attorneys, solicitors, barristers and judges learned the craft by professional practice at the Inns of Court rather than through academic training. Legal education was highly practical, initially under the direct supervision of the existing practitioners of the law, but from the thirteenth century onwards a collegiate system, with its corresponding lectures, evolved as well. Reports on cases, such as the Year Books, were produced for their analysis in class; students served in moot courts to acquire practice, and the observation of court proceedings at Westminster Hall was a basic component of legal education.

As of the sixteenth century, some legists very gradually adopted a more doctrinal approach to the common law. Faced with the evident difficulties of the common law, such as its rigidity, the overlapping jurisdictions of courts, and the lack of apparent order, as a consequence of the fact that the organic growth of the law centered around the system of writs, the English legists turned to doctrine in order to further the systematization of the common law. This scientific approach to the common law matches a similar evolution on the Continent, where from the sixteenth century jurists would approach the *ius proprium* in an increasingly scientific manner. It appears that early-modern English legal authors were well aware of the contemporary scientific movement in the rest of Europe.

Edward Coke (1552–1634) was Chief of Justice of the King's Bench until 1616, when James I dismissed him for his maintenance of positions hostile to the interests of absolute monarchy, at which point he dedicated himself to politics and the study of common law. Coke set about writing the *Institutes of the Law of England*, an extensive introduction to the common law, of which only the first part would be published: *A commentary upon Littleton*; "Coke on Littleton" would stand as the leading reference work on property law until the twentieth century. Even though Coke's book has the word *Institutes* in its title, the focus was thoroughly on the traditional English common law. Posthumously, a synopsis by Coke on the court system was published, along with another on criminal law, and, finally, a commentary on old legislation.

Matthew Hale (1609–76), also Chief Justice of the King's Bench, was the author of an introduction to criminal law which is still cited in English and American courts. He wrote, among other works, treatises on the historical law of England: *History of the Common Law* and the outstanding *History of the Pleas of the Crown*. Hale had thoroughly studied Roman civil law, and this familiarity probably helped him to improve the systematization of English law as proposed by Coke. Hale introduced the idea that the institutions of English law dated back to at least the Anglo-Saxon period.

William Blackstone (1723–80) was the author of the most important work on common law since Bracton: *Commentaries on the Laws of*

England, which acquired almost legendary status. It was the first successful attempt to systemize the entire common law within the scope of a single book. As such, it fit perfectly with the ideals of eighteenth-century Enlightenment. The author's achievement was particularly meritorious because he could only build on partial introductions to common law, such as those by Hale and Coke. The work's systematization and structure was, therefore, derived from the only possible reference work covering an entire system of law: Justinian's *Institutiones*. Particularly influential was Blackstone's reliance on natural law as an overall legal theory. Blackstone, who was familiar with the works of Grotius, Pufendorf and Barbeyrac, set out to prove that the principles of common law embodied the principles of natural justice. It was his approach to natural law that would ensure Blackstone's tremendous influence in the courts of the young United States. Post-revolutionary American courts struggled with the question of why they should continue to enforce the rules laid down in the past by judges appointed by a king they had abjured. Blackstone's combination of common law and natural law endowed it with a universality that provided the American judges with a theoretical framework that allowed them to continue to adhere to the common law.

While American federal and state courts cited heavily from Blackstone's *Commentaries*, in his own country he became the subject of ferocious mockery by Jeremy Bentham (1748–1832). Bentham was an eccentric genius whose work must be framed in the context of the Utilitarianism movement and the corresponding rejection of natural law theories. Bentham sought to develop an ideal system based on a principle of utility, providing the greatest possible good to the greatest possible number of people. Parting from this premise, he became an implacable critic of common law, with its unnecessary formalism, division into courts with overlapping competencies, the dualism between common law and equity, etc. While during his own life his legal ideas were not widely embraced, the succeeding generation would profoundly reform common law – the Judicature Act 1873 is just an example – in response to some of them.

VII. THE EXPANSION OF THE ENGLISH COMMON LAW

A. Europe

The global influence of the common law can be explained by its reception, in different degrees, in what were the colonies, protectorates, dominions and other overseas possessions established by England beginning in the seventeenth century. In Europe the English common law was received primarily in Ireland. Ireland had been under the firm dominion of the English kings since the sixteenth century at the latest, a situation which was formalized in 1801 when Ireland was constitutionally incorporated into the United Kingdom of Great Britain and Ireland. Under the English the common law gradually marginalized local customary laws and, after obtaining independence in 1922, the Irish kept the common law legal system. To a certain extent the common law was also received in Cyprus, a British colony between 1878 and 1960.

B. The United States of America and the British Empire

Outside Europe the common law was received in the North American colonies. However, contrary to what might be expected, it wasn't a wholesale reception. Colonial governments were allowed to establish their own laws, provided they were not contrary to the laws of England. This meant that, in practice, a substantial part of the common law was absorbed, but with a few important twists. There were, for instance, no ecclesiastical courts, and civil procedure was less technical because there were no writs. Inheritance law changed significantly to mirror the absence of a landed aristocracy; most colonies eliminated primogeniture and inheritances were more evenly divided among all children. These and other departures from the English common law can be explained by the specific circumstances of the colonies. In some of them the influence of the law of the original settlers from Dutch, French or Spanish origin was quite enduring. This legacy is today still felt most clearly in Louisiana and Québec, both featuring civil codes traceable to French origins. The American version of the common law has been influential outside the United States as well, having been adopted by countries and territories such as Liberia, the Marshall Islands and, mixed with its own Spanish legal tradition, Puerto Rico.

The vastness of the British Empire explains why the common law is today one of the world's most widespread legal systems. Major economies such as Australia, Canada, Hong Kong, India, New Zealand, Pakistan and Singapore adopted, after their independence, a legal system based on the English common law, sometimes incorporating provisions of local customary or religious (Islamic) law.

C. Scots Law

Scotland represents an interesting case of a mixed legal system; a system that, like others, such as South Africa, Québec, Louisiana and Puerto Rico, is a blend of the civil and common law traditions. Constitutionally speaking, Scotland and England did not form a union until 1707, when the United Kingdom of Great Britain was formed. Unlike Wales, which was absorbed into the common law system in the first half of the sixteenth century, Scots law managed to maintain its singularity up to this day, albeit under a growing shadow cast by English law.

During the Late Middle Ages Scots law was very similar to the law on the European mainland, based mainly on customary and feudal law. However, via the canon law the *ius commune* gradually seeped into Scotland. Following the wars of independence at the end of the thirteenth century, with its corresponding sentiments of antagonism towards the English, there were many Scottish students who went to law schools in Italy, France and Germany. When the students returned, ecclesiastical courts offered rich career opportunities for them. After the Reformation in the sixteenth century, in which Scotland broke with the pope and adopted a predominantly Presbyterian-Calvinist religion, students continued to travel abroad for their legal educations. Many ended up studying at other Protestant universities on the Continent, particularly in Leiden, in the Netherlands.

The legal education of Scottish students helps to explain the major influence of the *ius commune* in Scotland. The Romano-canonical procedure was implemented in lay courts during the Late Middle Ages. Gradually, from the sixteenth century onwards, substantial law of civilian origin also found its way into the Scottish legal system. The courts in Scotland were primarily to apply the rules of the *ius proprium* (statutes from the Scottish Parliament, and local customary and feudal law) but, in practice, the absence of officially codified customary law, along with the consequent uncertainty about the norms to be applied, at times opened the door to the use of Roman law and the writings of civilians in judicial proceedings. Unlike Germany, where Roman law was explicitly acknowledged as suppletive law in proceedings before the *Reichskammergericht*, there was no such official reception in Scotland, its use in judicial proceedings being more the consequence of a natural course of events. The influence of Roman law waned as of the eighteenth century, for two reasons. The first was a growing consciousness of the scientific respectability of Scottish law, a development similar to contemporary movements in other European countries. The second was the growing influence of the English common law after the House of Lords acquired appellate jurisdiction over civil matters through the Treaty of Union in 1707, as well as growing economic ties between Scotland and England due to industrial expansion and extensive trade opportunities in the British Empire.

Early-modern Scottish jurists, many of whom were trained by Dutch, German and French Huguenot scholars, were familiar with the objectives and methodology of the sophisticated Dutch school and the *usus modernus pandectarum*, which they did not hesitate to apply when they returned home. As a consequence, they were amenable to the absorption of Roman law concepts in their local law, but without ever forgetting its singularity. Mention should be made of James Dalrymple, Viscount Stair (1619–95), who was Lord President of the Court of Session (Scotland's supreme civil court), and the author of the landmark *Institutions of the Law of Scotland*. The work, very much like other contemporary works on the European continent, offered a comprehensive survey of Scots civil law, and was structured in the light of rational, natural law principles as they were thought to be embodied in the Roman law. Stair's book triggered a wealth of other works of legal scholarship; the eighteenth century saw the publication of many books that, together, confirmed the self-contained status of Scots law. The eighteenth century was, in any case, a century of exceptional brilliance in Scotland, producing Enlightenment philosophers of the caliber of David Hume (1711–76) and Adam Smith (1723–90), among others.

There is some disagreement among current scholars as to the correct sources of Scottish law, civil or common; many scholars would object to this discussion of Scots law under a chapter on "common law." And they would be justified, for, as a mixed system, it occupies a place of its own. It will come as no surprise to learn that Scottish law is sometimes presented as a potential source for a new European *ius commune*. For instance, it has an interesting civilian version of the English trust, and its law of obligations, featuring both civil and common law features, anticipates solutions adopted by the different study groups on European private law.

VIII. COMMON LAW AND *IUS COMMUNE*

While it is clear that the English common law was not influenced by the *ius commune* to the same extent as other *iura propia*, it would not be fair to deny its influence. During the Middle Ages ecclesiastical courts operated in England, as in all Christian countries, and, obviously, applied canon law. Equity, the jurisdiction of the Lord Chancellor, was based on a concept which lies at the heart of the canon law: *aequitas*. The procedure in the Court of Chancery was essentially Romano-canonical, as was that of the High Court of Admiralty. The universities of Oxford and Cambridge, just like any other medieval university on the Continent, had schools in both laws, training future clerks and officials. The works of Bracton, Hale and Blackstone evidenced an undeniable and sometimes explicit familiarity with Roman law. Norman custumals such as the *Grand Coutumier de Normandie*, rife with concepts and ideas from the *ius commune*, were also of interest in England because of the dynastical links between Normandy and England. The Magna Carta was probably drafted by people academically trained in the *ius commune*, which left its imprint on its text.

Nevertheless, until the early twentieth century most English jurists approached the *ius commune* with prejudice. Perhaps the difficult relations with the "Popish" Church of Rome, also during the Middle Ages, can explain, in part, this negative stance. But the main reason is probably that, in spite of the manifestations of the direct and, especially, indirect influence of the *ius commune* on the common law, the truth of the matter is that, as a system, there is a clear divide between the civil and the common law systems. Neither Roman law nor canon law had the same *permeating* influence on English law as on the rest of the European *iura propria*. The question is: why not?

At the beginning of the twelfth century the differences between legal trends on the island and on the Continent were barely noticeable, as customary law prevailed everywhere. Economic conditions and feudal systems were very similar. Moreover, the English kings – of Norman and, hence, Continental origin – kept one foot on each side of the Channel. English bishops, meanwhile, studied at Continental universities and applied papal decretals. In short, at the beginning of the twelfth century the ecclesiastical, political and economic framework in place in England was similar to that characterizing the rest of Western Europe. Why, then, did there develop in England, beginning in the twelfth century, a system of law so different from that which would govern the Continent?

Perhaps the key divergence is that a legal system of a national nature was established in England very early in its history. On the Continent, in contrast, the law would for a long time retain its local character, reflected in customary law. This was not the case in England. After conquering the island the Normans encountered a more or less centralized government apparatus based on a network of royal officials: the sheriffs. The Normans would contribute their particular talent as rulers; their kingdoms (Sicily, for example) were notable for their administrative efficiency. The

Normans also exhibited great acumen in the complex task of managing ethnic diversity in their realms; in England the fusion of Angles, Saxons, Jutes, Danes and Normans took place slowly, but decisively, and by the twelfth century it was complete. Henry II would be the first king to call himself "English." Something similar may be said of the way in which the Normans managed the feudal regime. Unlike what occurred on the Continent, England managed constantly and consistently to control the centrifugal forces inherent to feudalism. Thus, in England it was unnecessary to counteract tendencies leading to decentralization through the consolidation of a state apparatus by means of principles, ideas and traditions derived from Roman and canon law.

This strong, centralized government drew upon a national legal system that had materialized before any on the Continent. On the mainland, for a long time attachment to local customs and political fragmentation hampered the development of national law, and only the *ius commune* proved sufficiently complex and universal to overcome the diversity of local customary law. In England it was common law that offered an alternative to local customary law. In comparison to the reception of the *ius commune* on the Continent, common law was consolidated much earlier in England. We see the first decisive signs of the *ius commune* penetrating the *ius proprium* in the early thirteenth century, often via indirect routes. By that time, the common law was already up and running in England.

Not only was common law implemented earlier, but from its very inception it was able to respond effectively to the needs of society. While in the thirteenth century a limit was placed on the number of writs, the common law, with the development of actions on the case and, above all, equity, offered just enough flexibility to adapt to circumstances, in spite of the many complaints about rigidity and other defects. Basically, there was no doubt that it worked: once it had developed, there was no need to look for alternatives.

Common law exerted a constant and compelling intellectual attraction as well. Conceived as a set of procedural mechanisms applicable throughout the territory, it was always highly regarded for its richness, pragmatism and internal coherence. The quality of Glanvill's work rivaled that of contemporary glosses, and for centuries the English, following John Fortescue, considered their common law to be qualitatively superior to any other legal system.

In summary, by the end of the twelfth century, when on the Continent the principles of academic law were being explored, England already enjoyed a legal system featuring a national scope, one complex and consistent enough to avert the importation of Roman law. The fact that it was studied at Oxford and Cambridge was marginal to its practical impact. Canon law would have a somewhat greater impact, but soon common law assimilated it into its own structure and spirit.

Epilogue

Law has a strong backward-looking component. Judges apply laws that were promulgated months, years, decades, or centuries ago. Or they follow precedents established by courts in a distant or near past. And they have their archaic rituals, priestly attires, and abstruse terminology, discussing "originalism" and "constructivism" to come to terms with the historical dimension of ancient documents that are still normative today.

Legislation has a backward-looking component as well. Even if, by definition, legislative intent is to provide rules governing a certain area of life for the future, these rules do not fall from the sky. First, legislators look at what was wrong with past legislation, but they also look at what can be preserved from it. Then they look for improvements. To this end they may borrow from previously existing legislation from other countries, or look at guidelines drafted by transnational organizations, or what experts in the field have been saying, or they might consult with the groups and communities that will be affected by the changes. There is much borrowing when legislators make laws, and it is often from past materials.

By focusing on this backward-looking element we do not mean to say that law was better in some imaginary "golden age". Neither do we mean to assert that history can or should be *prescriptive*: that things should be done in a certain way only because that is the way they were done in the past. What we intend to offer is a framework for lawyers and other intellectuals who do not wish to be blind to this backward-looking aspect of the law. Legal tradition creates an inertia, a *path dependence* (to use Richard Posner's words), from which it is not always easy – or desirable – to break free. Even though the circumstances of the past have changed, the outcome of these past circumstances continues to shape our current choices.

Civil procedure offers an excellent example of this path dependence. In the ecclesiastical courts of the Late Middle Ages a new way of litigating was designed by introducing university-trained jurists at all levels, eliminating any popular or irrational elements, observing procedural guarantees, recording everything in writing, allowing appeal and, therefore, supervision by higher courts. The new system, itself based on the post-classical Roman *cognitio* procedure, proved better suited to the new hierarchical, bureaucratic organization of the Church than the customary popular procedures, which soon disappeared. This way of litigating remained practically intact down to the present day. Throughout history, most European countries have endeavored to allow for a more popular, decentralized, participatory administration of civil justice, such as trial by jury. All of them have failed. Even though today American movies have made us all familiar with the civil jury system, path dependence makes it seem virtually impossible for Europeans to adopt such an alien system. (The same applies vice versa: it would take no less than a complete revolution for the US to abandon its path dependence on the jury system in favor of what might be a more refined, technical, objective application of private law.)

Path dependence, indeed, lies at the heart of the consolidation of the two great legal traditions: civil law and common law. Different as they are in some regards, there is not, and never has been, an insurmountable wall between the two. The common law is not incomprehensible to a civil lawyer, and vice versa. Interaction between the two legal families is constant and possible. The differences – sources of law, methodology, concepts, procedure – are real, but sometimes the difference between a French and a German solution is more profound. Similarly, a modern solution in a civil law jurisdiction might be the exact opposite of the Roman solution, but that does not mean that Roman law is not at the heart of civil law. Path dependence narrows down the range of possible choices, but it does not erase them.

We continue to speak of "legal families," even if it is probably not very fashionable today. We use it as explanatory shorthand, which should not be abused or decontextualized. Probably the most accurate way to look at the law is to consider it a constantly renewed amalgam of materials inherited from the past, rather than a result of any one party's design. A largely separate class of jurists, then, takes care of making sense of the mixture and, in turn, prepares it for yet another renovation. This is a dynamic that has characterized Continental law from the Late Middle Ages up to today. It is this more or less *scientific* approach to the law that has commanded most of our attention.

Indeed, jurisprudence and doctrine have often fueled a critical assessment of existing law, thereby opening the door to organic improvement. That is still their role. It is essential that jurists have a clear understanding of parallel developments elsewhere. This comparative approach is more and more important in an increasingly global world. Today an understanding of legal history is more important than ever before. If the triumph of the nation-state some two centuries ago allowed lawyers to remain largely ignorant of legal issues outside their borders and national scopes of application, they will soon be required to pay less attention to such local expressions of the law, and called upon to translate them into the great, common legal language of Europe. And in most cases only history will teach them that language.

Further reading

In what follows the interested reader will find a non-exhaustive list of references to works that provide more information and further literature on the subjects handled in this book. Where possible we refer primarily to English-language versions that are still available; occasionally, however, we include works in other languages when we consider them particularly relevant or influential.

General surveys of continental legal history include: M. Bellomo, *The Common Legal Past of Europe, 1000–1800*, Washington (DC), The Catholic University of America Press, 1995; P. Grossi, *A History of European Law*, Malden (MA), Wiley-Blackwell, 2010; R. Lesaffer, *European Legal History: A Cultural and Political Perspective*, Cambridge, Cambridge University Press, 2009; O.F. Robinson, T.D. Fergus and W.M. Gordon, *An Introduction to European Legal History: Sources and Institutions*, 3rd edn., Oxford, Oxford University Press, 2000; P. Stein, *Roman Law in European History*, Cambridge, Cambridge University Press, 1999; A. Watson, *The Evolution of Western Private Law*, Baltimore (MD), Johns Hopkins University Press, 2001; and F. Wieacker, *A History of Private Law in Europe with Particular Reference to Germany*, Oxford, Clarendon Press, 1995. An overview of Western legal history approached from the perspective of legal scholarship and legal theory can be found in J. Gordley, *The Jurists: A Critical History*, Oxford, Oxford University Press, 2013, and J.M. Kelly, *A Short History of Western Legal Theory*, Oxford, Oxford University Press, 1992.

Useful introductions to the history of Roman law and its sources are offered by H.F. Jolowicz and B. Nicholas, *Historical Introduction to the Study of Roman Law*, 3rd edn., Cambridge, Cambridge University Press, 1972; G. Mousourakis, *The Historical and Institutional Context of Roman Law*, Aldershot, Ashgate, 2003; and O.E. Tellegen-Couperus, *A Short History of Roman Law*, London–New York, Routledge, 1993. A. Watson, *The Spirit of Roman Law*, Athens (GA)–London, University of Georgia Press, 1995, provides an insightful account of the central features, values and approaches of those who made the law in ancient Rome. Classic textbooks on Roman private law are J.A. Borkowski and P.J. du Plessis, *Textbook on Roman Law*, 5th edn., Oxford, Oxford

University Press, 2015; A. d'Ors, *Derecho Privado Romano*, 10th edn., Pamplona, EUNSA, 2004; M. Kaser and R. Knütel, *Römisches Privatrecht*, 20th edn., Munich, C.H. Beck, 2014; G. Mousourakis, *Fundamentals of Roman Private Law*, Heidelberg, Springer, 2012; B. Nicholas, *An Introduction to Roman Law*, Oxford, Clarendon Press, 1962. The Roman law of obligations was given extensive comparative and historical treatment by R. Zimmermann, *The Law of Obligations: Roman Foundations of the Civilian Tradition*, Oxford, Oxford University Press, 1996. The standard edition of the Latin text of the *Corpus Iuris Civilis* is still that of T. Mommsen, P. Krüger, R. Schöll and W. Kroll (Berlin, Weidmann, 1954, 3 volumes: 16th edition of *Institutiones* and *Digesta* (vol.1); 11th edition of *Codex* (vol.2) and 6th edition of *Novellae* (vol.3)). There are translations of (parts of) the *Corpus Iuris Civilis* in several modern languages. We mention here *Justinian's Institutes*, text and translation by P. Birks and G. McLeod, Ithaca (NY), Cornell University Press, 1987; and *The Digest of Justinian*, English translation edited by A. Watson, 2nd edn., Philadelphia (PA), University of Pennsylvania Press, 1998, 2 volumes.

For aspects of early medieval institutions and legal history, we refer to some of the contributions in J.H. Burns (ed.), *The Cambridge History of Medieval Political Thought, c.350–c.1450*, Cambridge, Cambridge University Press, 1988; R. Bartlett, *Trial by Fire and Water: the Medieval Judicial Ordeal*, Oxford, Clarendon Press, 1986; F.L. Ganshof, *Feudalism*, 3rd edn., New York, Harper, 1964; F. Kern, *Kingship and Law*, New York, Praeger, 1956 (reprint Lawbook Exchange, 2013); P.D. King, *Law and Society in the Visigothic Kingdom*, Cambridge, Cambridge University Press, 1972; M. Lupoi, *The Origins of the European Legal Order*, Cambridge, Cambridge University Press, 2000; J. Muldoon, *Empire and Order: the Concept of Empire, 800–1800*, Houndmills–London–New York, 1999; and F. Oakley, *Empty Bottles of Gentilism: Kingship and the Divine in Late Antiquity and the Early Middle Ages (to 1050)*, New Haven (CT)–London, Yale University Press, 2010.

A comprehensive account on the significance of the Gregorian reform on the evolution of the law in the Late Middle Ages can be found in H.J. Berman, *Law and Revolution: The Formation of the Western Legal Tradition*, Cambridge (MA)–London, Harvard University Press, 1983. Aspects of the development of late-medieval political and constitutional thought are covered by A. Black, *Political Thought in Europe, 1250–1450*, Cambridge, Cambridge University Press, 1992; E. Kantorowicz, *The King's Two Bodies: a Study in Medieval Political Theology*, Princeton (NJ), Princeton University Press, 1957; P. Legendre, *L'amour du censeur: Essai sur l'ordre dogmatique*, Paris, Seuil, 1974; S. Mochi

Onory, *Fonti canonistiche dell'idea moderno dello stato: Imperium spirituale, iurisdictio divisa, sovranità*, Milan, Pubblicazioni dell'Università Cattolica del Sacro Cuore, 1951; K. Pennington, *The Prince and the Law, 1200–1600: Sovereignty and Rights in the Western Legal Tradition*, Berkeley (CA), University of California Press, 1993; G. Post, *Studies in Medieval Legal Thought: Public Law and the State, 1100–1322*, Princeton (NJ), Princeton University Press, 1964 (reprint Lawbook Exchange, 2012); B. Tierney, *Religion, Law and the Growth of Constitutional Thought, 1150–1650*, Cambridge, Cambridge University Press, 1982; W. Ullmann, *Principles of Government and Politics in the Middle Ages*, 2nd edn., Oxon–New York, Routledge, 2010 (first published by Methuen in 1966). A recent update on the state of research on medieval jurists is provided by H. Lange, *Römisches Recht im Mittelalter. Vol. 1 Die Glossatoren. Vol. 2 Die Kommentatoren*, Munich, C.H. Beck, 1997–2007. The natural law and Aristotelian traditions in the Late Middle Ages are the subject of J. Finnis, *Aquinas: Moral, Political and Legal Theory*, Oxford, Oxford University Press, 1998; J. Gordley, *The Philosophical Origins of Modern Contract Doctrine*, Oxford, Clarendon Press, 1993; J. Gordley, *Foundations of Private Law: Property, Tort, Contract, Unjust Enrichment*, Oxford, Oxford University Press, 2007; B. Tierney, *The Idea of Natural Rights: Studies on Natural Rights, Natural Law and Church Law, 1150–1625*, Atlanta (GA), Scholars Press, 1997; and B. Tierney, *Liberty and Law. The Idea of Permissive Natural Law, 1100–1800*, Washington (DC), The Catholic University of America Press, 2014. More details on the history of the legal profession as from the twelfth century onwards can be found in J.A. Brundage, *The Medieval Origins of the Legal Profession: Canonists, Civilians and Courts*, Chicago–London, University of Chicago Press, 2008.

For the history of the sources of medieval canon law and the principal ecclesiastical institutions, see the general surveys of J.A. Brundage, *Medieval Canon Law*, Oxon–New York, Routledge, 2013 (first published by Longman in 1995); J. Gaudemet, *Église et cite: Histoire du droit canonique*, Paris, Cerf/Montchrestien, 1994. A massive multi-volume series on the history of canon law was produced under the direction of G. Lebras and J. Gaudemet (eds.), *Histoire du droit et des institutions de l'Église en Occident*, Paris, Sirey/Cujas, 1955–1981, 18 vols.; in English, several volumes in the series History of Medieval Canon Law cover the canon law sources, for example W. Hartmann and K. Pennington (eds.), *The History of Medieval Canon Law in the Classical Period, 1140–1234. From Gratian to the Decretals of Pope Gregory IX*, Washington (DC), The Catholic University of America Press, 2008. On the political and constitutional impact of medieval canon law theories, see F. Oakley, *The*

Conciliarist Tradition. Constitutionalism in the Catholic Church, 1300–1870, Oxford, Oxford University Press, 2003; K. Pennington, *Popes and Bishops. The Papal Monarchy in the Twelfth and Thirteenth Centuries*, Philadelphia (PA), University of Pennsylvania Press, 1984; B. Tierney, *Foundations of the Conciliar Theory: The Contribution of the Medieval Canonists from Gratian to the Great Schism*, enl. new edn., Leiden, Brill, 1998. Readers interested in the nature of medieval canon law should consult R.H. Helmholz, *The Spirit of Classical Canon Law*, Athens (GA)–London, University of Georgia Press, 1996. Recent research has brought to light some fascinating facts about Gratian and the different versions of one of the most important works in legal history: see, among others, A. Winroth, *The Making of Gratian's Decretum*, Cambridge, Cambridge University Press, 2000. Despite its shortcomings, the standard edition of the basic medieval canon law texts is still E. Friedberg (ed.), *Corpus Iuris Canonici*, Leipzig, Bernhard Tauchnitz, 1879–1881, 2 vols. (reprint Lawbook Exchange, 2000). There are no translations in modern languages of the full text, but the first 20 *distinctiones* of the *Decretum Gratiani*, together with their *glossa ordinaria*, have been translated into English: Gratian, *The Treatise on Laws (Decretum DD. 1–20)*, transl. A. Thompson, with the Ordinary Gloss, transl. J. Gordley, and an Introduction by K. Christiansen, Washington (DC), The Catholic University of America Press, 1993.

On the evolution of law and political thought in early-modern Europe, see H. Coing, *Europäisches Privatrecht, Vol. 1: Alteres gemeines Recht (1500 bis 1800)*, Munich, Beck, 1985; D.R. Kelley, *Foundations of Modern Historical Scholarship: Language, Law and History in the French Renaissance*, New York, Colombia University Press, 1970; K. Haakonssen, *Natural Law and Moral Philosophy. From Grotius to the Scottish Enlightenment*, Cambridge, Cambridge University Press, 1996; R. Tuck, *The Rights of War and Peace: Political Thought and the International Order from Grotius to Kant*, Oxford, Oxford University Press, 1999; and many useful articles in J.H. Burns (ed.), *The Cambridge History of Political Thought, 1450–1700*, Cambridge, Cambridge University Press, 1991.

For the history of law in the bourgeois period, see A.-J. Arnaud, *Les origines doctrinales du code civil français*, Paris, Librairie générale de droit et de jurisprudence, 1969; M. John, *Politics and the Law in Late-Nineteenth-Century Germany: The Origins of the Civil Code*, Oxford, Clarendon Press, 1990; D.R. Kelley, *Historians and the Law in Postrevolutionary France*, Princeton (NJ), Princeton University Press, 1984; P.A.J. van den Berg, *The Politics of European Codification: A History of the Unification of Law in France, Prussia, the Austrian*

Monarchy and the Netherlands, Groningen, Europa Law Publishing, 2007; J.Q. Whitman, *The Legacy of Roman Law in the German Romantic Era. Historical Vision and Legal Change*, Princeton (NJ), Princeton University Press, 1990; D. Wisner, *The Cult of the Legislator in France, 1750–1830. A Study in the Political Theology of the French Enlightenment*, Oxford, Voltaire Foundation, 1997; and R. Zimmermann, *Roman Law, Contemporary Law, European Law. The Civilian Tradition Today*, Oxford, Oxford University Press, 2001.

The history of the English common law is well documented in general surveys such as J.H. Baker, *An Introduction to English Legal History*, London, Butterworths, 2002; J.H. Langbein, R.L. Lerner, B.P. Smith, *History of the Common Law: The Development of Anglo-American Legal Institutions*, New York, Aspen, 2009; S.F.C. Milsom, *Historical Foundations of the Common Law*, London, Butterworths, 1981. *The Oxford History of the Laws of England*, under the direction of general editor J.H. Baker, provides in several volumes a detailed survey of the development of English law and its institutions from the earliest times until the twentieth century. Six volumes have been published so far at Oxford University Press.

Index